D1645507

Birds of
Heath and
Woodland

The Orbis Encyclopedia of Birds of
Britain and Europe
Volume Four

Birds of Heath and Woodland

Edited by John Gooders

ORBIS PUBLISHING

London

©1979 Orbis Publishing Ltd., London
©1971 Rizzoli Editore, Milan
Printed in Great Britain by Jarrold & Sons Ltd., Norwich
ISBN 0 85613 380 9

Frontispiece: Wren (J. A. Bailey/Ardea)

Contents

Editor's Preface

The single most important skill for the bird-watching beginner to acquire is that of putting a name to a bird. Nine out of ten questions one is asked are about identification. Not that there is anything surprising about that – the desire to name what one sees is not only natural, but also a prerequisite for moving on to more interesting things. Ornithology has a technical language, virtually incomprehensible to the outsider, but learning bird names is relatively uncomplicated. It just makes more sense to say that we saw a Kestrel hovering, than that we saw a long-winged, long-tailed bird of hawk-like propensities, hovering! Once we have mastered the name, then we can communicate easily with other bird-watchers and ornithologists and also check our own records as well as those of our birding forebears.

Birds are not difficult to identify. Most have bright patches of colour, or a particular pattern or marking, even a characteristic shape, that separates them from other species. Even those that look similar may have a distinctive call-note. Who, for instance, could mistake the flash of blue of a Kingfisher? Who could miss the white wing patches of the Woodpigeon? Is there anyone who could mistake the shape of the Swift for any other bird, except another swift? And who will ever forget the call of the Nightjar on a summer's evening? These examples may be carefully chosen from this volume, *Birds of Heath and Woodland*, to make points about colour, pattern, voice and so on, but the same criteria apply to all other species of birds. Certainly, there are hardly any really difficult groups of birds to be found in this volume. Warblers, waders and gulls can be a problem; but wagtails, woodpeckers and thrushes are not, provided one knows what to look for. In fact this is always more than half the battle and, at the same time, the spot where most beginners come unstuck. A black and white bird that climbs trees and hacks at the bark may be a woodpecker – but which one? There are several to choose from in Europe and unless one knows in advance what to look for, the diagnostic feature will be missed. So familiarity with the local field guide, especially one that makes a point of picking out the salient features, is of prime importance. When travelling to a new country for the first time, seeing new birds every day, the same problems have to be faced all over again – one simply does not know the 'field marks' of the birds one is seeing. So description after description is carefully recorded in the field note-book for checking-out later. Most birds get names put to them, but others are narrowed down to a small group of similar species and no further. Even on second visits to the same area, some birds will still get away without being named, but gradually skill improves and one knows more and more what to look for

among particular groups of birds. To the traveller, as to the beginner in his or her own country, only one piece of advice is really worthwhile – read the field guide and become familiar with the birds before you see them. Then when you enjoy a fortunate encounter you will know what you are looking for.

There then follows what can only be called the great 'hoodwink' phase of watching birds. You now have a mental record of the diagnostic features of most of the birds of your area, either having seen them or having dreamed of seeing them. Then, one day, you spot a 'difficult' bird and start searching for the features that you know you should see to make it rare, new for your life-list, or conceivably new for the region. Naturally enough if you look hard enough you will see what you want to see and another new bird is 'identified' and added to the list. In my travels I meet a lot of bird-watchers of very different levels of experience and expertise. Most, thank heaven, suffer from self-hoodwinking only in the mildest and most understandable of forms, and are quick to laugh at themselves and their mistakes. Just occasionally a self-confessed expert appears on the scene and sees ten or even twenty per cent more birds than anyone else – even on their first visit to the country. Strangely, no one else sees any of these elusive birds. Beginners beware!

Although I have written so much here about identification it is, after all, only a skill which allows people to put names to birds. In itself that may be quite satisfying, but it is in its application to our knowledge of birds that the skill becomes of use. Of course, it is not necessary to be able to name every bird you see in order to study the feeding behaviour of, for example, the Bee-eater. For that you only need to know a Bee-eater when you see one. But for studies of populations, distribution, ecology, migration and so on, the ability to identify birds quickly and accurately is essential.

In this five-volume series every bird that has ever occurred in Europe is fully detailed. The individual species is described under standard headings covering every aspect of its life from where it is found, to how many eggs it lays. Because identification is so important most birds are illustrated at least twice and several a good many more times. They are shown as adults in summer and in winter, as juveniles, as immatures and sub-adults, and in flight – not for every species but wherever appropriate. Identification guides usually fit into the pocket and suffer from too little information. This encyclopedia is a bit awkward to take into the field, but there is a wealth of information and reference awaiting the return of anyone who goes out a-birding.

John Gooders

Introduction

Gradually man will find ways (he has to if he cannot find quick and effective means to limit his population explosion) of utilising more and more marginal land. Marshes must be drained, estuaries reclaimed, heathland and moors made fertile, the sea harvested, the hills planted and the woods felled. Throughout the world man is being forced by pressure of numbers to take more and more marginal land into production. In the mountainous Kingdom of Nepal the problems can be seen remarkably clearly. In the uplands, and that is most of the country, land is so short that the terraces extend to the very tops of the hills. Tiny walled plots have been created and cultivated in the most unlikely spots and yet still there is not enough land to provide an adequate food supply. In the forested lowland region of the country known as the *terai*, settlements were few until a malaria eradication campaign made it possible for people to move in twenty years ago. Now most of the forests have gone. The birds of the area have gone too, their places taken by those ubiquitous species that are able to find a good living alongside man. In the few areas of original woodland that remain the birdwatcher will be enchanted with the wealth of species, but elsewhere the species found on the plains of India are all there is to see.

Nepal is remote from Europe, but in a less dramatic way the same things have been happening in Britain. Over the last thirty years agriculture has changed from a quaint rural affair to a modern, mechanised, cost-effective business. Machinery needs room and hedges and ditches have had to go. Equally important has been the effect on marginal land: heaths and hills have been ploughed, the chalk downlands have gone, poor marginal land has been brought into cultivation. Woodland has not done so badly, though the modern forestry industry seems intent on converting the forests into monotonous conifer plantations and removing all the old dead and fallen wood that provides so much food for birds. The resultant effect on bird populations has been to push some species further and further away from heath and woodland. Where, for instance, is the Woodlark now that so many marginal sandy areas have been ploughed? And the Red-backed Shrike that lived nearby? And what of the Nightjar – are there fewer than there used to be? Others may have done rather well out of the changes – certainly the Woodpigeon must see

(Below) Kingfisher *Alcedo atthis*

Marka

vii

modern agriculture with its huge fields and mechanised wastage along with modern forestry's deep and secure coniferous roosting sites, as a sort of pigeon-paradise. The colonising Collared Dove too must have been pleasantly surprised to find western Europe so accommodating. Farmers, of course, would prefer there to be rather fewer pigeons, but it is the very conditions they have created that have produced the problem.

It is still one of the greatest of pleasures to walk the marginal land, the heath and woodland of Britain. In the spring the trickling streams are inhabited by Kingfishers, Dippers and Grey Wagtails; and the surrounding woods are full of the songs of Wren and Blackbird. A Great Spotted Woodpecker beats against an old dead branch to produce a rapid drumming sound that acts as its song and territorial defence; and thus incidentally becomes one of the very few avian instrumentalists. The Green Woodpecker, in contrast, calls loudly, its 'yaffles' echoing through the woods. A Dipper, all brown and bulky and marked with a broad white chest, flies low over the stream and then off among the trees on a short-cut known only to itself. Confined to fast-running streams, Dippers feed by wading along the rocky bottom picking insect larvae from among the stones and at times submerging completely to do so. As a result it defends a territory that may be only a few metres wide, but as much as three kilometres in length.

As the stream gets narrower, the hills get steeper and the woodland becomes little more than scrub, we leave behind the lush greenness of spring and very soon take to the open moors. Here birds are thin on the ground and our most constant companions are Meadow Pipits. Small, dull, olive-streaked little birds, they are both common and unremarkable, yet they are among the most successful of species, nesting from sea-level to the slopes of the highest peaks. Another noticeably successful bird shares their home in more ways than one. The Cuckoo can be found on lowland marshes where it lives parasitically off Reed Warblers, through dry heathland and woodland up to the highest moors where the Meadow Pipit is its customary host. No European bird, one would guess, is as well known as the Cuckoo. Even small children quickly learn its characteristic call and the bare facts of its rogue life-style. Yet surprisingly few actually see the Cuckoo and the vast majority that do so, fail to recognise it. The same could also be said of that other famous songster – the Nightingale. Up among the hill moors the Cuckoo is an obvious bird as it flies low over the rank grasses searching out likely Meadow Pipit nests in which to deposit its own remarkably similar egg. Strange as it may seem, Cuckoos specialise in one type of foster parent or another, so that the eggs of a single female will resemble those of the host on which she regularly preys.

Once the woodlands have been left behind birds become much scarcer. Meadow Pipits, Cuckoos and another large raptor-like bird, the Short-eared Owl, are the most obvious inhabitants. Unlike most owls, the Short-eared hunts by day. Over the rank grasses it quarters like a harrier, hovering now and again when it catches sight of a movement below. Most often it turns away to continue its steady beating, but occasionally it will drop feet-first and disappear. If it is nesting it may soon re-emerge carrying its luckless prey, but at other seasons it will eat its food where it has been captured. Short-eared Owls are vole specialists and their numbers correlate closely with the population of these small rodents. Like lemmings, the population of voles is cyclical, varying year by year and reaching a peak every four to six years. In such peak years Short-eared Owls may become superabundant.

Owls form a very large family of birds ranging in size from the huge Eagle Owl to the diminutive Pygmy Owl, which is smaller than a Blackbird. They take a vast range of prey and have adapted to the most diverse of habitats – yet by far the largest number still inhabit the woodlands where doubtless they evolved. Being nocturnal predators they are wonderfully equipped for night-flying with extra-large eyes, splendid binocular vision and exceptional hearing. They also have the ability to fly on completely silent wings (save those species such as the fish-owls which have no need of a silent approach to their prey) and are camouflaged in mottled browns and greys to avoid the attentions of small birds while they sleep during the day.

By the very nature of their lives, they are not birds that we come into contact with a great deal, though no doubt there are many more human sightings by owls, than owl sightings by humans. They do, in fact, live all around us and two of the most common species, the Barn Owl and Tawny Owl, often take advantage of our constructions in which to build their nests. It is, however, by their calls that we are most aware of their presence among us. Tawny Owls, in particular, can be heard above the roar of traffic deep in our city centres and occasionally glimpsed flying over street lamps. These 'city owls' have changed their diet to move in with us. Instead of capturing small mammals, as they do in the countryside, they have switched to a diet of House Sparrows.

Every bird of heath and woodland that has ever appeared in Europe is featured in these pages. The range of species is enormous, from pigeons and doves, owls, nightjars, swifts and some of the most colourful of birds such as the kingfishers, bee-eaters and rollers, to the woodpeckers, swallows and thrushes. They include some of the best known and loved of our birds like the common Swallow which may nest year after year in our old shed or garage, to the virtually unknown, such as nightjars. It is remarkable that only a century ago one of the country names for the common Nightjar was 'Goatsucker', because it was believed that it fed from lactating she-goats after dark. In fact we now know this to be completely unfounded and that Nightjars feed on insects taken in the air, even if they are insects distributed by goats! Frankly there is so much of interest that it is difficult to know where to start – or where to stop if you are writing an introduction!

Birds of Heath and Woodland

FAMILY PTEROCLIDAE: Sandgrouse

D. C. Houston/Bruce Coleman

J. S. Wightman/Ardea

The sixteen species which constitute this family are the shape and size of a pigeon but the central tail-feathers and the flight-feathers are generally elongated. Although the common name for members of this family is 'sandgrouse', they are not in any way related to true grouse. According to current opinion, the Pteroclidae are closely related to the pigeons and doves of the family Columbidae in both structure and behaviour: both families are therefore placed in the order Columbiformes. There are, however, other authorities which consider that these birds should be placed in a separate order although their arguments are not always entirely convincing. However, authorities all agree that the sandgrouse should be classified after the order Charadriiformes and before the true pigeons.

All sandgrouse are terrestrial—that is they do not perch in trees—and the general coloration is sandy which allows the birds to merge well with their desert or semi-desert environment. The females are usually duller in colour than the males. Those species which live in deserts tend to have lighter-coloured upper parts than species which spend most of the day in the shelter of bushes and herbaceous vegetation, a clear example of cryptic coloration at work. The plumage is generally mottled and barred. The different calls of the various species are among the best means to distinguish them.

The primaries are very long and often pointed, consistent with the considerable power of flight required of these birds which must cover great distances every day to reach the few places where water is available. The legs are short and Pallas's Sandgrouse *Syrrhaptes paradoxus* has feathered toes and legs.

The nest is a hollow in the ground where normally three eggs (sometimes two or four) are laid. Both sexes incubate the eggs: the male usually incubates at night. The young hatch covered in down and are able to leave the nest soon after birth.

The diet consists mainly of vegetable matter,

(Above) Chestnut-bellied Sandgrouse *Pterocles exustus*; it breeds in Egypt and is one of the smaller sandgrouse although the tail feathers are elongated. (Facing page) Yellow-throated Sandgrouse *P. gutturalis* which lives in arid regions of Africa. (Preceding page, page one) Tawny Owl *Strix aluco*

(Above) Chestnut-bellied
Sandgrouse and (below)
world distribution of the
family Pteroclidae

especially the hard seeds of various leguminous plants; these are crushed in the bird's stomach by the large amounts of grit which they swallow.

As they live in areas sparsely supplied with water, sandgrouse must, in order to drink, fly for tens or even hundreds of kilometres every day and they gather in groups which may be enormous in size at the few waterholes in the district. They are very much creatures of habit and will rarely desert their chosen watering-place, even if water is temporarily available nearer home. This behaviour has some survival value, since in this way sandgrouse do not run the risk of relying on fluctuating water supplies and consequently dying of thirst if these fail. Naturally this behaviour also has its negative side and sandgrouse, which by day have little or nothing to fear from predators, are easy prey for carnivorous birds and mammals (including man) who lie in wait near the watering-place at sunset or just before dawn, the times of day when sandgrouse prefer to drink. As a rule, species living in open country water at dawn, and those living in bush or scrub do so at sunset. The birds arrive, sometimes thousands at a time, from all directions: near Baghdad, for example, at least eighty thousand birds have been counted watering at the Euphrates river. Like pigeons, sandgrouse drink without lifting their heads from the water, and each bird is capable of taking on sufficient water for its daily needs in a few seconds. Additionally the adults carry water among their breast feathers to quench the thirst of their young that remain at the nest. The Tibetan Sandgrouse *Syrrhaptes tibetanus* is an exception in this respect, being sedentary in habit and content to drink as and when it can, sometimes relying mainly on dew or on water from the melting snowfields near where it lives.

There are only two genera in the family Pteroclidae. The genus *Syrrhaptes* contains only the above-mentioned Tibetan Sandgrouse and Pallas's Sandgrouse *S. paradoxus*. The latter has, in the past, undertaken extraordinary irruptive migrations from the central Asian steppes to Europe and to China. Particularly massive invasions occurred in 1863, 1872, 1876, 1888 and 1908, when these birds were found as far away as Italy and England. They even remained and nested in the countries they invaded.

The other fourteen species all belong to the genus *Pterocles* and are found mainly in Africa. Many of them, however, have various sub-species which extend the range to some parts of Asia Minor and southern Asia, the Canary Islands, Spain, Portugal and southern France. One species, the Madagascar Sandgrouse *P. personatus*, is found only in Madagascar.

In Europe there are two resident species, the Black-bellied Sandgrouse *P. orientalis* and the Pin-tailed Sandgrouse *P. alchata*. Two species occur accidentally: the Spotted Sandgrouse *P. senegallus* and Pallas's Sandgrouse. The latter even bred in Britain in the nineteenth century, but invasions by Pallas's Sandgrouse have not occurred now for many years, perhaps because of massive changes caused by man in its homeland.

J. S. Wightman/Ardea

J. S. Wightman/Ardea

(Above) Lichtenstein's Sandgrouse *Pterocles lichtensteinii* which is small with a short tail and tends to be less gregarious than other sandgrouse. (Left) Black-faced Sandgrouse *P. decoratus* which is present in Africa

French: GANGA UNIBANDE
Italian: GANGA
Spanish: ORTEGA
German: SANDFLUGHUHN

Black-bellied Sandgrouse
Pterocles orientalis

(Above) Male Black-bellied Sandgrouse (foreground) and female. (Below right) Breeding areas (yellow), wintering areas (magenta) and areas where the Black-bellied Sandgrouse may be seen all year round (orange)

HABITAT Stony open and treeless areas and sometimes slightly hilly regions. Also grassy steppes, but avoids open desert.

IDENTIFICATION Length: 34 cm. Largest sandgrouse which breeds in Europe. Male adult: background colour of upper parts sandy with various grey, reddish, blackish and yellow spotting. The sides of the grey head are buff: conspicuous black patch on throat. Breast ash-grey, divided by a black band. Whole belly black: is the only sandgrouse with an all black belly although may sometimes be confused with Chestnut-bellied Sandgrouse whose dark brown belly may sometimes appear black. Central tail-feathers only slightly elongated. Female is more spotted and mottled than male, the throat and breast being spotted above as well as below the black band. Distinguished from Pallas's Sandgrouse, which is similar in size, by the much less elongated tail feathers and black belly.

Gregarious and often found with Pin-tailed Sandgrouse. In flight white underwing of male contrasts with black belly. See also page 10.

CALL A low gruff 'charr-rar-rar' or 'joor-joor-joor'; also whistling and croaking noises.

REPRODUCTION From April to June. Two or three eggs are laid in a hollow in the ground. The buff-coloured eggs are smooth and glossy, varying greatly in the intensity of the light to dark brown markings. Both parents incubate the eggs for about twenty-one days. Both also care for the nestlings.

FOOD Vegetable matter: berries, seeds and shoots.

DISTRIBUTION AND MOVEMENTS Breeds in the Canary Islands and North Africa eastwards to Asia Minor: also in Spain, Portugal and Cyprus. Accidental in Italy, Malta and Germany.

SUB-SPECIES Sub-species are present in Asia.

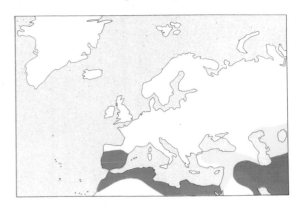

Pin-tailed Sandgrouse
Pterocles alchata

HABITAT Semi-desert areas or on desert edges with vegetation.

IDENTIFICATION Length: 32 cm. Male has a greenish-yellow patch extending from the crown over much of the back. Upper-tail coverts strongly barred black and central tail-feathers are long and filiform. In flight is distinguished chiefly by white belly as well as by wide red band, bordered black, on breast. The throat is black in the male and white in the female: the female's general coloration is paler with finer barring. She also has three 'collars' instead of two. In the male the upper parts are spotted yellow and the wing coverts are chestnut. See also page 10.

CALL A loud, frequent 'kattar-kattar'.

REPRODUCTION Late April onwards. Nests on the ground in the open in a shallow hollow like other sandgrouse. Two to three eggs which are cream-coloured with brown, red and grey spotting are laid. Both parents incubate the eggs for nineteen to twenty-one days. Both also tend the young who leave the nest shortly after hatching but remain with adults.

FOOD Vegetable matter.

DISTRIBUTION AND MOVEMENTS Breeds in North Africa, the Middle East, the USSR as far as southern Transcaucasia, reaching almost to Afghanistan and Mongolian borders. In Europe breeds in Spain, Portugal and southern France. The eastern populations migrate to Pakistan and parts of India.

SUB-SPECIES *P. a. caudacutus* breeds in Europe.

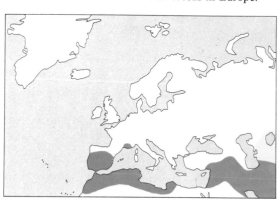

(Below) Male Pin-tailed Sandgrouse (foreground) and female. (Left) Breeding areas (yellow), wintering areas (magenta) and areas where the Pin-tailed Sandgrouse may be seen all year round (orange)

French: GANGA CATA
Italian: GRANDULE
Spanish: GANGA COMÚN
German: SPIESSFLUGHUHN

French: GANGA DU SÉNÉGAL
Italian: GRANDULE DEL SENEGAL
Spanish: GANGA MOTEADA
German: SENEGAL-
SPIESSFLUGHUHN

Spotted Sandgrouse
Pterocles senegallus

HABITAT Sparsely vegetated desert and semi-desert areas.

IDENTIFICATION Length: 33 cm. Male: pale reddish patch on the nape; ash-grey band which encircles the neck and extends from the neck to the bill. Throat, chin and upper neck yellow; breast grey. Remaining parts are pinkish-beige with dark patches on wings and lower belly. Female: closely spotted on upper parts and breast; like the male has dark patch on belly. Both male and female have filiform, very elongated central tail-feathers, although shorter than those of the Pin-tailed.

Flight swift, with rapid wingbeats. See also page 10.

CALL A very distinctive musical 'queeto-queeto'.

REPRODUCTION Begins late February or March: breeding season is prolonged. Nest is a hollow (often a natural one) in the ground. Two or three eggs are laid, buff and sparsely marked with reddish spots and blotches. Both sexes incubate the eggs, probably for about twenty days. Both parents tend the chicks.

FOOD Feeds on vegetable matter such as seeds of desert plants.

DISTRIBUTION AND MOVEMENTS Northern and east central Africa. Also occurs in Asia, from Israel to northern India. Sedentary, but may undertake some local movements and generally moves in smaller flocks than other sandgrouse. Accidental in Sicily.

(Below) Female Spotted Sandgrouse (foreground) and male

Pallas's Sandgrouse
Syrrhaptes paradoxus

HABITAT Sandy semi-desert and steppe. Also sandy beaches; occasionally in fields. On migration may be found in arid regions.

IDENTIFICATION Length: 35–40 cm. Distinguished from other sandgrouse by the black patch on the belly (less broad than Black-bellied's). Central tail-feathers long and filiform, like the outermost primaries. Male: orange head and throat, with a grey band descending from the eye to the sides of the neck; upper parts sand-coloured with darker bars and spots. Female has a grey edge to the patch on her throat, and sparse black spots on the crown and neck.

Gregarious, like other sandgrouse; lives in large groups. Rather cumbersome when taking off, fluttering its wings like a pigeon: however, once airborne flies very quickly. See also page 10.

CALL A resonant 'ker-kee-ker-kee' in flight. On land also utters a guttural 'kok-kok'. When fighting, Pallas's Sandgrouse emits a rapid 'crick-ti-crick'.

REPRODUCTION April to June. Nests in large colonies, in steppe or desert. Nests in a scrape in the ground, sometimes lined with a few wisps of grass, and lays three to four eggs, buff to greyish, with grey and brown spots. Both parents incubate the eggs for about twenty-four days and both tend the young. Probably breeds twice and possibly three times a year.

FOOD Plants: seeds and shoots of desert and steppe plants.

DISTRIBUTION AND MOVEMENTS The normal range is from the northern shores of the Caspian, across southern Siberia and Mongolia, to northern China. Is mainly sedentary but irregular migration and irruptions do occur when it may reach western Europe, India and Korea. Has been recorded in Norway, Britain, France, Spain, and south to Italy. The most significant irruptions, consisting of small flocks which reached many parts of Britain and Ireland, last occurred in 1908. A few pairs bred in Yorkshire and Moray in 1908. However since 1908 it has only been a very scarce visitor to Britain.

(Below) Male Pallas's Sandgrouse (foreground) and female

French: SYRRHAPTE PARADOXAL
Italian: SIRRATTE
Spanish: GANGA DE PALLAS
German: STEPPENHUHN

Sandgrouse in flight

1: **PALLAS'S SANDGROUSE** *(Syrrhaptes paradoxus)* Male from above (a): note orange colouring of cheeks and throat, the black rear border of the primaries, and the chestnut of the secondary coverts (seen only in this species). The secondary flight-feathers are ochre, not dark as in Pin-tailed or Black-bellied. Tail is very long, due to elongated needle-like central tail-feathers. The first primary is also long and needle-like, but this is seldom noticeable in the field. Female from above (b): sandy-yellow with fine spots. She has the palest wings of any sandgrouse; like the male, she shows the characteristic chestnut coloration of the wing-coverts. From below (c), male and female are very similar; this is the only sand-grouse species with pale underwing present in Europe.

2: **PIN-TAILED SANDGROUSE** *(Pterocles alchata)* Male from above (a): green and yellow markings, with an unmistakable 'scale'-like pattern. The upper breast is orange, and the central tail-feathers long and needle-like. On the proximal part of the wing are two or three black stripes. A russet patch is visible near the bend of the wing. From below (b), the orange band on the breast and the yellow throat and black chin are even more clearly seen. The rest of the underparts are white; so too are the wing

coverts, while the flight feathers and forward and rear edges of the wings are dark. Female, from above (c) has the closest and heaviest bars of any species. The wing shows the dark area of the secondaries and tertiaries, and the 'scales' of the coverts, contrasting with the paler primaries. From below (d) the three dark stripes on the neck and breast and the highly characteristic pattern of the wing (similar to the male's) are visible.

3: **BLACK-BELLIED SANDGROUSE** *(Pterocles orientalis)* Male from above (a) has a characteristic dappled look, short tail, and head markings reminiscent of Pallas's Sandgrouse but darker and with a black patch on the throat. Primaries and secondaries dark, contrasting sharply with the tawny patch on the wing coverts. Female from above (b): paler than male, with fine dark spots or linear markings extending over the crown. The pattern and colouring of the wings also resembles the male's; the tawny patch on the wing coverts is a distinctive feature. From below, male (c) and female (d) are very similar apart from colouring of head, throat and upper breast. A distinguishing feature is the black patch which covers much of the underparts. The wing coloration is reminiscent of Pin-tailed, but there is no dark leading edge.

(Below) Pin-tailed Sandgrouse *Pterocles alchata*

COLUMBIDAE: Pigeons and Doves

J. Burton/Bruce Coleman

The family Columbidae numbers two hundred and eighty species or more, and is of worldwide distribution; only in the Arctic and Antarctic, on a few ocean islands and in the most inhospitable regions of northern Asia and South America are members of the family absent. Many species have well-developed migratory habits, though many others are sedentary, or only migrate between high and low altitudes so as to escape the rigours of the mountain winter. The body is generally short and thickset, with a small head. Size varies from 18 to 83 centimetres among members of this family. The plumage is soft and very thick on the back, and is attached to a thin layer of skin in direct contact with the underlying bone. The bill may be thin or very heavy, but is always of medium length, often with a wattle covering the nostrils. The wings may be medium, long or short; the tail is square and of medium length, or else wedge-shaped and very long. The species vary in colouring from delicate shades of pearl or ash-grey to greens, russets, warm browns and violet hues. Many species show a metallic sheen especially on the neck and wings.

The food of pigeons and doves generally consists of plant matter, although some species will eat small snails and other invertebrates. Species that regularly feed on wild or cultivated cereal grains possess a powerful muscular gizzard, which often contains tiny stones or some other hard material for grinding up the grains, and a long intestine to aid in their digestion. Species living mainly on fruit, on the other hand, have a 'soft' stomach and a very short intestine in which only the pulp of the fruit is digested, leaving the kernel intact; when the kernel is passed, it may fall into suitable soil and grow into a new plant. It appears that pigeons are very efficient at dispersing seeds of certain plants, which, without their aid, might not spread at all.

A distinctive habit of species of the family Columbidae is their method of drinking: the bill is submerged in the water and they 'suck up' the water without raising their head. The only other species that drink in this way, as far as is known, are the sandgrouse—which belong to the same order—and hemipodes.

The nest is not built with particular care, though the platform on which it is constructed may be strong and compactly woven. The nest is usually rather flat, and generally contains one egg (sometimes two); the egg is white or it may be a uniform pale colour. The young hatch after an incubation period of about three weeks, during which both parents take turns incubating. During their first few days of life, the fledglings are fed on a secretion produced by the glands of the adult's crop, known as 'pigeon's milk'.

The family Columbidae has recently been subdivided into forty-three genera, twelve of which are

(Above right) Woodpigeons *Columba palumbus* and (right) Turtle Dove *Streptopelia turtur* with young at the nest. (Facing page) Palm Doves *S. senegalensis*

R. J. C. Blewitt/Ardea

L. Gaggero

(Right) Topknot Pigeon *Lopholaimus anctarticus*. (Below) Mourning Dove *Zenaida macroura* and (below right) Stock Dove *Columba oenas*

monotypic. The sub-family Columbinae not only contains the familiar doves, pigeons and turtle-doves (and practically all the European species), but also species such as the quail doves of the genus *Geotrygon*, confined to Central and South America, the Pheasant Pigeon *Otidiphaps nobilis* of New Guinea, and many other species such as the small South American turtle-doves and the Australian 'bronze-wing pigeons'. Also included in the sub-family Columbinae are a variety of species belonging to genera such as *Phaps*, *Histriphaps*, *Geophaps*, *Lophophaps*, *Ocyphaps* and *Petrophassa*. The bronze-wing pigeons provide a very good example of evolutionary radiation: although they have diverged in important respects in the course of their evolution, adapting to a variety of different environ-

ments, their plumage and especially their behaviour shows how closely akin they are.

The sub-family Columbinae also includes the Rock Dove *Columba livia*, indigenous to Europe, Asia and North Africa and the ancestor of all breeds of domestic pigeon. Another member is the Pink-headed Dove *Streptopelia roseogrisea*, ancestor of the domestic turtle-doves. A very similar species, the Collared Dove *Streptopelia decaocto*, which some authorities consider conspecific with the Pink-headed Dove, has recently invaded Europe from Asia Minor and successfully established itself in a number of north European countries, nesting from Britain, Ireland and Norway south to southern France and Italy. One of the reasons for its spectacular success appears to be the fact that it has chosen to settle in parks and gardens in towns and villages, particularly those rich in ornamental conifers. Here it is safe from hunters, and can always find something to eat.

The most famous species of this sub-family is the Passenger Pigeon *Ectopistes migratorius*. In the time of John James Audubon, millions—perhaps hundreds or even thousands of millions—of these birds lived in the North American forests. In his *Ornithological Biography*, Audubon described the overwhelming sight of hordes of these pigeons

K. Brate/Photo Researchers

(Above) Stock Dove *Columba oenas*

(wandering rather than migratory birds), darkening the sky, bending the treetops, and being attacked by man by any and every available means. 'Those who do not know these birds', writes Audubon, 'might naturally suppose that such terrible onslaughts should soon put an end to the existence of the species; but I have become convinced, after careful observation, that nothing but the gradual reduction in our forests can diminish the numbers of these birds; for they not infrequently quadruple their numbers each year, and never less than double it.' Less than a hundred years later, this prediction was to be proved totally wrong. On September 1st, 1914, the last Passenger Pigeon, a female named Martha, died in the Cincinnati Zoological Gardens. It is impossible to say whether the carnage wrought

on this species was the only reason for its extinction, but it certainly hastened it.

Another dove belonging to the sub-family Columbinae is the Namaqua Dove *Oena capensis*, an inhabitant of the African continent and the island of Madagascar. It has a fine long, tapered tail, and is one of the few species showing marked sexual dimorphism: the male has beautiful velvety black face and breast, edged with pale grey, while the female has much more sober colouring on these parts. It lives in open country, wanders endlessly across vast tracts of land, stopping to nest when the conditions are right. Among still extant American species of this sub-family, are the Mourning Dove *Zenaida macroura*, a smaller and less brightly-coloured version of the Passenger Pigeon which is

J. Six

found from North America to the West Indies and Central America; the White-winged Dove *Z. asiatica*, a native of the Antilles and of certain areas in the southern United States, Central and South America; and the Common Ground Dove *Columbina passerina*, which frequents gardens and towns.

The second most important sub-family of Columbidae includes almost all the tree-living and fruit-eating species, the so-called 'fruit-pigeons'. This is a somewhat artificial classification, covering pigeons with different origins, whose resemblance may be due to the phenomenon of convergent evolution. In the Ethiopian and Oriental faunal regions, the largest species belong to the genus *Treron* and are known as the 'green pigeons', so named because of the background colour of their plumage, often embellished with splendid yellows, oranges and violets, and with coloured wattle and palpebral ring. Unlike other members of the family, the green pigeons have a muscular gizzard, and can digest the seeds of the wild figs that are their chief item of diet. The Indo-Malayan and Pacific regions have other types of pigeon, that is the species of the genera *Ptilinopus* and *Ducula*, with frequently brilliant colouring, reminiscent of parrots. The Orange Dove *Ptilinopus victor* of the Fiji Islands has the most pronounced sexual dimorphism of the whole order Columbiformes: the male is brilliant

orange with a yellow head, while the female is dark green, except for her head which is the same colour as the male's.

The crowned pigeons of the genus *Goura* (three species) constitute the sub-family Gourinae, characterised by their large size (up to 83 cm in length) and by a laterally compressed crest on the head, made of loosely-woven spatulate feathers which is reminiscent of the Peacock's tail in shape. The crowned pigeons inhabit the Australasian faunal region. The Samoan Islands are the home of the Tooth-billed Pigeon *Didunculus strigirostris*, whose atypical features have caused it to be placed in a sub-family of its own, Didunculinae.

(Above) Plumed Pigeons *Lophophaps plumifera* of Australasia. (Left) Torres Strait Imperial Pigeon *Ducula spilorrhoa* and (far left) Victoria Crowned Pigeon *Goura victoria.* (Facing page top) Feral pigeons, a common sight in towns and cities. They are descended from domestic forms of the Rock Dove. (Facing page below) World distribution of the family Columbidae

J. R. Brownlie/Bruce Coleman

S. C. Bisserot/Bruce Coleman

G. Pizzey/Bruce Coleman

French: PIGEON COLOMBIN
Italian: COLOMBELLA
Spanish: PALOMA ZURITA
German: HOHLTAUBE

Stock Dove
Columba oenas

(Below right) Breeding areas (yellow), wintering areas (magenta) and areas where the Stock Dove may be seen all year round (orange)

HABITAT Woods, parks and also areas near sea coasts and on rocky terrain. Sometimes present in towns.

IDENTIFICATION Length: 32 cm. Rather small, compact shape. Distinguished from Woodpigeon by lack of white on wings and neck, shorter tail, darker and more blue-grey plumage. Flight-feathers and end of tail black. Has two short black wing-bars. Iridescent green patches on sides of neck. Is very easily confused with the Rock Dove but lacks the Rock Dove's pale or white rump. Display flight of the Stock Dove is circular and it sometimes glides on raised wings. See also page 24.

CALL A deep 'oo-oooo'.

REPRODUCTION From March onwards. Nests in a hole in a tree, building or cliff: rarely in a rabbit hole. May use the nest of other species. Eggs: usually two, sometimes one, white or creamy eggs are laid. There are two or three broods per year. Both sexes incubate the eggs for sixteen days, and both tend the young.

FOOD Leaves, seeds, peas, beans, grain, etc.

DISTRIBUTION AND MOVEMENTS Europe except for more northerly regions, western Asia, north-west Africa. Resident in western Europe and Mediterranean region. In Britain and Ireland breeds widely in most counties. Also occurs as a passage and winter visitor.

SUB-SPECIES Sub-species are present in Asia.

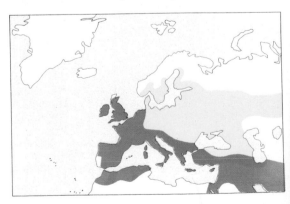

Woodpigeon
Columba palumbus

French: PIGEON RAMIER
Italian: COLOMBACCIO
Spanish: PALOMA TORCAZ
German: RINGELTAUBE

(Below left) Breeding areas (yellow) and areas where the Woodpigeon may be seen all year round (orange)

HABITAT Generally frequents areas fairly well covered with trees such as woods, thickets and plantations. Also present in meadows, cultivated land, open country, urban parks and gardens.

IDENTIFICATION Length: 40 cm. Larger than other European pigeons, and heavily built. Uniform grey-blue plumage, with a broad white wing-bar and (in adults only) a very pronounced white patch at the side of the neck. Head and rump darker than the rest of the plumage, flanks and belly pale, breast a cloudy wine-red colour, sides of neck iridescent purple and green. Tail and flight feathers black. From below, the tail has a paler grey bar along its length and a black terminal bar. Juveniles are paler and have no black on the neck. Legs pink; bill has pink base and yellowish tip.

Flight powerful, straight and fast, with rapid wing-beats sometimes followed by a brief glide. Feeds on the ground and in trees, eating new leaves, shoots, seeds and blossoms. On land, walks moving its head back and forth, holding the body horizontal. Gregarious: associates with domestic pigeons and Stock Doves. In winter often wanders in huge flocks. See also page 24.

CALL A subdued, rhythmical coo: 'coo-coooo-coo-coo-coo', repeated several times over.

REPRODUCTION April to September. Nests on hedges or in trees. Eggs: normally two, white, smooth, slightly shiny. Incubation is shared although the female undertakes the major part. The squabs or young pigeons are fed on 'pigeon's milk', secreted from the crop.

FOOD Plant matter: seeds, leaves, fruit, berries, nuts, flowers. Occasionally worms and insects.

DISTRIBUTION AND MOVEMENTS Europe except for most northerly regions, western and southern Asia, northwest Africa. May be resident, bird of passage or migratory. Birds ringed in northern Europe winter in large numbers in central and western Europe. In Britain and Ireland is a widely distributed resident breeder, and the Woodpigeon also occurs as a winter visitor from continental Europe.

SUB-SPECIES Sub-species are present in the Azores, Madeira and in Asia.

French: PIGEON BISET
Italian: PICCIONE SELVATICO
Spanish: PALOMA BRAVIA
German: FELSENTAUBE

Rock Dove
Columba livia

(Below right) Areas where the
Rock Dove may be seen all
year round (orange)

HABITAT By rocky coasts, gorges, precipitous rock-faces inland. Domestic species of the Rock Dove are common in city and countryside as are feral pigeons—domestic species which have gone wild.

IDENTIFICATION Length: 33 cm. Distinguished from Stock Dove by its much paler back, two very marked black wing-bars, and white or off-white rump, visible both in flight and at rest. From below, in flight, further distinguished by white (rather than grey) axillaries and underwing. Head, breast and belly grey-blue, darker than back; iridescent green or purple patches at sides of neck. Tail has terminal black band, and some white on outermost feathers. Juveniles duller in colour. Domestic forms have colours ranging from grey to white, cinnamon, black.

Smaller than Woodpigeon, flies faster and lower, often close to ground or water surface, often gliding. Alights on rocks, ground, buildings, very occasionally on trees. Almost always seen alone, in pairs or in small groups. See also page 24.

CALL 'Ur-roo-coo', 'ur-ur-roo-coo', and a deep 'urr-urr-urr', with variations which may be faster and softer.

REPRODUCTION April to July. Nests in crevices, clefts and among rocks. Domestic forms nest on urban buildings. Eggs: two or sometimes only one, oval, white, with a smooth and slightly shiny surface. Incubated by male and female for seventeen to nineteen days.

FOOD Seeds, grain, peas, beans, potatoes and plants.

DISTRIBUTION AND MOVEMENTS Western and southern Europe, north Africa, southwest and south Asia Minor. Mainly sedentary. In Britain and Ireland is a fairly numerous resident breeder. Pure, or apparently pure populations confined to northern and western coasts and islands of Scotland and Ireland. Feral populations predominate elsewhere.

SUB-SPECIES *C. l. livia*: Faeroes, Britain and Ireland, France, Iberian peninsula, western Mediterranean islands, Balkan peninsula, Rumania, USSR; also parts of Asia and Africa. *C. l. gaddi* (paler): eastern Mediterranean islands, Asia Minor, Near East; also parts of Asia. Other sub-species in the Canary Islands, Asia and Africa.

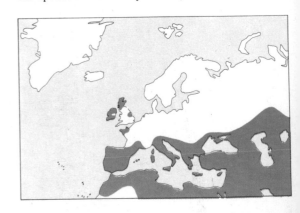

Collared Dove
Streptopelia decaocto

French: TOURTERELLE TURQUE
Italian: TORTORA DAL COLLARE
ORIENTALE
Spanish: TÓRTOLA TURCA
German: TÜRKENTAUBE

HABITAT Lives in regions with scattered trees and bushes, mainly in cultivated or urban areas.

IDENTIFICATION Length: 28 cm. Resembles a small slender Woodpigeon but plumage is more sober in coloration: grey-brown with a tinge of pink below, particularly on the breast. Also similar to a Turtle Dove but the Turtle Dove is smaller and shorter and also more chestnut in colour: it also has grey-brown rather than blackish wing tips. Black half collars of the Collared Dove are distinctive. Underside of the tail black at the base from underside whereas Turtle Dove's tail is black at base both from above and below. Primary coverts of Collared Dove grey-blue. Bill grey-black and legs dark pink. See also page 24.

CALL Male's call is a persistent trisyllabic 'coo-roo-coo-coockoo' which is reminiscent of the Woodpigeon's call: the accent is on the middle syllable.

REPRODUCTION Begins in March: may be prolonged until September. Builds a flat nest of twigs mainly on conifers but also on other trees, or very occasionally on the ledge of a building. Two drab yellow-white eggs are laid. It may breed twice a year or more—up to five times. Both parents incubate the eggs for approximately fifteen days.

FOOD Mainly grain and seeds: also fruits and berries.

DISTRIBUTION AND MOVEMENTS Breeds from Ireland east across Scandinavia, France, Italy, the Balkans and southwest Asia to Sri Lanka and Korea. Mainly sedentary but undertook a massive expansion northwest to Europe from about 1930. In Britain first arrived (and bred) in Norfolk in 1955. Is now a resident breeder in many British counties.

(Left) Areas where the Collared Dove may be seen all year round (orange)

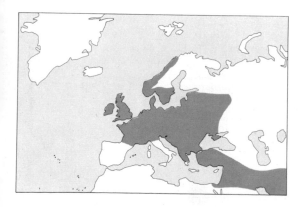

French: TOURTERELLE DES BOIS
Italian: TORTORA
Spanish: TÓRTOLA COMÚN
German: TURTELTAUBE

Turtle Dove
Streptopelia turtur

(Right) Breeding areas (yellow) and areas where the Turtle Dove may be seen on passage (pink)

HABITAT Open country: open woodland, edges of woods, thickets, parks, scrubland, bush, large gardens, hedgerows and farmland.

IDENTIFICATION Length: 27 cm. Distinguished from other doves and pigeons by its small size and more slender outline; tawny scapulars and wing coverts; black centres to feathers; longer tapered tail, black with a white edge, which is particularly conspicuous in flight. Plumage brown, back and rump brown; head, neck and outer wing coverts ash-grey. Throat and underparts pale wine-colour, shading into white on abdomen and undertail. Black and white patches at the sides of the neck. Juveniles duller with no neck patches. Bill black, legs deep pink.

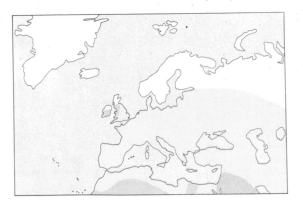

Flies quite fast. Alights on bushes and trees of medium height, rarely on buildings: usually breeds at lower heights than other members of the family. See page 24.

CALL A low-pitched singing 'rrurr-rrurr' repeated several times.

REPRODUCTION From mid-May to June or July. Nests on tall bushes, hedges, in orchards, etc. Nest is a thin platform of twigs: may use another bird's nest as a base. Eggs: one or two (exceptionally three), white, slightly shiny. Both male and female incubate the eggs for thirteen or fourteen days.

FOOD Plant matter: grain, leaves and seeds. Occasionally eats small molluscs.

DISTRIBUTION AND MOVEMENTS Europe except for most northerly regions, western Asia and north Africa. Migratory, wintering in tropical Africa. In Britain is a fairly numerous breeder, mainly in southern and central England although locally elsewhere. Breeds in small numbers in Ireland: seen on passage in Britain and Ireland.

SUB-SPECIES *S.t. turtur:* Europe, Asia, Canary Islands. *S.t. arenicola* (paler and smaller): Balearic Islands, north Africa and Asia. Other sub-species are present in Africa.

Rufous Turtle Dove
Streptopelia orientalis

French: TOURTERELLE ORIENTALE
Italian: TORTORA ORIENTALE
Spanish: TÓRTOLA ORIENTAL
German: ORIENT-TURTELTAUBE

HABITAT Lives in forested areas: usually breeds in thickets rather than in trees as it prefers a lower nesting site.

IDENTIFICATION Length: 33 cm. Very similar to Turtle Dove but larger and has much darker plumage: upper parts more heavily spotted and a deeper chestnut than the Turtle Dove's. Neck-patch is blue-grey instead of white like the Turtle Dove's. Undertail and bill grey. Legs pink. See also page 24.

CALL A deep singing 'coo-coo-caucurr'.

REPRODUCTION April to June. Lays two white, very shiny eggs. Both male and female incubate the eggs for about fourteen days. There are probably two or three broods per year.

FOOD Rice and other grains; shoots.

DISTRIBUTION AND MOVEMENTS Eastern and southern Asia from Afghanistan east to Formosa. Partially migratory: northern populations winter in the southern parts of the breeding range. In Britain is a scarce vagrant: also accidental in Scandinavia and in Italy.

SUB-SPECIES Sub-species are present in Asia.

Palm Dove
Streptopelia senegalensis

French: TOURTERELLE DU SÉNÉGAL
Italian: TORTORA DELLE PALME
Spanish: TÓRTOLA SENEGALESA
German: PALMTAUBE

HABITAT Lives in oases and gardens in urban areas.

IDENTIFICATION Length: 21 cm. Head wine-red, mantle warm brown, front of neck and breast speckled with dark spots. Belly white. Wings are brown with slate-grey, almost blue, outer coverts. Tail is brown and outer tail-feathers are white. Smaller than the Turtle Dove and may be distinguished by dark marking on the lower neck and, in flight, by the blue-grey forewing. See also page 24.

CALL A distinctive rising and falling gurgling note: 'oh-cook-coook-cook'.

REPRODUCTION February to June. Usually nests in cultivated or inhabited areas on a ledge of a building or in low bushes or trees. Eggs: lays two smooth white eggs which both parents incubate for about thirteen days. Both adults also care for the young.

FOOD Mainly cereals but also seeds.

DISTRIBUTION AND MOVEMENTS Breeds in North Africa and the Middle East east across Asia. In Africa it is known as the Laughing Dove while in Asia it is named the Little Brown Dove. In Europe it nests in Turkey and possibly also in Bulgaria.

SUB-SPECIES Sub-species are present in Asia.

(Left) Wintering areas (magenta) and areas where the Palm Dove may be seen all year round (orange)

Doves and Pigeons in flight

1: **COLLARED DOVE** *(Streptopelia decaocto)* Tail ends almost squarely. Characteristic coloration: the upper parts (a) are sandy-brown, with a grey area on the wing. The black collar is usually easily seen. The underparts (b) are pale, 'with wine-coloured breast and unmistakable tail pattern, with a broad white terminal band. The Collared may be confused with the Turtle Dove but it is larger, has more uniform colouring and is less chestnut in colour.

2: **TURTLE DOVE** *(Streptopelia turtur)* From above (a), the chestnut pattern of the back and scapulars, with dark patches, the grey on the wing and the white of the outer tail-feathers makes the Turtle Dove unmistakable. From below (b), note white tail and undertail. The bird's flight, with series of rapid wingbeats interrupted by glides, often with the body inclined alternately to right and left, enables it to be identified even against the light. Like other species of the genus *Streptopelia*, flight is fast and the wings are moved in a quick and jerky manner.

3: **RUFOUS TURTLE DOVE** *(Streptopelia orientalis)* Colouring very reminiscent of the Turtle Dove, but when seen in good light its distinctive features are immediately apparent. From above (a), the coloration of the upper parts is darker than the Turtle Dove's, including the head; collar is less apparent, and the edges of its feathers are grey-blue, not white. On the wing there is also a narrow pale band, and the outermost tail-feathers are grey rather than white. From below (b) the colouring is darker overall, and the tail coverts are grey like the outer tail-feathers, rather than white as in the common Turtle Dove.

4: **PALM DOVE** *(Streptopelia senegalensis)* Coloration is similar to a Turtle Dove's but darker and more blurred on the back and the collar is inconspicuous except at close quarters. The grey streak on the wing is very noticeable. The iridescent bronze-green highlights give a distinctive overall appearance to this bird, and its characteristic call is a further aid to identification.

5: **ROCK DOVE** *(Columba livia)* This species is the ancestor of all domestic pigeons including the familiar urban pigeons which in many cases have the same colouring. From above (a), there is a double black wing-bar, pale back and white rump, by which this species can be immediately distinguished from other European species. Unlike similar species, the Rock Dove has uniform coloration on back and wings. The dark terminal bar on the tail is thinner than in any other species. From below (b), the strikingly white underwing stands out. In general it can also be fairly easily recognised by the rocky habitat in which it is found.

6: **WOODPIGEON** *(Columba palumbus)* From above (a): distinctive features are its large size, longer tail and neck than those of other pigeons, white collar, and a clearly visible white patch on the wing. Also distinguished by fawn-coloured bill, visible at a considerable distance, and by its unmistakable call. Juveniles lack white collar, and their overall coloration is drabber but there are no major differences between them and adults. In flight seen from below (b) has dark wings.

7: **STOCK DOVE** *(Columba oenas)* From above (a): lacks pale rump. The middle of the wing is paler; the inner edge of the primaries is dark; also has two short black bars on the wing. From below (b), shows a grey, not white, under-wing.

8: **EASTERN STOCK DOVE** *(Columba eversmanni)* Something of a half-way species between the Woodpigeon and Stock Dove. From above (a): The coloration of the rump varies from pale grey to near-white. The most distinctive feature is the dark wine-colour of the head, including the crown. The black patches on the wing vary, but are generally less extensive than in the Stock Dove. The tail does not appear to have a dark terminal band; however, there are two bands but they are difficult to see. From below (b), a feature which distinguishes it from the Stock Dove is the pale underwing.

R. Longo

The order Cuculiformes is composed of two distinct families. One family, the Musophagidae or turacos, consists almost exclusively of African species, and as such are not discussed here. The second family—the Cuculidae or cuckoos—includes some species found in Europe, although most are of tropical and sub-tropical distribution.

The one hundred and twenty-seven species in this family are grouped in six sub-families. They vary in size from that of a sparrow to that of a large crow; the shape of the body is tapered, with a tail that is sometimes very long, sometimes graduated, or forked in one species. The wings are of medium length or long, depending on whether or not the species is migratory. The legs are short (except in species living on the ground), and possess zygodactyl toes, that is the outer toe can be turned backwards. The bill is moderately long, usually slightly decurved, and sometimes very powerful. The orbital ring is often coloured, and the presence of 'eyelashes' on the lids gives these birds a characteristic appearance. The plumage is coarse and rather sparse; in some species, the feathers are hair-like. An erectile or semi-erectile crest is often present on the head. The general coloration is tones of brown or grey, with various spots and bars. However some birds have splendid plumage of metallic or near-metallic green or bronze.

Cuckoos are generally arboreal, but there are some exclusively terrestrial species that rarely fly. The flight of migratory species, on the other hand, is fast and powerful, and some birds in this family migrate over phenomenal distances.

Species that build their own nests do so with a fair degree of care, and the eggs (usually two to six) are incubated by both parents. The greatest variation in egg colour is found in certain parasitic species that lay eggs indistinguishable from those of the host species, except for a difference in the

thickness of the shell.

The sub-family Cuculinae comprises forty-seven species grouped in sixteen genera which are brood parasites. This sub-family is confined to the Old World, and is widely distributed there, extending from northern Europe to Polynesia and New Zealand. The best-known species is the common Cuckoo *Cuculus canorus,* which breeds practically throughout the Palearctic region and migrates to Africa and southern Asia. A resident sub-species breeds throughout Africa except in true deserts and river-forests. Outside Africa,

(Above) Recently hatched Cuckoo *Cuculus canorus.* (Left) Great Spotted Cuckoo *Clamator glandarius.* (Facing page) Young Cuckoo *Acrocephalus palustris.* Cuckoos foster their young off to another bird — a phenomenon known as brood parasitism. By doing this each female can produce many more offspring as she is not responsible for feeding them all. The female Cuckoo removes an egg from the host's nest and lays one in its place: her egg may closely resemble that of the host. Once hatched, the fledgling cuckoo may eject the eggs or nestlings of the host birds or, through its insistence on being fed, cause the other nestlings to starve

other species of the same genus are found in Asia and Australia. The Great Spotted Cuckoo *Clamator glandarius* is the only European species of the genus *Clamator*. It is widespread in Africa and Asia, and is a parasite of various species of the family Corvidae: the young Great Spotted Cuckoos are reared in the host's nest without the host's own offspring being expelled from the nest (unlike the Cuckoo and similar species who expel the host's young). The genera *Urodynamys* and *Eudynamys* are monotypic composed of the Long-tailed Cuckoo *U. taitensis* and the Koel *E. scolopacea*. The latter is distributed from India to China and Australia, and is also a parasite of the House Crow *Corvus splendens*. The male Koel is metallic black in colour and the female brown with pale

P. Montoya/Jacana

(Right) Young Cuckoo being fed by a foster parent
(Below) World distribution of the family Cuculidae

spots; the young of both sexes are black, like the young crows whose nest they occupy and with whom they are confused by their adoptive parents. Another Asiatic species, the Drongo Cuckoo *Surniculus lugubris*, is parasitic on the Drongos (order Passeriformes, family Dicruridae), and resembles its host not only in its all-black plumage but also in its forked tail.

The sub-family Phaenicophaeinae comprises the true, non-parasitic cuckoos; it includes mainly tropical species, distributed in both the Old and New Worlds. The only African species is the Yellow-bill *Ceuthmochares aereus*; Asia has eight genera, and America three. Of the latter, one genus, *Coccyzus*, includes two species distributed in North America and accidentally encountered in Europe. These are the Yellow-billed Cuckoo *C. americanus* and the Black-billed Cuckoo *C. erythropthalmus*. Cuckoos of this sub-family build their own nests and lay two to six eggs.

The sub-family Protophaginae consists of only two genera: *Crotophaga* (three species) and *Guira* (monotypic). Both genera are restricted to the New World and are mainly tropical. Species of the genus *Crotophaga* are medium-sized birds with black plumage and a long tail; they are the only species of the family which are gregarious. They evidently build communal nests in which several females lay their eggs.

The sub-family Neomorphinae has five genera in the Americas and a single one, *Carpococcyx*, in southeast Asia. Three species the Striped Cuckoo *Tapera naevia*, Pheasant Cuckoo *Dromococcyx phasianellus* and Pavonine Cuckoo *D. pavoninus* are parasitic like the Cuculinae; the genus *Morococcyx* has five species, all neo-tropical. The most curious species of this sub-family is the Roadrunner *Geococcyx californianus*—a unique cuckoo in appearance being brown with black stripes. It is essentially a terrestrial bird and the long legs are adapted for running. The Roadrunner feeds mainly on lizards and other reptiles. A similar species, the Lesser Roadrunner *G. velox*, is found from Mexico south throughout Central America.

The ten species of the genus *Coua* constitute the sub-family Couinae and are native to Madagascar. One species is usually found in the island's forests, while the others live mainly in arid terrain and bush.

Another genus *Centropus*, which includes twenty-seven species, makes up the sub-family Centropodinae. Species are distributed from Africa (including Madagascar) to southern Asia, Australia and the Solomon Islands. The coucals (as these cuckoos are called) are basically terrestrial birds and are rather heavily built. They feed mainly on insects but also on small vertebrates. Coucals build a spherical nest among the grass or a little above ground-level. The Senegal Coucal *Centropus senegalensis* is one of the most common species of the west African savannah, but similar species are also present in eastern Africa. The White-browed Coucal *C. superciliosus* has once been observed rescuing its young from a savannah fire, flying them out of danger gripped between its thighs.

D. D. Burgess/Ardea

(Above) Roadrunner
Geococcyx californianus:
this fast-running and
terrestrial cuckoo is a tireless
predator. The Roadrunner
lives in arid regions of the
southwestern United States
and Central America. (Left)
Black Coucal *Centropus
toulou:* most coucals live in
open woods and grassland.
They run well but are poor
fliers

M. D. England/Ardea

French: COUCOU GRIS
Italian: CUCULO
Spanish: CUCO
German: KUCKUCK

Cuckoo
Cuculus canorus

HABITAT During the breeding season lives in wood-land, bushy or cultivated terrain or open treeless country. Winters mainly in bushy country but its habitat varies from tundra to farmland to urban areas.

IDENTIFICATION Length: 33 cm. Generally seen in flight; may sometimes be confused with a Sparrowhawk, though it does not have the latter's broad, rounded wings. Upper parts and breast grey-blue, underparts whitish with strong grey bars. In flight, the pointed wings and long graduated tail with white spots and tips are distinguishing features. Legs yellow. Both sexes are similar, but occasionally russet-coloured females are seen, resembling juveniles. The song is the most immediate distinguishing feature, and in Britain the sound of the Cuckoo is eagerly awaited as a sign that summer is not far off.

On land, hops along or walks with a swaying gait. Perches on bushes, branches, walls, rocks. Flies with rapid wingbeat, and glides before alighting. The wings are hardly raised above the horizontal plane in flight. During courtship, sings while it rhythmically raises and lowers its head. When facing the female the male moves his whole body up and down. See also page 34.

CALL Immediately distinguishable by its song which consists of a soft 'cuck-coo' which is constantly repeated. Sometimes a 'hoo-hoo-hoo'. The female also has a long-drawn-out warbling note. Both male and female make coughing and choking notes when they are excited.

REPRODUCTION From mid-May onwards. The Cuckoo is a brood parasite, laying its eggs in the nests of other species, including warblers, pipits, chats, Redstart and Robin. Each female has a well-demarcated territory, which she quarters on the wing looking for a suitable nest in which to lay. When she finds it, she removes one egg from it in her bill and drops it some distance away, leaving one of her own in its place. If the nest is too small or the entrance too narrow, she will stand above the nest holding her wings outstretched and tail erect; in this posture she drops her own egg (not always success-fully) into the nest. When the young Cuckoo hatches, it is immediately driven by instinct to push the other eggs or fledglings out of the nest, finally remaining alone in it.

The Cuckoo lays from eight to twelve eggs (although sometimes many more) which vary greatly in colour: some may show close mimicry in colour and markings to that of host species.

FOOD Generally feeds on insects, chiefly large cater-pillars. Also earthworms.

DISTRIBUTION AND MOVEMENTS Breeds in Eurasia and northwest Africa from Britain and Ireland, Iberia and Morocco east across Asia to Japan and central Burma. Winters in tropical Africa and sub-tropical Asia. In Britain and Ireland is a widespread breeder although irregular in Shetland. Resident from April to July or August. Also occurs as a passage visitor.

SUB-SPECIES *C. c. canorus*: throughout Europe except for the Iberian peninsula and Balearic islands. Also east to China and Japan. *C. c. bangsi* (smaller) Iberian peninsula, the Balearic islands and northwest Africa. Other sub-species are present in Asia.

(Above) Adult Cuckoo (foreground) and juvenile. (Below) Breeding areas (yellow) and areas where the Cuckoo may be seen on passage (pink)

Oriental Cuckoo
Cuculus saturatus

French: COUCOU DE L'HIMALAYA
Italian: CUCULO ORIENTALE
German: WALDKUCKUCK

HABITAT Woods, especially pine and spruce forests, and also marshes. Tends to live far from human habitations and farmland.

IDENTIFICATION Length: 39 cm. Very similar to Cuckoo from which it is distinguished by much sparser and broader bars on underparts and by paler underwing. Juveniles resemble females in brown phase; they can be distinguished from juvenile Cuckoos by the dark, almost black upper parts. In the grey phase, breast and head are more intense grey than the Cuckoo's. The bastard wing or alula is whitish-cream without spots, or with very faint markings, according to some authorities; while that of the Cuckoo is strongly barred. The Oriental Cuckoo is a shy skulking species, especially in the breeding season. See also page 34.

CALL The call of the Oriental Cuckoo is a 'du-du-du-du' which is repeated six or eight times.

REPRODUCTION From May to July lays its eggs mainly in nests of ground-nesting species, such as warblers and pipits. The coloration of the eggs is often similar to those of the host species and is extremely variable; egg size also varies a great deal. Further details on reproduction are lacking.

FOOD Insects and their larvae.

DISTRIBUTION AND MOVEMENTS Nests from eastern Europe across Siberia to Kamchatka, southwards to the Himalayas, Burma, southern China, Taiwan and Japan. Winters from Indonesia south to New Guinea, the Bismarck Archipelago, Australia and the Solomon Islands.

SUB-SPECIES *C. s. horsfieldi* (larger) nests in eastern Europe.

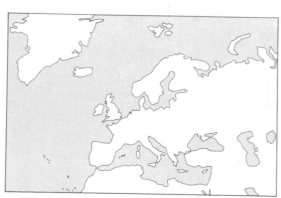

(Above) Adult Oriental Cuckoo (foreground) and juvenile. (Left) Breeding areas (yellow) of the Oriental Cuckoo

Great Spotted Cuckoo
Clamator glandarius

French: COUCOU-GEAI
Italian: CUCULO DAL CIUFFO
Spanish: CRIALO
German: HAEHERKUCKUCK

HABITAT Lives in bushy country with scattered trees, on edges of woods, olive-groves, savannahs and other lightly wooded areas.

IDENTIFICATION Length: 39 cm. Distinguishable by its thick crest and long grey tail with white edges. Plumage is brown with distinctive white spots above, cream below and at sides of head. Bright orange orbital ring. Both sexes alike. Juveniles have almost black head, smaller crest, and bright chestnut primaries: their underparts are buffer.

In flight, distinguished by long graduated tail, resembling Magpie's. Certain postures adopted by this cuckoo also resemble those of Magpies and the Magpie is often a host to this species. Flight is powerful and direct. See also page 34.

CALL Similar to a tern's: 'kittera-kittera-kittera'; also a high-pitched 'jree', and a crow-like 'cark' when alarmed. These harsh and noisy cries are frequently repeated.

REPRODUCTION End of April onwards. Parasitic on certain species of the family Corvidae, especially Magpies. Eggs are mimetic of the Magpie's. The eggs generally hatch before the host's, but the young cuckoo does not attempt to eject the host's own eggs from the nest. Fifteen or sixteen eggs may be laid, and there may be several Great Spotted Cuckoo and host fledglings in the host's nest.

FOOD Insects and their larvae.

DISTRIBUTION AND MOVEMENTS Southern Europe, Asia Minor, and Africa. Partially migratory: Palearctic breeders winter in tropical Africa. Accidental in northern Europe as far north as Britain, Ireland, Denmark and the USSR.

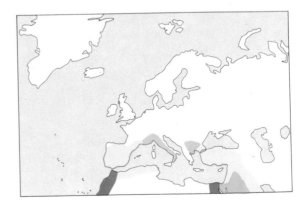

(Above) Adult Great Spotted Cuckoo (foreground) and juvenile. (Right) Breeding areas (yellow), wintering areas (magenta), areas where the Great Spotted Cuckoo may be seen all year round (orange) and on passage (pink)

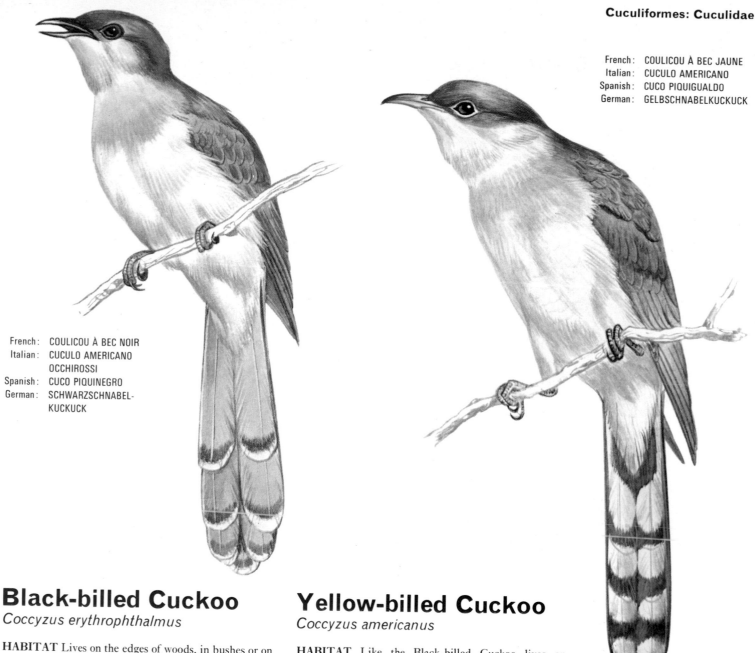

French: COULICOU À BEC JAUNE
Italian: CUCULO AMERICANO
Spanish: CUCO PIQUIGUALDO
German: GELBSCHNABELKUCKUCK

French: COULICOU À BEC NOIR
Italian: CUCULO AMERICANO
         OCCHIROSSI
Spanish: CUCO PIQUINEGRO
German: SCHWARZSCHNABEL-
        KUCKUCK

Black-billed Cuckoo
Coccyzus erythrophthalmus

HABITAT Lives on the edges of woods, in bushes or on cultivated land.

IDENTIFICATION Length: 29 cm. Resembles Yellow-billed Cuckoo from which it can be distinguished by the absence of rufous coloration on its wings, the colour of its tail (no black and very little white), its black bill and its red eyelids. Spots on tail also smaller.

CALL Song is similar to the Yellow-billed Cuckoo's but with more babbling notes.

REPRODUCTION From mid-May to July. Builds its own nest, like the Yellow-billed Cuckoo, of twigs and roots. The nest is lined with soft plant matter. It lays from two to seven marbled, blue-green eggs. Incubation is carried out by both sexes.

FOOD Insects and their larvae.

DISTRIBUTION AND MOVEMENTS Breeds in North America from southern Canada to the southern United States. Winters in South America as far south as Peru. The Black-billed Cuckoo is accidental in France, Italy, Britain and Germany.

Yellow-billed Cuckoo
Coccyzus americanus

HABITAT Like the Black-billed Cuckoo lives on cultivated land and by the edges of woods.

IDENTIFICATION Length: 30 cm. Resembles the Cuckoo but is smaller and more elongated. The yellow lower mandible, the rufous feathers on its wings and its black tail feathers with bold white spots are distinctive features.

CALL A very rapid, guttural sound which decreases in volume: 'kay-kay-kay-kay-kay-cow-cow-cow-cow'.

REPRODUCTION Late June to early July. Builds a grass and moss-lined nest of twigs on the branches of trees. Lays three or four blue-green eggs. Incubation is carried out mainly by the female for about fourteen days.

FOOD Insects and their larvae: berries in the autumn.

DISTRIBUTION AND MOVEMENTS Breeds in North and Central America and winters in South America. Accidental in Iceland, Britain, Ireland, Denmark, France, Italy and Belgium.

SUB-SPECIES Sub-species are present in America.

(Above) Black-billed Cuckoo (left) and Yellow-billed Cuckoo

Cuckoos in flight

1: **CUCKOO** *(Cuculus canorus)* Female Cuckoos have two colour phases while males have only one. In the grey phase (a), the upper parts are a fairly uniform grey which is slightly paler on the back (especially the rump which contrasts with the dark, graduated tail). The underparts are barred and it resembles a Sparrowhawk. This would appear to help the female by enabling her to frighten the owners of the nest where she intends to lay her eggs. In the reddish phase the female looks more like a Kestrel than a Sparrowhawk, with analogous advantages. Figure (b) shows a juvenile cuckoo during the reddish phase in which it resembles the female though its rump is conspicuously orange-brown. Figure (c) shows one of the positions in flight and (d) shows an adult seen from below. The low-wing flight of the Cuckoo, in which the wings are not raised above the horizontal plane is distinctive.

The Oriental Cuckoo *Cuculus saturatus* is so similar to the Cuckoo that a flight illustration would be virtually identical to the Cuckoo's. The Oriental Cuckoo is slightly smaller and differences in barring can only be detected by direct comparison and vary from one individual to another. These two species can best be distinguished by their different calls.

2: **GREAT SPOTTED CUCKOO** *(Clamator glandarius)* Its shape is typical of a cuckoo but the tail is much longer and the general appearance more streamlined than the Cuckoo's. Juveniles (a) can be easily recognized by their black hoods and the reddish-brown marking on their wings. These characteristics are lacking in adults (b) and the coloration of their upper parts is generally more uniform; in fact even their heads are grey. In flight the white spots on the feathers are less conspicuous. Figure (c) shows an adult seen from below; juveniles lack the marking at the end of the tail.

3: **YELLOW-BILLED CUCKOO** *(Coccyzus americanus)* Although it resembles the Cuckoo, it may be identified by its smaller size and by the lack of bars on its underparts. In flight its yellow bill is not always clearly visible, which makes it difficult to distinguish from the Black-billed Cuckoo—another transatlantic vagrant to Europe. Seen from above (a) the Yellow-billed Cuckoo can be recognized by the reddish flash on its open wings. Seen from below (b) the distinction between it and the following species is easier because of the characteristic pattern of white markings on its tail feathers and by its generally paler coloration.

4: **BLACK-BILLED CUCKOO** *(Coccyzus erythrophthalmus* It is easiest to identify from below when its much more uniform tail pattern can be seen. Figure (a) shows the bird from above and (b) shows it from below when it is easily distinguishable from the Yellow-billed Cuckoo because of its more uniform tail. Less rufous coloration on wings than Yellow-billed Cuckoo. As indicated by the English name, the bill is all black.

(Below) Cuckoo
Cuculus canorus

ORDER Strigiformes
FAMILY **TYTONIDAE: Barn Owls**

D. Middleton/Bruce Coleman

The order Strigiformes—or nocturnal birds of prey as owls are sometimes called—consists of a group of species with fairly well-defined characteristics. They are sometimes included in a single family—the Strigidae—but this classification is not universally accepted. In this encyclopedia the barn owls (and bay owls) are kept separate as they are distinct in terms of morphology although their anatomical differences (which are mainly to do with bone structure and so forth) are negligible.

The eleven or twelve currently recognized species in the family Tytonidae range in length from 30 to 54 centimetres. They have soft plumage, often with a dark and a light phase in the same species. The coloration of the upper parts varies from brown with white speckles to grey-brown or rufous-orange with grey-brown and white spots and fine, wavy markings. The underparts may be buff, grey-brown or uniform white, speckled, barred or covered with fine, wavy white, grey or brown markings. Their facial discs (characteristic formations of the facial feathers which are found throughout the order) are elongated and heart-shaped and may be white, grey or rufous-coloured. The long, hooked bills are almost hidden by the semi-stiff, thread-like feathers of the facial discs. The tails are comparatively short and generally barred like the wings. The legs are fairly long with the tarsi completely or almost completely covered with short feathers; the strong toes have a fine coating of 'fur'. And the outer toe is reversible—it can be turned outwards and backwards. Barn owls' claws are strong and hooked; the claw on the middle toe is pectinated on the inside. The eyes are relatively small and the irises are black in spite of the nocturnal habits of these species.

The posture of barn owls, which is often erect, and their slender bodies gives them a characteristic appearance. Nine of the eleven species of the family Tytonidae are barn owls of the genus *Tyto*: the others are the so-called bay owls. Five species belong to the Australasian faunal region: three are exclusive to Australia and New Guinea—the Masked Owl *Tyto novaehollandiae*, the Sooty Owl *T. tenebricosa* and the New Britain Barn Owl *T. aurantia*. One species, the Grass Owl *T. capensis* is also distributed in southeast Asia and southern Africa. And the fifth, the common Barn Owl *T. alba*, is virtually cosmopolitan in distribution although it is not found in the northernmost regions of America and Eurasia or in some areas of Africa and Central America. Of the remaining species, the Madagascar Grass Owl *T. soumagnei* is limited to the island of Madagascar and the Minahassa Barn Owl *T. inexpectata* and Celebes Barn Owl *T. rosenbergii* are confined to the islands of the Celebes.

G. D. Plage/Bruce Coleman

H. Tomanek/Bruce Coleman

(Above) Barns Owls *Tyto alba*. (Below) World distribution of the family Tytonidae. (Preceding pages, 36-7) Barn Owls

The best known species however is undoubtedly the common Barn Owl which has been sub-divided into at least thirty-two sub-species within its vast distribution area, mainly on the basis of different coloration.

Bay owls are sometimes placed in a separate sub-family Phodilinae, and may be viewed as a link between barn owls and the other owls of the family Strigidae. However the heart-shaped pattern of their facial discs, the comparatively short tails, the pectinated claw on the middle toes and certain other characteristics justify their placement with the barn owls. Of the two species, only the Bay Owl *Phodilus badius* from southeast Asia and the Sunda Islands is well-known. There is only one recorded example of the second species, the Tanzanian Bay Owl *P. prigoginei* which was discovered in 1951 in mountain forests of the Congo region.

During the daytime barn owls remain hidden in barns, attics, among ruined building, in hollow tree-trunks and even in underground caves. It is easy to see them, especially on moonlit nights, as they fly around searching for food. Their diet consists mainly of small mammals (particularly rodents), small birds, insects, amphibians, shell-fish and also fish. They swallow their prey whole and, like many other predators, regurgitate the bones and other indigestible parts in the form of pellets. Their flight is quiet, due to the special structure of their outer flight feathers which reduces vibration caused by the movements of their wings. This structure is also found in the majority of birds of the family Strigidae.

Three to eleven eggs are laid per clutch: they are often laid over a considerable period of time. The female incubates the clutch for about a month or slightly longer and the male brings food to his mate who rarely leaves the nest. The nestlings are covered with white down when they hatch. This is soon replaced by a second downy plumage which is only later replaced by real feathers which grow from the same feather-bearing papilla or 'goose-pimples'.

Bay owls are strictly nocturnal forest-dwelling species which feed on small prey. Insects probably form the bulk of their diet. However their presence close to pools or rivers indicates that they may eat aquatic creatures as well.

Barn Owl
Tyto alba

HABITAT Lives in open and often arid country with scattered trees. Frequently nests in churches, barns and other old buildings.

IDENTIFICATION Length: 34 cm. Upper parts golden rufous colour with dense, small markings. White underparts and face: when seen from below in flight may appear all white. The dark-breasted race *T. a. guttata* is deep buff below and marked grey-blue above. When perching the large head and long legs are characteristic. Hunts at night but may also be seen during the day. Usually catches its prey on the ground.

The Barn Owl generally lives alone or in pairs. During courtship the male flaps its wings under its body as it flies. In defence posture it flattens itself on the ground with wings spread horizontally. When annoyed it lowers its head and arches its wings. See also page 58.

CALL A long eerie screech: also whistling and grunting notes.

REPRODUCTION From April onwards but may begin as early as February. Nests in old buildings, tree-trunks, crevices in rocks and in abandoned nests. The Barn Owl lays between four and seven smooth white eggs. Incubation is carried out by the female (who is brought food by the male) for about thirty-three days. The young are tended by both parents and are independent in about ten weeks.

FOOD Small rodents and birds.

DISTRIBUTION AND MOVEMENTS Europe, Asia Minor and southern Asia, Africa, North, Central and South America and Australia. Mainly sedentary although northern populations may migrate southwards. Is a widely distributed resident breeder in Britain and Ireland. *T. a. guttata* occurs as a scarce visitor.

SUB-SPECIES *T. a. alba*: Britain and Ireland, western and southwest Europe and the Mediterranean region. *T. a. ernesti* (paler): Corsica and Sardinia. *T. a. guttata* (darker): the rest of Europe. Other sub-species are present in the Americas, Asia and Africa.

French: CHOUETTE EFFRAIE
Italian: BARBAGIANNI
Spanish: LECHUZA COMÚN
German: SCHLEIEREULE

(Above) Dark colour form of the Barn Owl (foreground) and paler form. (Left) Areas where the Barn Owl may be seen all year round (orange). (Overleaf) Barn Owl with prey.

M. Barnfather/Bruce Coleman

R. Allin/Bruce Coleman

G. Hansson

All nocturnal birds of prey belong to the family Strigidae except for the barn owls and bay owls of the family Tytonidae. In practice both families are the night-flying equivalents of species of the order Falconiformes whose predatory role they take over when night falls. Yet contrary to popular belief, the majority of the one hundred and twenty-five species of the family Strigidae can see perfectly well in daylight. There are species which hunt readily during the day and night—several pygmy owls of the genus *Glaucidium*—and others, such as the Hawk Owl *Surnia ulula*, which only hunt in daylight.

Owls may be as small as sparrows or as large as eagles; they appear rotund, with large heads and rather short tails. The eyes are situated at the front of the head and are surrounded by characteristic facial discs which are formed by the distinctive arrangement of the facial feathers. The hooked bills are turned down and are usually covered by the feathers of their facial discs which meet between the eyes. The nostrils are surrounded by soft tissue (the cere) like those of day-flying birds of prey. The ear-tufts which are present in a few species do not represent true ears. The outer toe is reversible but is nearly always turned sideways rather than back.

Although the coloration of owls' plumage is highly variable—a shade of brown or white with darker markings—it nearly always provides camouflage and makes them practically invisible in day-

S. C. Porter/Bruce Coleman

light in the places where they shelter. As a rule the sexes are alike although the females are usually larger: the female often has more dark bars on her upper parts.

The retina of an owl's eye contains an extremely large number of cells. The majority of these cells are rods, and they are the cells which give black and white or night vision. However, it has been ascertained that certain species which are also active during the day can also perceive colour. The frontal position of their eyes (which have limited scope for independent movement unlike those of most other birds) gives them precise stereoscopic vision but only in a limited visual field. However, the limited mobility of owls' eyes is largely compensated for by the extreme mobility of their heads. Their hearing is highly developed and this enables them to locate their prey even in almost complete darkness. This has been demonstrated in various species including the Barn Owl *Tyto alba*. The ears of several species are placed asymmetrically on their heads, and experiments have shown that by

having their ears on different levels these birds hear stereophonically. This enables them to locate the exact distance and direction from which the sounds come.

In order to approach their victims without being heard owls fly very quietly, this quiet flight being facilitated by their exceptionally soft flight feathers and the pectinated border of the outer flight feathers. This adaption is lacking in the few species which feed almost exclusively on fish or other forms of aquatic life.

Most nocturnal birds of prey are tree-dwellers, but some species live on open ground, among rocks, in marshes or in deserts where tall cacti grow. There are underground-dwelling species in both families, such as the Burrowing Owl *Speotyto cunicularia* of the North American prairies which lives in burrows with prairie dogs.

Most of the one hundred and twenty-five species of the family Strigidae are sedentary and solitary, and only a very few are truly migrant. The Scops Owl *Otus scops* from Europe, the Oriental Hawk Owl *Ninox scutulata* from Asia and the Short-eared Owl *Asio flammeus* from Eurasia and America are among the few which migrate.

The diet of owls appears to be exclusively animal and consists mainly of small mammals, particularly rodents. In fact owls provide a highly effective means of rodent control but unfortunately this is not wholly appreciated, especially in shooting

(Facing page) Tengmalm's Owl *Aegolius funereus* peers from a tree hole (left) and (right) Little Owl *Athene noctua*. (Preceding page) Snowy Owl *Nyctea scandiaca*: its huge size and predominantly white plumage make it easy to identify

(Left) Eagle Owl *Bubo bubo*. (Below and below left) Short-eared Owl *Asio flammeus*: it is the only medium-sized brown owl which is likely to be seen in the day. (Bottom) Hawk Owl *Surnia ulula*: its long tail and hawk-like appearance are distinctive

estates on the continent where the wholesale slaughter of both day-flying and nocturnal birds of prey still continues. Many people are convinced that owls are harmful to game whereas the reverse is true.

The majority of owls of the family Strigidae have no fixed nesting season but nest when food is most abundant. The populations of many species of rodent are known to fluctuate cyclically and the nesting habits of many owls are tied to these cycles. When the rodents are plentiful, the owls are able to rear many more young than when their prey is scarce; indeed if the rodent populations drop below a certain level owls may not nest at all. When

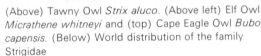

(Above) Tawny Owl *Strix aluco*. (Above left) Elf Owl *Micrathene whitneyi* and (top) Cape Eagle Owl *Bubo capensis*. (Below) World distribution of the family Strigidae

there is an abundance of rodents, some owls such as the Short-eared Owl *Asio flammeus* and the Snowy Owl *Nyctea scandiaca* literally invade territories outside their normal habitat in pursuit of hordes of voles or lemmings.

Owls usually borrow the nests of other species or lay their eggs in holes in tree trunks, in cavities among rocks or on the ground. They also nest in structures such as old buildings, the roofs of farmhouses and towers. As a rule only the female incubates the eggs but both parents rear the young. The chicks hatch with soft downy plumage which is often barred or marked. This quickly gives way to a second coat of semi-plume feathers which are later replaced by proper feathers.

There are about twenty-five genera in the family Strigidae which are widely distributed through many areas of the world, with the exception of the polar regions. Some species are found in a number of desert regions, sometimes in the form of very light coloured sub-species. The Elf Owl *Micrathene whitneyi* nests in cavities in giant cacti in Central America and in the more arid central regions of North America.

Among the Holarctic species is the Hawk Owl *Surnia ulula* which is predominantly day-flying and looks more like a falcon than an owl because of its long tail and fairly slender wings. Among the largest species is the Eagle Owl *Bubo bubo* which is widely distributed in North Africa and Eurasia but is disappearing from an increasingly large number of places because it is so extensively hunted and its habitat is being destroyed.

D. Sudia/Photo Researchers

(Above) Barred Owl *Strix varia* from North and Central America. (Left) Tawny Owl *S. aluco* at its tree-hole nest

B. Bevan/Ardea

French: CHOUETTE HARFANG
Italian: GUFO DELLE NEVI
Spanish: BÚHO NIVAL
German: SCHNEE-EULE

Snowy Owl
Nyctea scandiaca

(Above) Male Snowy Owl
(foreground) and female.
(Right) Wintering areas
(magenta) and areas where the
Snowy Owl may be seen all
year round (orange)

HABITAT Nests on tundra and northern moorlands. In winter frequents dunes, marshes and coasts.

IDENTIFICATION Length: 52–65 cm. Large size and mainly snow-white plumage make it unmistakable. Female has more blackish bars on upper parts than the male.

Flight more like a buzzard's than an owl's: often glides. Usually perches on rocks or on high vantage points from which it can survey its surroundings and locate its victims. See also page 58.

CALL During the breeding season emits a loud 'crow-ow' or a repeated 'reek'.

REPRODUCTION Nesting season ranges from mid-April to May or June, depending on the latitude. Nests on the ground in a hollow scrape which is sometimes lined with moss and feathers. Nest is usually sited on a raised area, occasionally on a boulder or crag. The Snowy Owl lays from four to ten white eggs on alternate days. May lay up to fifteen eggs but size of the clutch is dependent on the food supply. Incubation is carried out by the female, who is fed by the male, and takes thirty-two or thirty-three days.

FOOD Mainly lemmings and birds about the size of an Oystercatcher (including geese, ducks and gulls). Also consumes rabbits, mice and other rodents.

DISTRIBUTION AND MOVEMENTS The arctic: breeding distribution circumpolar from Novaya Zemlya, arctic islands of Canada, Greenland, Eurasia and Bering Sea islands. The Snowy Owl sometimes travels south to the United States, the Jan Mayen Islands, Iceland, Britain and Ireland, Scandinavia, central Europe and Asia. However these are irregular or eruptive movements which are related to food supply. In Britain the Snowy Owl is an irregular visitor mainly in winter, chiefly to the Scottish Highlands and the Shetlands. Also a scarce visitor to Ireland. A pair bred successfully in the Shetlands from 1967 to 1975. However in general the Snowy Owl has occurred less frequently in this century than in the nineteenth century.

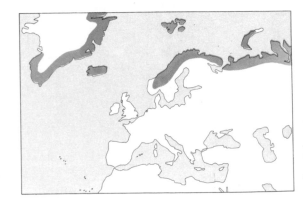

Eagle Owl
Bubo bubo

French: HIBOU GRAND-DUC
Italian: GUFO REALE
Spanish: BÚHO REAL
German: UHU

HABITAT Lives in a wide range of habitats including dense forests, also rocky areas, on mountainsides and in deserts.

IDENTIFICATION Length: 65–70 cm. Along with the Snowy Owl is one of the largest owls present in Europe—almost the size of an eagle. Its large ear tufts make it easily recognisable and, along with the facial disc distinguish it from diurnal birds of prey. Rufous-brown upper parts with dark brown markings; rufous breast with broad streaks; large orange eyes.

Lives alone and hunts at dawn and dusk, capturing prey the size of a Capercaillie. During the day sleeps in hollow trees or fissures in rocks or else roosts on branches close to the trunk. Slow, silent flight. See also page 58.

CALL A short, deep 'oo-oo-oo' and a strident 'kvek-kvek'.

REPRODUCTION From mid-March to May. It does not build a nest but lays its eggs in a shallow unlined scrape, on ledges of crags or cliffs or sometimes in hollow tree trunks or other birds' abandoned nests. It lays two or three oval white eggs. Incubation begins after the first egg has been laid and takes between thirty-four and thirty-six days: the female alone incubates the eggs. The male brings food to the nest. The young birds leave the nest after five weeks but do not fly well until about fourteen weeks of age.

FOOD Mammals such as mice, and rabbits, birds (including other owls), lizards, frogs, fish and large insects.

DISTRIBUTION AND MOVEMENTS Breeds from Scandinavia, France, Germany and Iberia east across Eurasia and south to the southern Sahara in Africa, Arabia and southern India. Mainly sedentary, and has decreased in numbers over much of its range. The few British records may all be erroneous or refer to escapes from captivity.

SUB-SPECIES *B.b. bubo*: continental Europe. *B.b. hispanus* (paler): the Iberian Peninsula. *B.b. ruthenus* (paler and greyer): eastern Russia. *B.b. interpositus* (darker than *B.b. ruthenus*, more yellowish): southern Ukraine, the Crimea and the Caucasus. There are other sub-species in Asia and Africa.

(Below) Areas where the Eagle Owl may be seen all year round (orange)

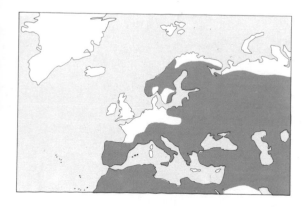

French: HIBOU MOYEN-DUC
Italian: GUFO COMUNE
Spanish: BÚHO CHICO
German: WALDOHREULE

Long-eared Owl
Asio otus

HABITAT Prefers coniferous forests, but it also inhabits areas with scattered trees, heaths and marshland. Also occasionally found in larger gardens.

IDENTIFICATION Length: 35 cm. A medium-sized brown owl like the Tawny Owl but differs in being smaller and in having very conspicuous ear-tufts. Face is thinner and more elongated than that of the Short-eared or Tawny Owls. Eyes are orange-yellow rather than black as in the Tawny Owl. Wings are long, and lacks the Short-eared Owl's dark patch on the upper wing. See also page 58.

CALL A deep and more mournful 'oo-oo-oo' than the hoot of the Tawny Owl.

REPRODUCTION March–April. It usually nests in the abandoned nests of other birds, squirrels' nests and rarely on the ground under a tree or vegetation. It lays four or five oval white eggs: when food is abundant there may be two broods. Incubation takes twenty-seven or twenty-eight days. The female alone incubates the eggs and feeds the fledglings with food brought by the male.

FOOD Small mammals, birds and insects.

DISTRIBUTION AND MOVEMENTS Breeds in central Asia, northwest Africa and North America. Partially migratory: travels south to northern Egypt, northern India and Mexico. In Britain is a resident breeder distributed widely although sparsely in Scotland and northern England. Breeds locally elsewhere in England and in Wales. Also occurs in Britain as a winter and passage visitor. Breeds throughout Ireland although it is rather thinly spread.

SUB-SPECIES Sub-species are present in the Canary Islands and North America.

(Left) Long-eared Owl. (Below) Breeding areas (yellow), wintering areas (magenta) and areas where the Long-eared Owl may be seen all year round (orange)

French: HIBOU DU CAP
Italian: GUFO DI PALUDE DEL CAPO
Spanish: LECHUZA MORA
German: KAPOHREULE

Brown Fish Owl
Ketupa zeylonensis

French: CHOUETTE PÊCHEUSE
BRUNE
Italian: GUFO PESCATORE
German: BRAUNFISCHEULE

HABITAT Forests, bushy vegetation and rocky areas by water.

IDENTIFICATION Length: 56 cm. Similar in size and coloration to the Eagle Owl but may be distinguished by shorter ear-tufts and unfeathered tarsi and feet. Rufous-brown coloration is more uniform than that of the Eagle Owl, and the coloration varies between geographical races. Orange-yellow iris is less striking than that of the Eagle Owl. Wings create noise in flight, unlike those of most other owls, because the outer margins of the primaries are not pectinated. Remains on the ground for long periods.

CALL A low long 'hoo-oo-oo'.

REPRODUCTION Begins in February and March. The nest consists of a platform or hollow in a tree formed by the joining of large branches. May also nest on ledges and in hollows in rocky outcrops. Does not build a true nest but may line the hollow with twigs. Both sexes incubate the eggs probably for about thirty-five days. Further information on breeding and nestlings is not available.

FOOD Mainly fish: generally fishes at night. Also reptiles, birds and large insects.

DISTRIBUTION AND MOVEMENTS Southern Asia, from Turkey east to China and north as far as the Sakhalin Islands and the coastal regions of eastern Siberia.

SUB-SPECIES Sub-species are present in Asia.

African Marsh Owl
Asio capensis

HABITAT Open areas, especially damp meadowland, swamps and marshes.

IDENTIFICATION Length: 30 cm. Smaller than Short-eared Owl and plumage darker and more uniform. Upper parts and upper breast dark brown and its under-parts are white with buff markings. Eyes brown. Its head is lightly barred and its wings and tail are barred. Black bill and legs. The coloration of juveniles is warmer and richer than that of adults.
The African Marsh Owl is a sociable bird which is rarely seen on its own and tends to form small groups. Prefers to hunt at dusk and may be seen quartering the ground like a harrier.

CALL A hoarse 'craw-ak' reminiscent of the cry of a crow.

REPRODUCTION April onwards. Nest is a shallow unlined hollow in the ground, under low vegetation or bushes. Lays two to four smooth white eggs. Incubation takes about thirty days, and both parents care for the young.

FOOD Mainly large insects; also eats scorpions, frogs and lizards.

DISTRIBUTION AND MOVEMENTS An essentially African species present especially in western regions south of the Sahara, and from Ethiopia to the Cape. It is believed to have nested in southern Spain and is also present as a resident breeder in coastal regions of northwest Morocco.

SUB-SPECIES The sub-species *A.c. tingitanus* is occasionally found during the autumn in Portugal and southern Spain; it nests from northern and central Morocco to northern Algeria. The nominate sub-species *A.c. capensis* occurs from Ethiopia to Cape Province and *A.c. hova* is found in Madagascar.

(Facing page, bottom) African Marsh Owl. (Above) Brown Fish Owl. (Overleaf, pages 50–51) Long-eared Owl *Asio otus* feeding its young

Ardea/Sdim

Short-eared Owl
Asio flammeus

HABITAT Open plains and moorland; also heaths, marshes and dunes.

IDENTIFICATION Length: 37 cm. Is the medium-sized brown owl most likely to be seen in the day. Light rufous plumage with large streaks on its underparts and barred wings. Its clearly defined brown facial disc is darker round the eyes. Ear-tufts difficult to see in the field. Wings very long: has a soaring flight like a harrier besides the normal slow and flapping flight typical of owls. See also page 58.

CALL Emits a harsh barking note in flight; also a deep triple 'hoot'.

REPRODUCTION Late April onwards. Nest is a shallow unlined hollow in the ground. Lays from four to eight white eggs: may lay up to fourteen eggs and have a second brood when food is plentiful. The female incubates the eggs and tends the young.

FOOD Small mammals, birds and insects.

DISTRIBUTION AND MOVEMENTS Wide breeding distribution: Europe, Asia and the Americas. Northern populations migrate south to northern Africa, southern Asia and Guatemala. In Britain it is a resident and migratory breeder, some British birds migrating south and west within Britain. Breeds in Scotland and northern England, locally in north Wales and eastern England. Irregular elsewhere. Has also bred occasionally in Ireland. Occurs as a passage and winter visitor in both countries.

SUB-SPECIES Sub-species are present in South and Central America and in the Pacific islands.

(Facing page, top) Short-eared Owl. (Right) Breeding areas (yellow), wintering areas (magenta) and areas where the Short-eared Owl may be seen all year round (orange)

French: HIBOU PETIT-DUC
Italian: ASSIOLO
Spanish: AUTILLO
German: ZWERGOHREULE

Scops Owl
Otus scops

HABITAT Open woodland, orchards, parks and farmland. Also present in villages and small towns.

IDENTIFICATION Length: 19 cm. Its small size, small ear-tufts and its delicately coloured grey-brown plumage with fine wavy markings are distinctive characteristics. The toes are unfeathered. It often appears slimmer and more elongated than other owls. See also page 58.

CALL A monotonous 'piu' which is insistently repeated.

REPRODUCTION Late April to mid-June. Nest is an unlined cavity in a tree, wall or building. May also use the old nest of another bird. Eggs: usually lays four or five smooth and slightly glossy white eggs. The female alone incubates the eggs for about twenty-four days and tends the young on food brought by the male. The young leave the nest after about three weeks.

FOOD Mainly insects.

DISTRIBUTION AND MOVEMENTS Central southern Europe, Africa and Asia. Partially migratory: European populations winter south to tropical Africa. Accidental in northern Europe including Britain and Ireland where it is a very scarce visitor mainly in spring.

SUB-SPECIES Sub-species are present in Iberia and in Asia.

(Right) Breeding areas (yellow), wintering areas (magenta), areas where the Scops Owl may be seen all year round (orange) and on passage (pink)

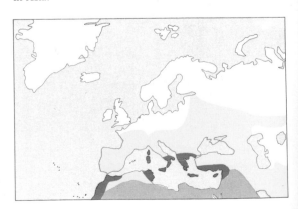

French: HIBOU DES MARAIS
Italian: GUFO DI PALUDE
Spanish: LECHUZA CAMPESTRE
German: SUMPFOHREULE

French: CHOUETTE CHEVÊCHE
Italian: CIVETTA
Spanish: MOCHUELO COMÚN
German: STEINKAUZ

Little Owl
Athene noctua

HABITAT Usually open country, woodland with scattered trees, farmland and dunes. Also present in semi-desert and rocky areas.

IDENTIFICATION Length: 21 cm. Due to its diurnal habits it is one of the most familiar small owls of Europe. Head noticeably flattened. Brown upper parts with white bars and speckles. Underparts off-white with dark streaks. Often perches on posts and other positions which serve as good look-outs. Flight is bounding and light: hovers searching for insects at dusk. See also page 62.

CALL A 'koo-koo-yoo' which is generally uttered in the daytime.

FOOD Small rodents, small birds, reptiles, insects and earthworms.

REPRODUCTION Mid-April onwards. Nest is an unlined cavity in a tree or building or a crevice in a cliff. May also nest in a burrow in the ground or in the old nest of another bird. Usually lays three to five white eggs (occasionally as many as eight). The female alone incubates the eggs for about twenty-nine days, although both parents tend the young.

DISTRIBUTION AND MOVEMENTS Breeds from western Europe and North Africa east to China. Mainly sedentary. Introduced to Britain (and New Zealand) in the late nineteenth century and is now a widespread breeder in England and Wales, also less commonly in southern Scotland. Only occurs as a vagrant in Ireland.

SUB-SPECIES *A.n. noctua*: central and western Russia and central southern Europe. *A.n. vidalii*: western Europe. *A.n. indigena*: southeast Europe. Other sub-species are present in Africa and Asia.

(Below right) Areas where the Little Owl may be seen all year round (orange)

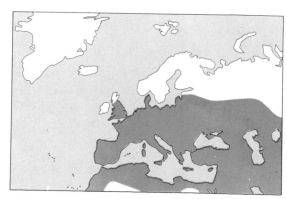

Tengmalm's Owl
Aegolius funereus

HABITAT Usually coniferous forests; also found in mixed forests in some areas.

IDENTIFICATION Length: 25 cm. Resembles the Little Owl, but slightly bigger and with brown rather than grey-brown coloration. Its head is much rounder and it has a darker facial disc (which is not flattened on the eyes as it is in the Little Owl) and broad white supercilia. Its legs and feet are covered with long white feathers. Its underparts are speckled with white, not streaked as in the

Little Owl. Immatures are chocolate brown with a few white markings. In repose it is more erect than the Little Owl; its flight is more like the Long Eared Owl's, though its wingbeats are quicker. It is only active at night (except in arctic regions). During nuptial flight it sings as it hovers over the treetops. See also page 62.

CALL Its song is distinctive, consisting of a series of rapid hoots—'hoo-hoo-hoo'—often rising and falling in volume, almost like a trill.

REPRODUCTION Mid-April. It nests in cavities in trees, either natural holes or those made by woodpeckers. It lays between three and six finely pitted white eggs. Incubation takes twenty-five days and is probably carried out by the female alone.

FOOD Small mammals and birds. Occasionally frogs and sometimes insects.

DISTRIBUTION AND MOVEMENTS Breeds in Scandinavia east across the USSR. Also breeds in central Europe and in North America. Mainly sedentary. In Britain is an accidental visitor chiefly to Scotland and eastern England.

SUB-SPECIES *A.f. caucasiaus* (darker): northern Caucasus region. Other sub-species are present in Asia and North America.

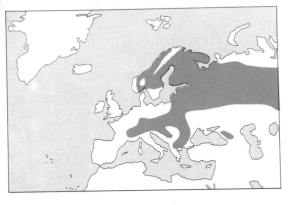

French: CHOUETTE DE TENGMALM
Italian: CIVETTA CAPOGROSSO
Spanish: LECHUZA DE TENGMALM
German: RAUHFUSSKAUZ

(Above) Areas where Tengmalm's Owl may be seen all year round (orange)

Hawk Owl
Surnia ulula

HABITAT Coniferous forests and birch woods in mountainous areas: also present on tundra.

IDENTIFICATION Length: 35–40 cm. Pale facial disc edged black make it (along with the long tail) easily recognisable. Upper parts are speckled and barred with dark and white coloration; white underparts with dense black bars. Whitish face with black border. Long tail is distinctive. In appearance and behaviour is the most hawk-like of the owls. Wings more short and pointed than other owls'. Seen mainly during the day and often searches for its prey from a prominent perch such as a conifer. See also page 62.

CALL Emits a 'kee-kee-kee-kee' rather like the cry of a falcon.

REPRODUCTION Usually April-May. Nests in holes in trees or in the old nests of other birds. Lays from three to four white eggs, depending on the food supply. Both male and female incubate the eggs for twenty-five to thirty days although the female takes the larger part. Both tend the young.

FOOD Small mammals and birds and will occasionally also consume some insects.

DISTRIBUTION AND MOVEMENTS Northern Europe, northern Asia as far as the Kamchatka Peninsula, the northern United States and western Canada. Partially migratory—also irruptive—sometimes reaching as far south as central Europe. In Britain is a very rare vagrant.

SUB-SPECIES Sub-species are present in Asia and North America.

(Facing page bottom) Hawk Owl. (Right) Areas where the Hawk Owl may be seen all year round (orange)

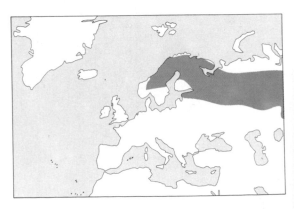

French: CHOUETTE HULOTTE
Italian: ALLOCCO
Spanish: CÁRABO
German: WALDKAUZ

French: CHOUETTE ÉPERVIÈRE
Italian: ULULA
Spanish: LECHUZA GAVILANA
German: SPERBEREULE

Tawny Owl
Strix aluco

HABITAT Open woodland (mainly deciduous) and parks. Also present in large gardens and in urban areas.

IDENTIFICATION Length: 38 cm. Is the most common medium-sized brown owl in Europe. May be distinguished from the Barn Owl by its darker brown face, densely speckled mantle and dark underparts. May be distinguished from the Long and Short-eared Owls by the absence of ear-tufts and its black eyes: also larger and stouter. Wings appear more rounded and shorter in flight than those of other owls.
   Mainly nocturnal in habits, and in the daytime may be seen roosting huddled up in a tree. Juvenile plumage is barred. See also page 62.

CALL Most well-known note is a long wavering 'hoot'. Also emits a sharp 'ke-wick'.

REPRODUCTION Usually from late March onwards. Nest is a hole in a tree, rarely in the ground or in a crevice in rocks. Also uses the old nest of other birds or a squirrel's nest. May occasionally nest in nest boxes and on rocks or the ledges of buildings. Eggs: from two to four (sometimes one to seven) white eggs are laid. The female alone incubates the eggs for about twenty-eight to thirty days. The female tends the young while the male brings food, but after about twenty days both hunt. The young leave the nest after about thirty-five days.

FOOD Mainly small birds and rodents.

DISTRIBUTION AND MOVEMENTS Breeds from western Europe and northwest Africa across Europe and Asia to southern China and south to southern Iran and the Himalayas. Sedentary. In Britain is a widely distributed resident breeder on the mainland. Absent from the Isle of Man, Orkney, Shetland and many Hebridean islands. Does not occur in Ireland even as a vagrant.

SUB-SPECIES *S.a. aluco*: continental Europe (except for areas where *S.a. sylvatica* is found) and Sicily. *S.a. sylvatica*: Britain, southwest France and the southern part of the Iberian Peninsula. *S.a. siberiae* (paler and greyer): the Urals and western Siberia. *S.a. willkonskii* (darker): the Caucasus. There are other sub-species in northwest Africa and Asia.

(Top) Tawny Owl. (Below) Areas where the Tawny Owl may be seen all year round (orange)

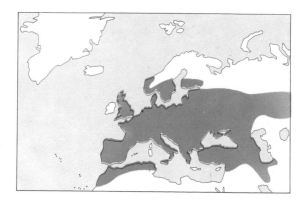

Strigiformes: Strigidae

French: CHOUETTE DE L'OURAL
Italian: ALLOCCO DEGLI URALI
Spanish: CÁRABO URALENSE
German: HABICHTSKAUZ

French: CHOUETTE LAPONE
Italian: ALLOCCO DI LAPPONIA
Spanish: CÁRABO LAPÓN
German: BARTKAUZ

(Above) Ural Owl and (above right) Great Grey Owl. (Right) Areas where the Ural Owl may be seen all year round (orange) and (far right) areas where the Great Grey Owl may be seen all year round (orange)

56

Ural Owl
Strix uralensis

HABITAT Mixed or coniferous forests, taiga and forests or partially wooded areas in mountainous regions.

IDENTIFICATION Length: 56 cm. A large owl with a long tail and dark eyes. It lacks ear-tufts. Resembles the Tawny Owl, but paler (almost buff), with large blackish streaks running down its underparts and broad bars on its wings and tail. Whitish grey facial disc without any distinguishing characteristics. It could be mistaken for the Great Grey Owl, though the latter is greyer, with dark concentric circles on its facial disc and a yellow rather than dark iris. Distinguished from pale colour forms of Tawny Owl by larger size and longer tail. See also page 62.

CALL A sharp, baying 'oo-ow-oo-ow-oo-ow' emitted at regular intervals and a harsh 'ko-vek'.

REPRODUCTION March onwards. It nests in tree cavities or sometimes on the ground or in abandoned birds' nests. Three or four white eggs are laid. Incubation and the rearing of the young each take about a month: the female alone incubates. As with most owls, incubation begins when the first egg is laid and consequently the chicks hatch at different dates and vary in size.

FOOD Mainly rodents: also birds and insects during the summer months.

DISTRIBUTION AND MOVEMENTS Northern Europe and northern Asia eastwards as far as Japan. There are isolated populations in the Balkans.

SUB-SPECIES *S.u. liturata* occurs almost everywhere in Europe; the nominate sub-species is present in the USSR and is found east of Moscow as far as the Urals and western Siberia. Other sub-species are present in Asia.

Great Grey Owl
Strix nebulosa

HABITAT Length: 57 cm. Almost as large as the Eagle Owl from which it can easily be distinguished by its grey plumage, its longer tail, large round head, the absence of ear tufts and the yellow rather than orange iris. Its dirty grey plumage is covered with irregular white and blackish markings on the upper parts and wide, dark streaks on the underparts. Its large facial disc is clearly marked with dark concentric rings; conspicuous dark patch on its chin. A light band across the base of the primaries is visible in flight. See also page 62.

CALL A low 'hoo-hoo-hoo' repeated at regular intervals, similar to that of the Tawny Owl but deeper.

REPRODUCTION Mid-April onwards. Its nest is generally situated on the top of broken off tree trunks although it often uses the abandoned nests of other large birds. It lays from three to five eggs, but nesting may not occur at all in unfavourable years when food is scarce. Its dirty white, somewhat elongated eggs are incubated for about a month by the female alone. She also tends the young and feeds them with food brought by the male.

FOOD Mainly small rodents such as voles and lemmings.

DISTRIBUTION AND MOVEMENTS Northern Eurasia and North America. It is predominantly a resident species with a tendency to travel nomadically from time to time, sometimes going north in the autumn and south in the winter. Cyclical fluctuations in the populations of its prey affect both its breeding habits and its distribution. When food is plentiful outside its normal range, it travels to these areas.

SUB-SPECIES The sub-species *S.n. lapponica* is present in Eurasia.

Pygmy Owl
Glaucidium passerinum

HABITAT Forests in hill districts and taiga.

IDENTIFICATION Length: 16 cm. It is the smallest European owl. Easily identified, not only because of its size, but also because of its small head and its long tail which is often held cocked like that of a flycatcher. Facial disc less well marked than that of other owls. Hunts by both day and night. See also page 62.

CALL A loud whistling 'kew-kew-keet-cheek'.

REPRODUCTION March-May. Lays from two to seven white and slightly glossy eggs. Incubation takes twenty-eight days and is undertaken by the female alone. She feeds the young on food brought by the male.

FOOD Small rodents and birds.

DISTRIBUTION AND MOVEMENTS Breeds from northern Europe across Russia and central Asia to the eastern shores of Siberia. There are isolated populations in the Pyrenees, the Alps, and mountainous areas of eastern Europe.

SUB-SPECIES A sub-species is present in Asia. The Pygmy Owl of North America is now regarded as a separate species.

(Below) Areas where the Pygmy Owl may be seen all year round (orange)

French: CHOUETTE CHEVÊCHETTE
Italian: CIVETTA NANA
Spanish: MOCHUELO CHICO
German: SPERLINGSKAUZ

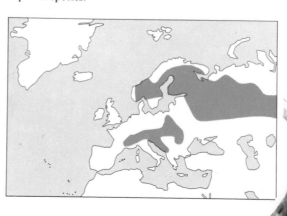

Owls in flight

1: **BARN OWL** *(Tyto alba)* The identification of this species presents few problems because of the generally sandy-orange coloration of its upper parts (the delicacy of the fine, wavy markings and speckles is not readily apparent in flight, especially when visibility is poor or at dead of night). It is the only nocturnal bird of prey with a white face, and its completely white underwing (which is even found in forms with dark underparts) is also distinctive. Can be distinguished in flight from the Tawny Owl by its longer wings.

2: **SNOWY OWL** *(Nyctea scandiaca)* A huge owl with predominantly white plumage. The male is very lightly speckled with black, while the female is much more heavily marked and appears grey from a distance. The Snowy Owl has very long wings. Flight resembles that of a buzzard rather than the typical slow and flapping flight of the large owls. Often glides in flight and frequently alights on the ground.

3: **EAGLE OWL** *(Bubo bubo)* One of the largest members of the family Strigidae. It is instantly recognizable because of its great size and prominent ear-tufts. Large orange eyes also distinctive. May be seen hunting at dawn and dusk.

4: **LONG-EARED OWL** *(Asio otus)* The long, erectile ear-tufts which are such a distinguishing feature when this species is perched, cannot be seen in flight because they are held down against its head feathers. It is a medium-sized, fairly pale owl with streaks on its underparts. The only species for which it could be mistaken is the Short-eared Owl, but all its bars and streaks are much lighter and less clearly defined, the proximal part of the trailing edge of its wing is greyish and its dark carpal patch is not followed by a pale marking. Seen from below, the overall appearance of its underwing is less white than the Short-eared Owl's. Hunts mainly over open country.

5: **SHORT-EARED OWL** *(Asio flammeus)* The only species with which it may be confused in flight is the Long-eared Owl but the Short-eared has clearly defined white markings on the coverts of its secondary and tertiary flight feathers, heavy barring on the latter and on its tail and a dark carpal patch which contrasts with a pale marking at the base of the primaries. The iris is yellow and the ear-tufts are much less conspicuous than those of the Long-eared Owl. Wings are markedly long, and it wheels, soars and glides in flight like a harrier. Also has the more typical slow and flapping flight of an owl.

6: **SCOPS OWL** *(Otus scops)* A small owl, similar to the Little Owl but with a more slender build, narrower head and ear-tufts which are not always erect. Wings are comparatively narrow and its flight is less bounding and not as quick as that of the Little Owl.

(Below) Long-eared Owl *Asio otus* alighting with prey for its young. (Overleaf, page 60) Tawny Owls *Strix aluco*

Werner Curth/Ardea

einhard/ZFAG

(Left) Snowy Owl *Nyctea scandiaca* and (below) young Great Horned Owls *Bubo virginianus:* this species takes the place of the Eurasian Eagle Owl *B. bubo* in the New World

7: GREAT GREY OWL *(Strix nebulosa)* Huge size, the large, barred head and pale markings on the wing like a speculum, and the black on the chin are characteristics which make this species easy to identify. The concentric dark rings around the yellow eye are also distinctive. Often hunts by day.

8: URAL OWL *(Strix uralensis)* In size only slightly smaller than the Great Grey Owl. Long tail and pale coloration are conspicuous and distinguish it from the Great Grey Owl and from pale forms of the Tawny Owl. Further distinguishing features are the pale, streaked back, barred tail, white 'epaulettes', light patch on the fold of the wing and regular, heavy barring on the flight feathers. Often hunts by day—feeds on mammals up to the size of a squirrel and on birds up to about 35 centimetres in length.

9: PYGMY OWL *(Glaucidium passerinum)* The smallest species of owl in Europe and fairly active even during the day. When seen in a good light, resembles a miniature Little Owl, with conspicuous white markings on the fold of the wing and on the primaries. Smaller head and less well marked facial disc are also good field characteristics.

10: TENGMALM'S OWL *(Aegolius funereus)* Generally similar to Little Owl, but with browner and more distinct coloration. The tail is spotted, not barred like the

Little Owl's. Black edge of facial disc and broad white eyebrows give Tengmalm's Owl a distinct facial expression—as if it is perpetually somewhat surprised. In contrast the Little Owl appears to be frowning.

11: LITTLE OWL *(Athene noctua)* One of the most common species of owl in much of Europe and also one of the species most often associated with man. Small to medium size, dull brown upper parts, the pattern of spotting and barring (visible mainly on the wings) and short tail are characteristic of the Little Owl. Easily identified in flight by its conspicuous up and down bounding motion.

12: HAWK OWL *(Surnia ulula)* On the wing and due to the tail which is unusually long for an owl, the Hawk Owl is reminiscent of a falcon. It is the only owl with barred underparts. One of the more diurnal owls, and often seen flying low and then sweeping upwards to perch: sometimes hovers.

13: TAWNY OWL *(Strix aluco)* In flight the following features are particularly conspicuous: all-brown coloration (in both light and dark phases), large head, black eyes (the absence of yellow or orange is more striking than the actual dark coloration of the iris), wide, barred wings. The Tawny Owl is predominantly nocturnal and in the day time may be seen hunched or in a tree roost.

(Below) Tawny Owl *Strix aluco*

Werner Curth/Ardea

ORDER Caprimulgiformes
FAMILY **CAPRIMULGIDAE: Nightjars**

R. K. Murton/Bruce Coleman

This family includes close to seventy species which are fairly uniform in structure, with flattened, rather large heads and small, delicate bills which can nevertheless be opened extremely wide. The nightjars are nocturnal birds, and their large eyes and gape, and long wings make them agile and efficient hunters as they prey on flying insects by night. The plumage is soft, varying in colour from brown to tawny-buff (almost sand-coloured), grey and black. This coloration provides good camouflage in their semi-desert and open woodland habitats. The upper parts are usually strongly spotted and vermiculated, while the underparts are more often barred or at the most spotted, but with conspicuous white areas on the chin and throat in at least one of the sexes. White patches are also often observed on the wings and the tips of the outer tail feathers. Some species have two colour phases: one grey and one rufous. The sexes are similar, differing mainly in the amount of white in the tail. The Standard-winged Nightjar *Macrodipteryx longipennis* has conspicuously elongated secondaries which give it a distinctive shape. Species with elongated tail feathers or secondaries are restricted to the savannahs of Africa and South America.

The legs are short, sometimes with feathered tarsi, and the middle toe of the foot may be pectinated in keeping with their nocturnal habits; indeed the nightjars, from an ecological viewpoint, replace swallows and swifts at dusk as hunters of insects in flight. By day they prefer to settle on the ground or on a branch or old tree-trunk, perching horizontally so that their coloration harmonises perfectly with the bark of the tree.

The flight of the nightjars is very quick and agile. They glide and wheel, then dart suddenly after prey: they are usually silent in flight.

The eggs are generally laid on the ground; a proper nest is not built and at most a few twigs and dry leaves are gathered together. Two eggs are generally laid which are incubated by both parents.

The family is divided into two sub-families consisting of about eighteen genera in all. On the basis of minor anatomical differences those species which lack the semi-rigid, thread-like plumes surrounding the base of the bill are classed in the sub-family Chordeilinae which is found only in the New World. In North America the two most common species present are: the Common Nighthawk *Chordeiles minor* and the Lesser Nighthawk *C. acutipennis*. In Central and South America other

J. M. Pearson/Bruce Coleman

(Above) Dusky Nightjar *Caprimulgus pectoralis* from Africa, and (left) Common Nighthawk *Chordeiles minor*. (Facing page) Nightjar *Caprimulgus europaeus*

K. W. Fink/Ardea

(Right) Nightjar *C. europaeus*: just before sunset the male flies to a regular perch to emit his churring note. (Below) World distribution of the family Caprimulgidae

F. V. Blackburn

species of the same genus are found as well as the Semi-collared Nighthawk of the monotypic genera *Lurocalis*.

The sub-family Caprimulginae contains over half the species of nightjars. Most are grouped in the genus *Caprimulgus* which includes all the species which nest in Europe and some which occur as accidentals. The differences in size and coloration between the various species may be very subtle and identification is often not easy even for the specialist. The habitat and call may, however, differ considerably from species to species. Some nightjars live in desert or semi-desert regions, such as the Egyptian Nightjar *Caprimulgus aegyptius*, which is very light in colour. Not all species fly long distances or hawk along the edges of woods after insects: the Fiery-necked Nightjar *Caprimulgus pectoralis* of southern Africa perches on a branch from which it flies up to capture any prey passing within its reach.

The family Caprimulgidae is very widely distributed; nightjars are absent only in the extreme north and south of the Americas, the far north of Asia, in New Zealand and in many ocean islands where flying insects are not abundant. The species which breed in the more northerly areas of Eurasia and America migrate south in winter to areas where insects are plentiful. The order Caprimulgiformes contains, besides nightjars, a further three families with a limited number of species. The most unusual of these is the Oilbird *Steatornis caripensis*, the sole member of the family Steatornithidae. It lives in caves in Central and South America and only comes out to feed on the fruit of some palms. The Oilbird navigates in the darkness of the caves by its own echo-sounding abilities.

Nightjar
Caprimulgus europaeus

French: ENGOULEVENT D'EUROPE
Italian: SUCCIACAPRE
Spanish: CHOTACABRAS GRIS
German: NACHTSCHWALBE

HABITAT Nests in open woodlands, clearings, on heathland and in arid zones. Winters in areas with scant vegetation.

IDENTIFICATION Length: 26 cm. Best distinguishing features are the song, the characteristic silhouette with long tail and wings and the free, silent, wheeling flight. Grey-brown in colour, closely spotted and barred tawny and dark brown. The male has white patches on the wing-tips and outer tail feathers, particularly visible in flight. The head is flattened, with a short straight bill but extremely wide gape.

Takes wing at sunset. By day is inactive, perching horizontally on a branch or on the ground, with almost closed eyes: like other nightjars is protected by the perfect camouflage of its coloration. In the breeding season the male produces a clap by beating the wings together, up to twenty-five times at a stretch. Before mating both birds sway their tails and the hind part of their bodies from side to side.

CALL A soft but insistent 'cuu-icc'. Also emits a 'queek-queck-queek' alarm note.

REPRODUCTION Mid-May onwards. Does not build a nest but lays in a slight scrape in the ground. Eggs: normally two, varying from grey-white to creamy, streaked or spotted yellow-brown or dark brown. Two broods per year. Both sexes incubate for eighteen days. Young are tended by both parents, and are independent after about thirty days.

FOOD Insects.

DISTRIBUTION AND MOVEMENTS Breeds in Europe, except for the far north, Asia east as far as Lake Baikal and Afghanistan and southwest Africa. Winters in eastern and southern Africa. In Britain breeds widely but in small numbers throughout England and Wales. Also breeds, although sparsely, in Scotland and in Ireland. Occurs in small numbers on passage at most coastal areas although widely scattered and in small numbers.

SUB-SPECIES *C. e. europaeus*: northern and central Europe, Asia. *C. e. meridionalis* (smaller): southern Europe, Asia, northwest Africa. Other sub-species are present in Asia.

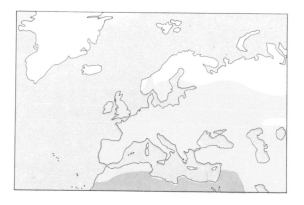

(Above) Female Nightjar (foreground) and male: the male has white tips to the outer tail feathers and three white spots on the outer wing-tips. (Left) Breeding areas (yellow) and areas where the Nightjar may be seen on passage (pink)

67

French: ENGOULEVENT À COLLIER
ROUX
Italian: SUCCIACAPRE
COLLOROSSO
Spanish: CHOTACABRAS PARDO
German: ROTHALSNACHT-
SCHWALBE

Red-necked Nightjar
Caprimulgus ruficollis

(Above) Red-necked Nightjar.
(Below) Breeding areas
(yellow) and areas where the
Red-necked Nightjar may be
seen on passage (pink)

HABITAT Scrubland and forested ridges and hillsides.
Also open desert areas.

IDENTIFICATION Length: 31 cm. In appearance
similar to the Nightjar, but may be distinguished by
larger size, lighter coloration, rufous collar and white
throat-patch. Both male and female have more conspicuous white patches on wings and tail.

CALL A distinctive loud 'kufuk' which is repeated
rapidly.

REPRODUCTION Early May onwards: may be
double-brooded. Does not build a nest but lays its eggs
on the ground, sometimes in a slight scrape. Eggs: two,
elongated, grey-white with brownish spots. No information is available on incubation or nestlings.

FOOD Insects.

DISTRIBUTION AND MOVEMENTS Breeds in
Iberia and northwest Africa; also in Tunisia. Winters in
Senegal and possibly elsewhere in Africa south of the
Sahara. Is a very scarce visitor to Britain.

SUB-SPECIES A sub-species is present in northwest
Africa.

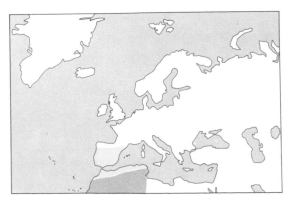

American Nighthawk
Chordeiles minor

HABITAT Sometimes nests in woods, but generally
lives in open country, fields and moorland.

IDENTIFICATION Length: 29 cm. Differs from other
species, both American and European, in having longer
wings and a forked tail. White marking on primaries is
conspicuous as is white patch on chin. White bar on tail
present in male only.
   Habits similar to those of the Nightjar but more
gregarious. Begins to be active even before sunset and
sometimes hunts by day. During courtship, the male will
dive from a height of several hundred metres to within a
metre or two of the ground, head down and wings half-
closed, and then pull out and soar upwards. He also
produces a booming sound, probably by vibrating the
primaries and thrusting the wings downwards.

CALL A nasal 'peent'.

REPRODUCTION From mid-May onwards in the
south, June in the north. Nests on the ground; like other
nightjars does not build a nest. Eggs: two, varying from
creamy to grey, spotted with grey, olive and lilac.

FOOD Insects.

DISTRIBUTION AND MOVEMENTS Breeds from
northern Canada south to Mexico and the Bahamas.
Winters in South America from Columbia to Argentina.
Accidental in Britain, Iceland and Yugoslavia.

SUB-SPECIES Sub-species are present in the breeding
range (North America).

Egyptian Nightjar
Caprimulgus aegyptius

French: ENGOULEVENT D'EGYPTE
Italian: SUCCIACAPRE ISABELLINO
Spanish: CHOTACABRAS EGIPCIO
German: ÄGYPTISCHE
          NACHTSCHWALBE

HABITAT Desert and semi-desert regions.

IDENTIFICATION Length: 25 cm. In appearance similar to Nightjar but much paler and more sandy in coloration and the white patches on wings and tail are either absent or obscure. Also lacks black barring on back. White underside of primaries conspicuous in flight. May be seen hunting near nomad encampments in the deserts.

CALL A harsh 'tukl-tukl' and other notes like those of Nightjar.

REPRODUCTION April to mid-June. Nests on the ground in open desert. Lays two eggs, paler than those of Nightjar, white or creamy mottled olive-brown and grey. Both sexes incubate the eggs for about eighteen days, and both tend the young.

FOOD Insects.

DISTRIBUTION AND MOVEMENTS Northern Africa and southwestern Asia. Winters in the southern Sahara and in northern Sudan. Accidental in Britain, Germany, Sicily and Malta.

SUB-SPECIES Three sub-species are present in Asia and Africa. *C. a. aegyptius* and *C. a. saharae* are found in northern Africa and are probably the sub-species found as accidentals in Europe. The Asian sub-species is *C. a. arenicolor*.

(Above) Egyptian Nightjar and
(left) American Nighthawk

French: ENGOULEVENT
          D'AMÉRIQUE
Italian: SUCCIACAPRE AMERICANO
Spanish: CHOTACABRAS YANQUI
German: AMERIKANISCHE
          NACHTSCHWALBE

APODIDAE: Swifts

A. Christiansen

(Above) Swift *Apus apus:* like all swifts the plumage is dark, and the curved narrow wings and short tail are adapted to fast flight

Swifts form a very homogeneous, well-defined group with unique characteristics; they are grouped together with hummingbirds in the order Apodiformes. There are about sixty-five species in the family Apodidae. Authorities differ as to whether or not swifts and hummingbirds should be placed in the same order, but hummingbirds are undoubtedly the closest to swifts in structure. The shape of the wings in particular is very similar: they are narrow, slightly curved, but whereas hummingbirds have primaries of normal length, swifts have extremely elongated primaries—an ideal adaptation for a life spent almost entirely on the wing. Hummingbirds, on the contrary, are particularly well adapted for hovering and are

practically the only birds capable of flying backwards. Swifts and hummingbirds differ considerably from each other both in breeding behaviour and in diet, and the resemblance between swallows and martins (of the family Hirundinidae) and swifts is usually regarded as convergent evolution.

Swifts are said to be the most aerial of all birds: they invariably take their food in flight. They mate in flight (though also on the nest); drink and bathe flying low over the surface of the water; and except during the breeding season, spend the night on the wing. They do not normally settle on the ground or on trees, although some swifts occasionally rest clinging to vertical rock faces or more rarely, to tree-trunks.

Swifts vary in length from nine to twenty-three centimetres. Almost all species have sooty-black or brown plumage, sometimes with white or pale grey patches. The very short legs have toes with hooked claws, useful for gripping: the legs are reduced as swifts rarely settle except at nest-sites. The bill is small although with a wide gape. The sexes are similar. The wings are narrow and pointed, and the short tail is usually forked.

Swifts mix their nest materials, which consist of stems and leaves of plants and feathers, with saliva from their well-developed salivary glands. This nest building material is collected as it is blown about in the air. The clutch varies from one to six eggs, depending on the species, and the incubation period is unusually long given the size of bird. Among species of the genus *Apus* incubation may take up to twenty days. The young also stay in the nest for a long time (up to eight weeks) although this period may vary considerably depending on the availability of food.

The family is usually divided into two subfamilies: the Chaeturinae and Apodinae. The Chaeturinae includes species with spiny tips to the tail-feathers: these help them to cling to sheer surfaces. Seventeen species of this sub-family are distributed in Asia, Africa and America. By far the most common is the Chimney Swift *Chaetura pelagica* of North America. In the wild it nests in hollow trees but has also taken to building its nest which is a half cup shape, on the inner walls of chimneys. There are about twenty species of the genus *Collocalia* in southeast Asia and some islands of the Pacific and Indian Oceans. Many of the species—known as swiftlets—nest in huge caves, sometimes in colonies of hundreds of thousands. They find their way easily in the darkness by means of echo-location: they utter high-frequency sounds which are bounced back from surrounding objects so that the swift can judge the distance of an obstacle by the time it takes for the sound wave to return to it.

The nest of the Grey-rumped Swiftlet *Collocalia francica* consists entirely of hardened saliva: it is the famous 'birds nest' so much prized in Chinese cooking. There are approximately twenty species altogether which are known as the edible-nest swiftlets.

The sub-family Chaeturinae is from Central and South America (although one species is found as far north as Alaska). These swifts build cup-shaped nests of moss on rock ledges, often behind waterfalls.

The sub-family Apodinae includes all swifts which lack 'spiny' tails. The most common genus is *Apus* with ten species in the Old World, chiefly in Africa and Eurasia. Members of this sub-family usually nest in holes in rocks or in buildings,

(Right) Three phases in the development of Swifts *A. apus*. The two or three smooth white eggs are laid at two or three day intervals: after an incubation period of fourteen to twenty days the nestlings hatch naked. The young are fed by both parents but become independent when they can fly—five to eight weeks after hatching

U. Berggren/Ardea

(Right) Little Swift *Apus affinis*. (Below) World distribution of the family Apodidae

although one species bores tunnels in sandbanks and others occupy nests abandoned by swallows. The Palm Swift *Cypsiurus parvus* is a small Asian and African species with a long forked tail. It builds a cup-shaped nest which is attached to the underside of palm leaves; and the single egg is safely glued into the nest with saliva to prevent it being dislodged by the wind.

Undoubtedly the best known and most studied species is the Common Swift *Apus apus*. It is often seen in cities, filling the skies in spring and early summer with its cries.

Detailed research has revealed interesting adaptations to a particular food, that is the insects which constitute the aeroplankton. These insects are plentiful in fine, warm weather but are almost non-existent on cold, windy, wet days: on such occasions swifts will travel hundreds of kilometres in search of them. The interval between the laying of the one to six eggs may also be as much as three days, if food is scarce. Normally the parents take turns to incubate, but the eggs may be abandoned for several days without any harm coming to the embryo when the parents are forced to be absent. The young may also be left untended for long periods, relying entirely on their reserves of fat. If their fast is even further prolonged, the chicks temporarily lose control of their body temperature: that is, they become 'cold-blooded' and lapse into a sort of torpor which enables them to survive until nourishment is once more available. It appears that the adults also become torpid when food is scarce.

Pallid Swift
Apus pallidus

HABITAT Tends to nest at warmer regions near the sea than the Swift.

IDENTIFICATION Length: 16 cm. In flight virtually indistinguishable from the Swift, unless seen in good light, when paler, browner, more mouse-coloured plumage and more conspicuous white patch on the throat may be observed. Often seen in association with Swift, which does make identification difficult. Flight outline somewhat different: head of the Pallid Swift appears broader and the wingbeats are slower. See also page 138.

CALL A shrill harsh scream like that of the Swift.

REPRODUCTION From April onwards. Breeds on rock outcrops and cliffs and on buildings: the nest is stuck to a vertical face. Nest is a shallow, cup-shaped structure of straw and feathers which is stuck together with saliva. Two smooth white eggs are laid, but the incubation period is not known.

FOOD Insects, invariably taken in flight.

DISTRIBUTION AND MOVEMENTS Breeds in Africa, Asia Minor and southern Europe including Iberia, Italy and Greece. A partial migrant, wintering southward to the Sahara desert.

SUB-SPECIES The two sub-species nesting in Europe are *A. p. brehmorum*, also found throughout northwest Africa and in southern Arabia, and *A. p. illyricus*, found mainly in Yugoslavia. Other sub-species are present in Africa.

(Below) Breeding areas (yellow) of the Pallid Swift

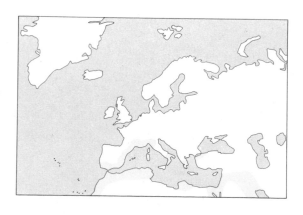

Swift
Apus apus

HABITAT Found in huge flocks in a wide range of habitats. An aerial species which feeds over open country, fresh water and built up areas. Nests on rocks, cliffs and sometimes in trees.

IDENTIFICATION Length: 16 cm. Easily distinguished from other swifts by smoky black plumage, whitish chin, long, crescent-shaped wings and short, rather forked tail. Juveniles have more white as well as a narrow white border to the wing-feathers. Easily distinguished from Swallows by short tail and long curved wings.

The vigorous, rapid flight is characterised by wide wheelings and glidings; a series of wingbeats alternates with gliding on fully extended wings. Almost always seen in flight although may be observed perching on walls, rocks, etc. Does not like settling on the ground, its short legs being more suited for clinging than for walking: it was once thought that swifts were unable to take flight from the ground, but this has been disproved. Particularly noisy in the breeding season, when whole groups will fly round in circles chasing one another and uttering excited cries. See also page 138.

CALL A shrill, penetrating 'sree-sree-sree'.

REPRODUCTION Late May onwards. Nests in colonies under eaves, in rock crevices and sometimes in abandoned nests of House Martins or in woodpecker holes. The nest, shaped like a shallow cup, is lined with straw, grass, seeds and feathers, collected in flight and glued together with saliva. Eggs: usually three, white and elongated: the female apparently incubates for a period of fourteen to twenty days, but the eggs are able to withstand some cooling and periods of up to twenty-seven days have been recorded. Both parents tend the young and feed them with insects which they carry to them in their throats.

DISTRIBUTION AND MOVEMENTS Breeds in Eurasia from the Atlantic coast to eastern China. Also breeds in northwest Africa. Winters in Africa south of the Sahara. In Britain and Ireland is a numerous and widely distributed breeder and is resident from late April to August.

SUB-SPECIES Sub-species are present in Asia.

(Right) Breeding areas (yellow) and areas where the Swift may be seen on passage (pink)

Alpine Swift
Apus melba

French: MARTINET ALPIN
Italian: RONDONE ALPINO
Spanish: VENCEJO REAL
German: ALPENSEGLER

HABITAT Breeds mainly on high, rocky, mountainous regions; occasionally on marine cliffs and old buildings.

IDENTIFICATION Length: 21 cm. Is the largest swift present in Europe. Distinguished from Swift by larger size and lighter brown upper parts, white belly and brown pectoral band. Flight and behaviour very similar to those of Swift although flight is even more vigorous and powerful. However, when gliding wings are often held pointing downwards. See also page 138.

CALL In flight utters a loud trill, rising and falling in pitch, much more melodious than Swift. Often sings in chorus in flight over nesting areas.

REPRODUCTION End of May onwards. The cup-shaped nest is built in rock crevices or under roofs and is used year after year. Nest material, such as grass, leaves, straw is gathered in flight by both sexes and glued together with saliva. Usually lays three smooth white eggs. Both sexes incubate for eighteen to thirty-three days and both tend the young.

FOOD Extremely voracious, feeding on large quantities of insects.

DISTRIBUTION AND MOVEMENTS Breeds in southern Europe, southwest Asia and Africa. Winters in tropical and southern Africa and southern Asia. Is a scarce visitor to Britain and Ireland. The majority of sightings have been in England and in particular on coasts from the Scilly Isles to Norfolk.

SUB-SPECIES Sub-species are present in Asia and Africa.

(Below) Breeding areas (yellow) and areas where the Alpine Swift may be seen on passage (pink)

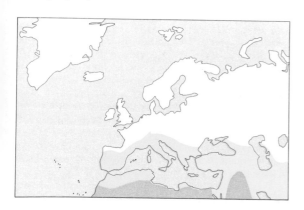

French: MARTINET CAFRE
Italian: RONDONE CAFRO
Spanish: VENCEJO CAFRE
German: KAFFERNSEGLER

French: MARTINET À DOS BLANC
Italian: RONDONE INDIANO
Spanish: VENCEJO CULIBLANCO
German: WEISSBÜRZLSEGLER

White-rumped Swift
Apus caffer

HABITAT Like all other swifts is aerial and only alights on land to breed.

IDENTIFICATION Length: 14 cm. Very similar to Little Swift but slightly larger and uniformly darker than the Little Swift. Markedly forked tail and narrow white rump. See also page 138.

CALL A guttural twittering note: less noisy than other swifts.

REPRODUCTION Generally uses the nests of other birds, especially of species such as the Red-rumped Swallow which builds a tunnel entrance. Adds some down and straw to the old nest but if necessary can build its own nest. Lays two to three white eggs which are incubated by both sexes for nineteen to twenty-three days. Two or three broods per year.

FOOD Insects.

DISTRIBUTION AND MOVEMENTS An apparently sedentary species, performing only sporadic movements. Breeds mainly in Africa south of the Sahara but has nested in Morocco and southern Spain.

SUB-SPECIES The sub-species *A. c. streubelii* is present in central Africa.

Little or House Swift
Apus affinis

HABITAT Like that of other swifts: frequently seen in inhabited areas.

IDENTIFICATION Length: 13 cm. Smallest swift present in Europe. Head, wings and tail sooty black with some green gloss; black upper and underparts, white rump. Both the White-rumped and Little Swift have broad white rumps, but the square shaped tail distinguishes it from White-rumped. See also page 138.

CALL Like that of the Swift, but higher pitched and more twittering.

REPRODUCTION Prolonged breeding season: may be double brooded. Nests in cities in Africa and Asia where it virtually replaces the Swift, but also far from inhabited areas, among rocks and in caves. Usually nests in colonies. May build a half-cup-shaped nest or sometimes uses abandoned swallows' nests. The nest is built by both male and female and the same nest may be replaced and used year after year. Usually lays two or three white eggs, sometimes up to six which both sexes incubate for eighteen to twenty-six days. Both tend the young who leave the nest after about forty days.

DISTRIBUTION AND MOVEMENTS Breeds throughout Africa and in southern Asia east to southern China. Accidental in Europe, in Iberia and Ireland.

SUB-SPECIES Sub-species are present in Africa.

(Above) White-rumped Swift and (above right) Little Swift. (Right) Breeding areas (yellow) of the White-rumped Swift

White-throated Spinetail Swift

Chaetura caudacutus

French: MARTINET ÉPINEUX
Italian: CHETURA CODACUTA
Spanish: RABITOJO
German: STACHELSCHWANZSEGLER

HABITAT Breeds in rocky and mountainous areas; sometimes also on plains.

IDENTIFICATION Length: 19 cm. Also known as the Needle-tailed Swift. Distinguished from other swifts by larger size, very short tail and a horseshoe-shaped white mark on the underparts. Dark brown plumage, glossed green, with white forehead, throat and flanks. The tail is not forked, distinguishing it from most swifts of the genus *Apus*. Hunts the insects on which it feeds in large groups, sometimes in company with martins and swallows, flying low over the surface of water or over the tops of trees. Flight is more rapid than that of other swifts. See also page 138.

CALL Emits a shrill cry.

REPRODUCTION Early June in Siberia; from July elsewhere. Nests in rock crevices and probably in hollow trees. The nest, like that of other swifts, is built from materials collected on the wing and glued together with saliva. Eggs: lays two to three white eggs. Further information is lacking.

FOOD Insects taken in flight.

DISTRIBUTION AND MOVEMENTS Eastern Asia: breeds discontinuously from western Siberia east to Japan. Winters in Australia and Tasmania. Accidental in Europe in Britain and Finland.

SUB-SPECIES Sub-species are present in eastern Asia.

ORDER Coraciiformes
FAMILY **ALCEDINIDAE: Kingfishers**

(Above) Kingfisher *Alcedo atthis:* kingfishers are among the most colourful birds present in Europe

The family Alcedinidae forms a homogeneous group consisting of about eighty species with a cosmopolitan distribution. They vary in length from ten to forty-six centimetres, but the general shape is almost identical in all species: a large head, large eyes, rather stumpy body, short legs with either three or four (depending on the species) markedly syndactyl toes. The bill is long and stout.

The most interesting characteristic of the kingfishers is the wide variety of plumage displayed by the various species and above all the dazzling coloration, often with a metallic gloss and an 'enamelled' effect. Blue, green, purple and red predominate, often together with white or dark markings. The legs and bill are also almost always brilliantly coloured. Both sexes have similar coloration and where sexual dimorphism is present it is not always the male who is the more vividly coloured. In some species the central tail-feathers are exceptionally elongated.

Although the kingfishers may be considered cosmopolitan, most of the species are found in the Old World. They are grouped into three subfamilies—Cerylinae, Alcedininae and Daceloninae —although only the sub-family Cerylinae is represented in the Americas, mainly in South America. The common Kingfisher *Alcedo atthis* is found throughout the Palearctic region: it is a 'tropical intrusion' into the European avifauna like the Roller *Coracias garrulus* the Hoopoe *Upupa epops* and bee-eaters of the family Meropidae which all belong to the order Coraciiformes, like the kingfishers.

Kingfishers are generally solitary in habit. They

78

usually perch on branches—generally in an upright position—from which they dart out in pursuit of their prey. Many species feed mainly on fish or at any rate on aquatic animals which they capture by diving, sometimes from flight. Some kingfishers even 'fly' under water. However, despite the name, some species do not fish, but feed on insects or even small vertebrates. One large species the Shovel-billed Kingfisher *Clytoceyx rex* of New Guinea, digs in the ground for earthworms and has a rather flattened, spoon-shaped bill perfectly adapted for this purpose. Many attempts have been made to correlate the shape and size of the bill with the feeding habits, but no viable relationship has emerged along these lines.

It is thought that species of the family were originally mainly terrestrial in habit and that proficiency in fishing was a secondary and later adaptation of the more developed species, rendered feasible by the peculiarly suitable shape of the bill.

Kingfishers nest in holes or burrows, in river banks, in the ground, in termites' nests or even in natural cavities in trees. The 'nesting chamber' is virtually bare and the two to seven pure white eggs which are laid are incubated by both parents, both of whom also tend the chicks.

The sub-family Cerylinae contains four species of the genus *Chloroceryle* as well as the Belted Kingfisher *Megaceryle halcyon*. They are present in Central and South America, although the Belted Kingfisher is also widely distributed in North America. Species of the sub-family found in the Old World include the Pied Kingfisher *Ceryle rudis* which is abundantly distributed in Africa and

(Top) White-breasted or Smyrna Kingfisher *Halcyon smyrnensis*. (Above left) Malachite Kingfisher *Alcedo cristata* and (above) a bird of the Malagasy race *A.c. vintsioides*

79

(Right) Kookaburra *Dacelo gigas:* this large kingfisher is found only in Australia, mainly in woodland. Its laughing call and snake-killing have made it a well known species. (Below) World distribution of the family Alcedinidae

J. R. Brownlie/Bruce Coleman

southwestern Asia. The brilliantly coloured Giant Kingfisher *Megaceryle maxima* is also common in tropical Africa.

The typical example of the sub-family Alcedininae is the Kingfisher, whose numbers are slowly dwindling in many parts of Europe due to increasing pollution of the waters where it hunts small fish and crustaceans. This genus also includes eight other species of similar coloration; they form the only group in the sub-family which is fundamentally fish-eating. Other species feed mainly on insects: for example the African Dwarf Kingfisher *Myioceyx lecontei* and the Pygmy Kingfisher *Ispidina picta* of tropical Africa. They are also the smallest species, less than ten centimetres in length. Madagascar is the home of the Madagascar Pygmy *Ceyx madagascariensis* which is unique in having entirely rufous upper parts. About ten species, currently grouped in the genus *Ceyx*, have only three toes and are found from southeast Asia and Indonesia to the Australo-Papuan area.

The sub-family Daceloninae contains the so-called 'tree kingfishers', some of which take insects in flight, like flycatchers, while others pounce on their prey on the ground, like shrikes. The Australian Kookaburra *Dacelo gigas* belongs to this sub-family. It is a large bird, lacking the brilliant coloration typical of most kingfishers, notorious for its hysterical laughing call and its ability to imitate weird noises, including steam whistles. Three other *Dacelo* species occur in the Australo-Papuan region. The Stork-billed Kingfisher *Pelargopsus capensis* is a species of southern Asia and is also fairly large, feeding both on fish and on prey found on the ground.

Four monotypic genera of this sub-family are the Banded Kingfisher *Lacedo pulchella*, the Shovel-billed Kingfisher *Clytoceyx rex*, the Hook-billed Kingfisher *Melidora macrorhina* and the Celebes Blue-eared Kingfisher *Cittura cyanotis*. The seven species of the genus *Tanysiptera*, all from the Australo-Papuan area, have elongated, racket-shaped central tail-feathers. The genus *Halcyon* contains about forty species, almost all terrestrial in habit. The White-collared Kingfisher *H. chloris* is found in coastal areas from the Red Sea to Samoa, even though it is not a true fisher. The Sacred Kingfisher *H. sancta*, with mainly yellow plumage, is the only representative of the family in New Zealand. As is evident, the distribution of kingfishers is worldwide: they are absent only from the more extreme latitudes and from some oceanic islands.

Lesser Pied Kingfisher
Ceryle rudis

French: ALCYON PIE
Italian: MARTIN PESCATORE
BIANCO E NERO
Spanish: MARTÍN PESCADOR PIO
German: GRAUFISCHER

HABITAT Always lives near water, generally by fresh water although not at high altitudes or in heavily forested regions.

IDENTIFICATION Length: 25 cm. Easily distinguished by striking black and white plumage. Adult male: black upper parts, with feathers edged and streaked white especially on tail and wings. Underparts white with black pectoral bands. Female very similar to male, but has only one incomplete pectoral band. Bill long and stout: both bill and legs black. Juveniles have duller coloration, but in both juvenile and adult plumage the sexes may be distinguished by the pectoral bands.

Like other kingfishers, the Lesser Pied makes a tunnel in which to nest. The tunnel is dug with the well developed bill and the loose earth removed with the feet. No actual nest is made, but there is a wider chamber at the end of the tunnel in which the eggs are laid: however, food castings such as bones may line the tunnel. There is no nest sanitation and the tunnel becomes foul before the young leave the nest.

CALL Emits a shrill 'kweek-kweek', also a whistling note.

REPRODUCTION From March onwards. Bores a tunnel over a metre long and about six centimetres wide ending in an unlined nest chamber where three to six eggs are laid. Both sexes dig the tunnel and both incubate the eggs. Sometimes several pairs may form a loose colony. Further details are not available.

FOOD Mainly small fish and aquatic invertebrates.

DISTRIBUTION AND MOVEMENTS A predominantly African species, found south of the Sahara and along the Nile valley. Extends eastwards to Asia Minor, India and southeast Asia. Accidental in Europe, Greece, Poland, and the Crimea.

SUB-SPECIES Sub-species are present in Asia.

(Below) Areas where the Lesser Pied Kingfisher may be seen all year round (orange)

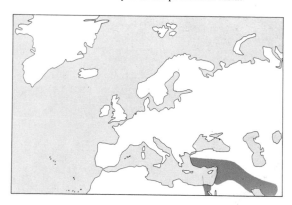

Coraciiformes: Alcedinidae

Belted Kingfisher
Ceryle alcyon

French: ALCYON À COLLIER
Italian: MARTIN PESCATORE
AMERICANO
Spanish: MARTÍN PESCADOR
ALCÍON
German: GÜRTELFISCHER

(Left) Male Belted Kingfisher
(foreground) and female

French: MARTIN-PÊCHEUR DE
SMYRNE
Italian: MARTIN PESCATORE
PETTOBIANCO
German: BRAUNLIEST

HABITAT Lives by fresh and salt water.

IDENTIFICATION Length: 34–37 cm. A large king-fisher with dark head and crest, blue-grey upper parts, white underparts, a white collar extending to the back of the neck and a blue-grey pectoral band on the upper breast. Female has chestnut breast band and flanks. Flight feathers are brownish-black; tail barred and bill is blackish.

Generally perches upright near water, on a branch or other support, ready to dive after fish.

CALL Emits a harsh grating sound.

REPRODUCTION Bores a tunnel in a river-bank, one to four metres long which ends in a nesting chamber where five to eight eggs are laid. Incubation lasts about twenty-three days.

FOOD Small fish, crustaceans, very small mammals; occasionally fruit.

DISTRIBUTION AND MOVEMENTS Breeds in North America: migrates south to Central America and the Carribean but some individuals winter in southern Canada. Accidental in Europe in Iceland and also in the Netherlands.

SUB-SPECIES Sub-species are present in North America.

82

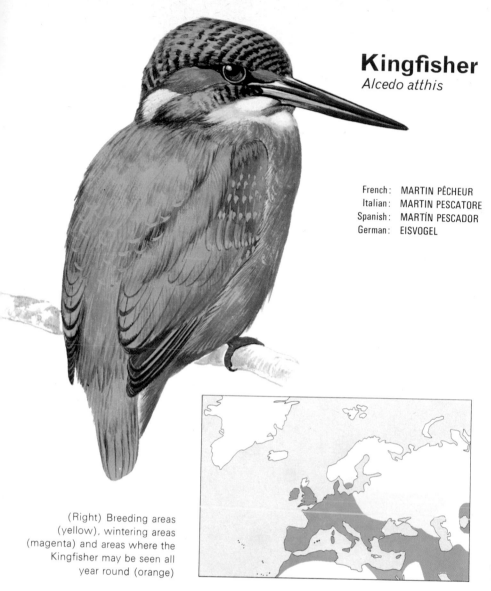

Kingfisher
Alcedo atthis

French: MARTIN PÊCHEUR
Italian: MARTIN PESCATORE
Spanish: MARTÍN PESCADOR
German: EISVOGEL

HABITAT Found near lowland fresh water: streams, rivers, canals and lakes. In winter also frequents sea-coasts, salt-marshes near coasts and estuaries.

IDENTIFICATION Length: 16 cm. Unmistakable vivid colouring, stumpy body, large head and long, flattened, dagger-shaped bill. Upper parts appear cobalt blue or emerald green, depending on the angle at which the light strikes them; underparts light chestnut, throat white, legs bright red. Tail short; bill black; legs reddish.

Perches on branches or roots near water and dives in to catch small fish, aquatic insects or crustaceans. Sometimes hovers above water and then dives. Usually flies low over water. During courtship male will follow female for long distances, flying among trees sometimes at considerable height.

CALL A high-pitched, whistling 'chee-kee'.

REPRODUCTION Late April onwards. Nest is a tunnel ending in a nesting-chamber, bored out by both male and female in river banks or sand-pits. Six or seven, glossy white eggs are laid. Both sexes incubate the eggs for nineteen to twenty-one days. Young hatch naked and are tended by both parents until they are able to fend for themselves.

FOOD Fish, insects, small molluscs and worms.

DISTRIBUTION AND MOVEMENTS Present in the Palearctic, Oriental and Australasian faunal regions. Northern populations winter in the south of the range and beyond to northeast Africa, Arabia and Indonesia. Is widely distributed in Europe except for the northern regions: in Britain (except for Scotland where it is local) and Ireland is a widespread resident breeder.

SUB-SPECIES *A.a. attis:* southern Europe. *A.a. ispida* (darker and larger): northern and central Europe. Other sub-species are present in Asia and the Pacific islands.

(Right) Breeding areas (yellow), wintering areas (magenta) and areas where the Kingfisher may be seen all year round (orange)

White-breasted Kingfisher
Halcyon smyrnensis

HABITAT The White-breasted Kingfisher generally occurs by inland or coastal waters but also is often found on dry ground, such as gardens, cultivated land, open plains and sometimes in forests.

IDENTIFICATION Length: 27 cm. Unmistakable colourful and contrasting plumage. Bright chestnut crown, nape and sides of the head; blue-green mantle, pale turquoise upper tail coverts, turquoise wings, chestnut shoulders and blackish wing coverts; white chin, throat and central part of the breast; remaining underparts chestnut. Dark iris; deep red bill; dark orange legs. The sexes are alike; juveniles have duller coloration.

CALL Emits a loud laughing cry.

REPRODUCTION April onwards. Like all kingfishers, it lays its white eggs in a cavity at the end of a tunnel. It lays between four and six eggs and incubation, by both male and female, takes three weeks.

FOOD Its diet is varied, consisting of insects, lizards and also fish and amphibians.

DISTRIBUTION AND MOVEMENTS Breeds in Turkey, Syria, Israel and southeast Asia. Has occurred accidentally in Arabia and east of the Jordan river as well as in southeast Europe (Greece and possibly Cyprus).

SUB-SPECIES *H.s. fusca* (India, Sri Lanka and east China); *H.s. saturatior* (Andaman Islands) and *H.s. gularis* (Philippines).

(Facing page, bottom) White-breasted Kingfisher. (Right) Areas where the White-breasted Kingfisher may be seen all year round (orange)

FAMILY MEROPIDAE: Bee-eaters

P. Slater/Photo Researchers

Bee-eaters are found only in the Old World, especially in tropical parts of Asia and Africa. Although they vary in coloration and size, ranging in length from 15 to 35 centimetres, they are a homogeneous family of insect-eating birds whose diet consists mainly of bees and wasps which they catch in the air. The twenty-three species of bee-eaters hunt either in flight like swallows or by launching themselves from perches like flycatchers. Like kingfishers they nest in burrows excavated in crumbly ground. Some species frequent woods or wooded areas, while others prefer open ground: they are often found by rivers.

Their bills are distinctive, being long, slender, laterally compressed, pointed and curved downwards. Their feet are small with the toes partly joined (syndactylous). The long pointed wings enable bee-eaters to fly quickly and gracefully. The long tails often have projecting pointed central tail

(Above left) Carmine Bee-eaters *Merops nubicus* and (above) Little Bee-eater *Melittophagus pusillus*. (Left) Bee-eaters *Merops apiaster*. (Facing page) Rainbow Bee-eater *Merops ornatus* at the entrance to the nest

W. T. Miller/Frank Lane

H. Chaumeton/Jacana

(Above and above right) Bee-eater *Merops apiaster*.
(Below) World distribution of the family Meropidae

feathers. Plumage is usually brilliantly coloured with green, yellow and blue being the principal colours, but some species are predominantly red. The sexes are similar.

Bee-eaters are generally gregarious and noisy and often nest in huge colonies. The eggs (from two to five are laid depending on the species) are white. Both parents share incubation and build the tunnel leading to the nesting chamber where their offspring hatch naked. No nest is made but the cavity is lined with insect castings. Species which nest in temperate zones are migrant and spend the winter in the tropics; some of the tropical species are also migrant.

Three of the seven genera of bee-eaters are monotypic: four genera and fifteen species are completely African; two genera and six species are exclusively Asiatic and one species is a native of Australia. The most widespread and numerous genus is *Merops* which includes the common Bee-eater *M. apiaster* from Europe. The Blue-cheeked Bee-eater *M. superciliosus* of North Africa and the Middle East to New Guinea also occurs accidentally in Europe. The Carmine Bee-eater *M. nubicus* of Africa is among the most beautiful species: it is red with a bright blue-green head. The Rainbow Bee-eater *M. ornatus* is the only Australian member of the family; after the breeding season it migrates north to New Guinea and the Celebes. The eight species of the genus *Melittophagus* are found in Africa and include the smallest bee-eaters such as the Little Bee-eater *M. pusillus*.

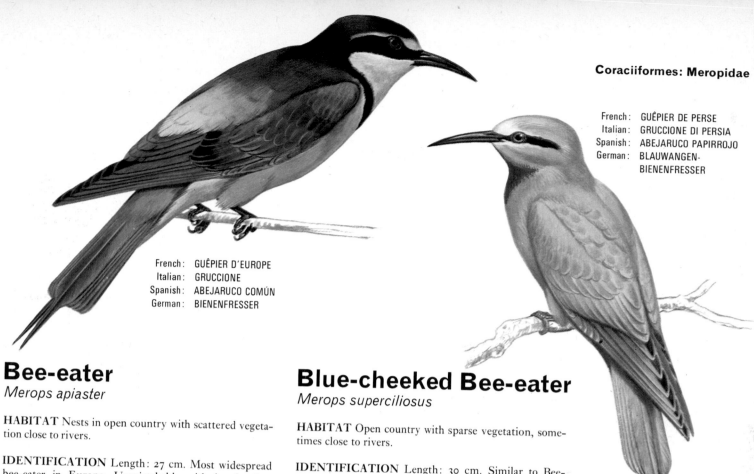

French: GUÊPIER D'EUROPE
Italian: GRUCCIONE
Spanish: ABEJARUCO COMÚN
German: BIENENFRESSER

French: GUÊPIER DE PERSE
Italian: GRUCCIONE DI PERSIA
Spanish: ABEJARUCO PAPIRROJO
German: BLAUWANGEN-
BIENENFRESSER

Bee-eater
Merops apiaster

HABITAT Nests in open country with scattered vegetation close to rivers.

IDENTIFICATION Length: 27 cm. Most widespread bee-eater in Europe. Unmistakable with its dazzling coloration, curved bill and pointed tail. In flight it is easily identified by its pointed wings and its narrow, elongated central tail feathers which project well beyond the rest of its tail. Both sexes are mainly blue-green with chestnut head and mantle shading into golden yellow at the back. Bright yellow throat; blue-green underparts, tail and wings.

CALL Emits a liquid 'proo-eek'.

REPRODUCTION Nests in colonies in tunnels often dug in river banks. The tunnel ends in a chamber where the eggs are laid. Both sexes excavate the tunnel which is one to two and a half metres long. The Bee-eater lays between four and seven glossy white eggs. Incubation is carried out by both parents and both tend the young.

FOOD Insects.

DISTRIBUTION AND MOVEMENTS Breeds in southern Europe, northern Africa, the Middle East and Asia. Northern populations winter in the southern part of the breeding range and further south to Cape Province in Africa and Arabia. Accidental in Britain, Ireland and Scandinavia. Recorded almost every year in England and has also bred on at least one occasion.

Blue-cheeked Bee-eater
Merops superciliosus

HABITAT Open country with sparse vegetation, sometimes close to rivers.

IDENTIFICATION Length: 30 cm. Similar to Bee-eater in shape and size but central tail feathers longer and basic coloration is a soft green which can be paler or darker depending on the sub-species concerned. Black-edged flight feathers shade into brown. There is a black streak from the bill across the eye to the ear-coverts. Bright chestnut throat. The front of the forehead, the cheeks and a rather indistinct supercilium are pale blue. The bill is dark. Lacks the Bee-eater's dark breast band.

CALL Emits similar but less sonorous notes than the Bee-eater.

REPRODUCTION The white eggs are indistinguishable from the Bee-eater's. The two species often nest in mixed colonies. The nest is a tunnel with a nesting chamber at the end containing five or six eggs. Both sexes incubate the eggs.

FOOD Insects which are caught in flight.

DISTRIBUTION AND MOVEMENTS Breeds from north Africa and southwest Asia east to India and north to the Caucasus. It is accidental in Europe in Greece, Yugoslavia, Italy, Malta, France, the Netherlands and Britain.

SUB-SPECIES There are sub-species in Africa and Asia.

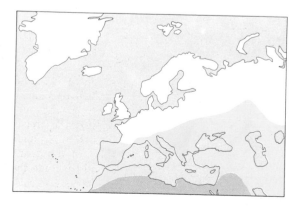

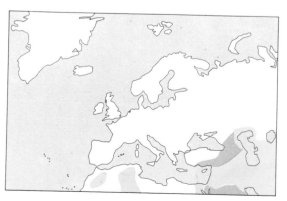

(Above left) Bee-eater and (right) Blue-cheeked Bee-eater. (Far left) Breeding areas (yellow) and areas where the Bee-eater may be seen on passage (pink). (Left) Breeding areas (yellow) and areas where the Blue-cheeked Bee-eater may be seen on passage (pink)

FAMILY CORACIIDAE: Rollers

The family Coraciidae, which consists of the rollers, has given its name to the entire order Coraciiformes.

Rollers are medium sized crow-like birds with large heads, short necks and heavy, rather wide, slightly hooked bills. Their legs are of medium length and the wings and tails are large and fairly long. The tail is either squarish or forked and in some species the outer tail feathers are elongated and thread-like. The bill is stout and slightly hooked. The brightly coloured plumage of the rollers is a combination of different shades of green, blue and chestnut; in some cases brown and purple are the principal colours. The sexes are more or less similar.

Rollers are remarkably skilled fliers and perform spectacular aerobatics: indeed their English name is derived from their somersaulting movements which are performed in courtship display. They are generally solitary and perch on branches, posts or telegraph wires from which they dive down to capture their prey which consists of insects and small vertebrates. When fire breaks out in vegetation, particularly in the savannah, rollers congregate in large flocks on the edge of the burnt ground with other insect-eating birds where their prey is exposed to attack as it flees from the fire.

Rollers nest in holes in trees, in banks of earth or among rocks; they sometimes even use the old, abandoned nests of other species. Their eggs, from three to six per clutch, are white, like those of most members of the order Coraciiformes and of many birds which nest in holes or burrows where white eggs are more easily seen.

The twelve species of the family are distributed in the tropical and temperate zones of the Old World—particularly in Africa. According to Wetmore's classification, which is followed here, the so-called ground-rollers are not included in this family. There are only two genera: *Coracias* and *Eurystomus*. The only European species is the common Roller *Coracias garrulus* which is mainly found around the Mediterranean, though it travels as far as southern Sweden to nest. The Abyssinian Roller *C. abyssinicus* is very similar, except that its two outer tail feathers are elongated and thread-like. There are four other species of the genus in Africa: the Indian Roller *C. benghalensis* is found in Asia from Arabia to Cambodia and Temminck's Roller *C. temminckii* is a native of Celebes and neighbouring islands. The species of the genus *Eurystomus* are smaller and do not perform the nuptial aerobatics of the genus *Coracias*, although they do capture their prey in flight. The Broad-billed Roller *E. orientalis* is widely distributed from India to Manchuria and east towards the Solomon Islands: the sub-species *E.o. pacificus* nests in Australia and New Guinea.

(Above) Roller *Coracias garrulus:* at rest it resembles a small blue-green crow whereas in flight the bright blue wing-patch is reminiscent of a Jay. (Below) World distribution of the family Coraciidae

Roller
Coracias garrulus

French: ROLLIER D'EUROPE
Italian: GHIANDAIA MARINA
Spanish: CARRACA
German: BLAURACKE

HABITAT Deciduous or coniferous woods or on plains where old trees, walls or buildings suitable for nesting are situated. Winters on open ground with scattered trees and bushes.

IDENTIFICATION Length: 30 cm. Similar in appearance to the Jay from which it differs in its pale blue plumage and chestnut-coloured back; dark blue wings with black margins; blue-green tail with brown central feathers. The sexes are similar. Bright blue wing-patch conspicuous in flight: flight is direct and resembles that of the Woodpigeon.

The Roller usually perches on branches, telegraph wires, bushes or buildings from which it dives after insects which it captures in flight. It hops awkwardly on the ground. During the breeding season it lives in pairs but at other times of the year it is gregarious. During the nuptial flight the male nosedives from considerable heights, tumbling and rolling in the air. Male and female perch close together during courtship, emitting call notes in turn.

CALL A loud, deep, crow-like 'krak-act'.

REPRODUCTION From mid-May. The nest is situated in holes in trees, crevices in rocks, gaps in old walls and sometimes in abandoned nests of other birds. The Roller lays four or five white eggs. Incubation is carried out by both parents for eighteen or nineteen days and both also tend the young.

FOOD Mainly insects. Occasionally scorpions, small lizards, small birds, frogs and fruit.

DISTRIBUTION AND MOVEMENTS Breeds from Iberia and France east across Eurasia to Kashmir. Winters in eastern and southern Africa and Arabia. Accidental in northern Europe including Britain and Ireland.

SUB-SPECIES A sub-species is present in Asia.

(Below) Breeding areas (yellow) and areas where the Roller may be seen on passage (pink)

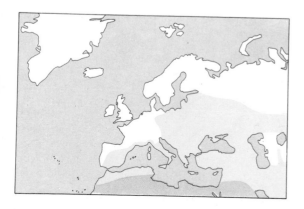

R. Austing/Frank Lane

G. J. H. Moon/Frank Lane

R. Austing/Frank Lane

R. Austing/Frank Lane

A. J. Deane/Bruce Coleman

Bruce Coleman

J. M. Pearson/Bruce Coleman

(Above) Hoopoe *Upupa epops* and (left) Abyssinian Roller *Coracias abyssinicus.* (Facing page far left sequence) Belted Kingfisher *Ceryle alcyon* diving into water. (Facing page, top left) Kingfisher and (bottom left) Lesser Pied Kingfisher *Ceryle rudis*

ORDER Coraciiformes
FAMILY **UPUPIDAE: Hoopoe**

C. Loke/Photo Researchers

P. Jackson/Bruce Coleman

Although it clearly belongs to the order Coraciiformes, the Hoopoe *Upupa epops* constitutes a separate family. It is about thirty centimetres long, and its striking plumage with different shades of pink and cinnamon, the black and white bands on its wings and tail and the distinctive crest make the Hoopoe quite unmistakable. The dark bill is long and curves downward. It is generally a solitary bird except on migration when it forms small flocks. The Hoopoe's English name is derived from its call note, which is heard mainly during the nesting season and has been interpreted by different writers and poets as being a good omen or a portent of evil. The Hoopoe certainly occupies an important position in the folklore of many countries in the Old World and has frequently been depicted in popular art since the time of the ancient Egyptians.

The Hoopoe spends most of its time on the ground hunting for the worms, insects and spiders which form its basic diet. From time to time it also eats small vertebrates such as lizards, mice and occasionally the young of other species of bird. Its long, curved bill is ideal for extracting its prey from fissures in the ground or from the bark of trees.

The Hoopoe likes fairly hot climates and lives in thinly wooded areas. It is equally at home in farmland, orchards, gardens and parks. It nests in holes in trees or in crevices in walls or rocks; it sometimes digs a burrow in a bank of earth, a sandbank or a nest of termites. Between four and six eggs (or sometimes more) are laid which range in colour from pale blue to olive and are usually without markings. Incubation, which begins before the clutch is completed, is carried out by the female only and she is fed regularly by the male throughout this period. Both parents rear the young. A rather unusual aspect of the Hoopoe's behaviour is that the nest is not cleaned and consequently the nestlings' excreta soon transforms it into a small, fetid dungheap giving off a powerful smell of musk. There is nearly always a purpose for everything that happens in nature, and the stench from the Hoopoe's nest is believed to keep enemies at bay most effectively. The smell of musk is in fact due to a special secretion from the uropygial gland which is situated at the base of the tail of young birds and incubating females.

The Hoopoe is essentially a tropical bird which has not always lived in temperate zones in the Palearctic region. Its distribution is sporadic, from central Europe, Asia to the Baltic, South Africa, Madagascar and southeast Asia. The northernmost populations are migrant but the others are sedentary. A number of sub-species have evolved, and they differ mainly in the intensity of coloration and are sometimes mistakenly regarded as separate species.

(Above and facing page)
Hoopoe *Upupa epops:* the
long decurved bill, prominent
crest and striking plumage
make this species unmistakable.
(Left) World distribution of
the family Upupidae

93

Hoopoe
Upupa epops

French: HUPPE FASCIÉE
Italian: UPUPA
Spanish: ABUBILLA
German: WIEDEHOPF

(Above) Hoopoe with erect crest and folded-down crest. (Below) Breeding areas (yellow), areas where the Hoopoe may be seen all year round (orange) and on passage (pink). (Facing page) Hoopoe at its tree-hole nest

HABITAT During the nesting season it lives in wooded areas, orchards and parks where there are old, hollow trees suitable for nesting. It winters on bushy ground and on plains.

IDENTIFICATION Length: 27 cm. Unmistakable due to its pink-brown plumage, long curved bill, black-edged crest, and the heavy black and white bars on its wings and tail. In flight its broad, rounded wings with black and white bars and slow, languid movements are distinctive. Its crest is lowered in repose, but erect when

the Hoopoe is excited. It almost invariably feeds on the ground where it runs and walks with ease. Flight is more powerful and agile than it appears, enabling it to escape quickly from danger. It perches on trees, walls and buildings. The Hoopoe usually lives alone or in pairs but forms small flocks on migration.

CALL A deep 'hoo-hoo-hoo'.

REPRODUCTION Late April onwards. It generally nests in holes in tree-trunks and sometimes in holes in walls. The cavity is usually unlined. It lays between four and six oval, grey-white or olive-yellow eggs. Incubation is carried out by the female—who is fed by the male—for eighteen days.

FOOD Insects.

DISTRIBUTION AND MOVEMENTS Europe, except for the northern regions; central and southern Asia and Africa. It winters in tropical Africa. Accidental in Britain and Ireland (where it occasionally stays on to breed), the Faeroes, Iceland, Spitsbergen, Scandinavia, Finland and the northern USSR.

SUB-SPECIES There are sub-species in Asia and Africa.

Mike Price/Bruce Coleman

ORDER Piciformes
FAMILY PICIDAE: Woodpeckers

B. Campbell/Bruce Coleman

R. Kinne/Bruce Coleman

H. M. Barnfather/Bruce Coleman

(Above) Grey-headed Woodpecker *Picus canus.* (Above top right) Downy Woodpecker *Dendrocopos pubescens* and (above right) Lesser Spotted Woodpecker *D. minor*

Woodpeckers are compact, sturdily built birds. Their coloration is generally white, black, yellow, red, brown or green, and often various combinations of these colours. It is unusual for a woodpecker to have mimetic plumage, but many species have markings, bars or streaks, especially on the upperparts. Some species have crests. As a rule the sexes are alike, the only difference being the presence of a red or yellow patch on the male's head.

Woodpeckers' tails, which are generally wedge-shaped, have stiff feathers which provide highly effective supports when the birds are climbing tree-trunks. So important is this function that the central tail feathers are the last to be moulted and are not shed until the new outer tail feathers have grown, thus ensuring that the birds are never deprived of their invaluable props. Only wrynecks of the genus *Jynx* lack this sort of tail. Most woodpeckers usually have twelve tail feathers, but woodpeckers of the genus *Verreauxia* have only eight and those of the genus *Sasia* and the Powerful Woodpecker *Phloeoceastes pollens* have ten. Their flight

feathers are also fairly stiff, making their flight strong and undulating though not very sustained.

The woodpecker is a woodland bird and its arboreal habits are also demonstrated by other unusual morphological adaptations, the most characteristic of which is its incredibly long and mobile tongue. The bones supporting the tongue are particularly long and are usually wrapped round the back of the cranium, ending near the base of the bill. The stiff tip of the tongue is often edged with bristles or hooked barbs. Glands secreting a viscous mucus coat the tongue with a sticky substance which makes it an ideal instrument for catching ants and other insects and their larvae and for sucking sap from trees.

True woodpeckers have powerful, straight, scalpel-shaped bills, while those of the wrynecks and the so-called piculets are weaker and more rounded. The nostrils are covered with bristle-shaped feathers which protect them from sawdust as most species chisel holes in the trunks of old trees, hunting for the larvae of wood-eating insects.

Woodpeckers' legs are also well adapted to their way of life. They are short and powerful, with strong toes and very sharp, curved claws which enable them to grip firmly. When woodpeckers are climbing, they hold their toes in a curious way, with the second and third toes pointing forward and the fourth sideways; the first toe—if it is present—is also pointed sideways, but some species only have three toes. When they are perching or hopping on the ground, two toes point forwards and two backwards in the typical fashion of most climbing birds (zygodactylous toes).

Besides insects and sap, woodpeckers eat fruit and sometimes also hard-shelled nuts. Sometimes they store food in the summer to be eaten later when it is scarce. Some species normally feed on the ground and even nest on the ground if they live in treeless regions in America and southern Africa. In such cases the nest is situated in a tunnel dug in a

(Above and above left) Great Spotted Woodpecker *Dendrocopos major* at its tree-hole nest. (Left) Spotted-throated Woodpecker *Campethera scriptoricauda* and (far left) young Green Woodpecker *Picus viridis*

(Right) Lesser Spotted Woodpecker *D. minor* flying from its nest hole. (Below right) Grey-headed Woodpecker *P. canus* and (below) world distribution of the family Picidae

Eric Hosking

W. Schramil/Jacana

bank of earth or in a termites' nest instead of in a hole in a tree. The nest cavity is unlined, and the four to nine shiny white eggs are incubated by both parents for eleven to seventeen days. The young hatch blind and naked but are capable of abandoning the nest and climbing before they can fly. Woodpeckers' voices are generally deep and many species produce a characteristic drumming noise by beating their bills rapidly against branches or the hollow trunks of dead trees. This drumming forms part of the nuptial ceremony.

There are about two-hundred species in the family Picidae which is distributed almost everywhere apart from the extreme latitudes, Madagascar, Australia and most of the islands east of the Philippines, Celebes and Alor. Almost all species are solitary and do not travel far. Only the Wryneck *Jynx torquilla* and species of the genera *Colaptes* and *Sphyrapicus* are migrant. From the systematic point of view the family is usually divided into three sub-families.

There are only two very similar species in the sub-family Jynginae: the common Wryneck from the Palearctic region and the Red-breasted Wryneck *Jynx ruficollis* from tropical Africa. Their tails and bills are like other birds, but they have typical woodpecker tongues. The coloration of wrynecks is distinctly mimetic and similar to that of nightjars. Although they are primarily tree-dwellers, they rarely climb like true woodpeckers. Their diet consists mainly of ants. They assume a characteristic pose when alarmed, stretching their necks and undulating them from side to side. This movement together with their coloration is reminiscent of the defensive attitudes of certain snakes.

Small woodpeckers are allocated to the sub-family Picumninae. Their upper parts are grey or olive green and their underparts are white with black bars or markings. There are twenty-nine of these species which are also known as piculets. The genus *Picumnus* (consisting of five species) is distributed in South America and southeast Asia, but the other species occur in Africa and Asia. Haiti has its own species—the Antillean Piculet *Nesoctites micromegas*. Although their bills are less powerful than a true woodpecker's, they are adequate for probing rotten wood in search of insects.

The one-hundred-and-seventy-nine species of true woodpecker belong to the sub-family Picinae. The majority are natives of North, Central and South America and the Indo-Malaysian region but the sub-family is also well represented in the Palearctic region and in Africa. The Ivory-billed Woodpecker *Campephilus principalis* is one of the most beautiful species. It is probably extinct in the southern United States but occasional pairs may still be present in the most remote mountain regions of Cuba. The felling of old trees and the destruction of the forests where the Ivory Woodpecker lives has contributed to its decline.

(Right and overleaf) Green Woodpecker *P. viridis*: the black moustachial stripe is more conspicuous than the Grey-headed's although both species have red crowns

David Hosking

Wryneck
Jynx torquilla

French: TORCOL FOURMILIER
Italian: TORCICOLLO
Spanish: TORCECUELLO
German: WENDEHALS

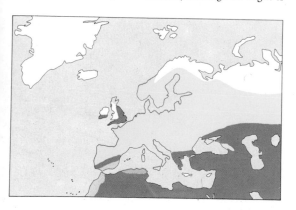

HABITAT During the breeding season it lives in spacious parks, gardens and deciduous woods.

IDENTIFICATION Length: 16 cm. Slightly elongated body with grey-brown plumage and fine wavy markings on the upper parts which are reminiscent of the plumage of a nightjar. Although it is similar to a woodpecker, it looks and behaves like a passerine. Adults and juveniles are alike. The Wryneck usually perches on branches but it is sometimes seen on the ground where it moves with small hops in search of food. It sometimes climbs tree-trunks in true woodpecker fashion, although its flight is less undulating than that of other woodpeckers.

CALL A nasal 'kew-kew-kew'.

REPRODUCTION From late May. The nest is situated in holes in trees, in cracks between tiles, in Sand Martins' nests or in nesting boxes. It lays between seven and ten dull white eggs. Incubation is carried out by both parents for twelve days, and both take part in rearing the offspring.

FOOD Insects and spiders: occasionally eats berries in the autumn.

DISTRIBUTION AND MOVEMENTS Europe and northwest Asia. It is predominantly a migrant, and spends the winter in tropical Africa, India, southern China, southern Japan, Vietnam, Laos and Cambodia. A very few pairs breed in southeast England and in the last decade a few have bred in the Scottish Highlands. Occurs on passage, mainly to coasts, in Britain and Ireland.

SUB-SPECIES *J.t. torquilla*: Europe, except for mainland Italy, Sicily and Sardinia. *J.t. tschusii* (darker and smaller): Italy, Sicily and Sardinia. There are other sub-species in Asia and Africa.

(Below left) Breeding areas (yellow), wintering areas (magenta), areas where the Wryneck may be seen all year round (orange) and on passage (pink)

French: PIC VERT
Italian: PICCHIO VERDE
Spanish: PITO REAL
German: GRÜNSPECHT

Green Woodpecker
Picus viridis

HABITAT Lives in deciduous forests, parks, thinly-wooded areas and along hedgerows.

IDENTIFICATION Length: 31 cm. It can be distinguished by its green plumage which is vivid on the upper parts and paler on the underparts, red crown and yellow rump. Its moustachial stripe is red in the male and black in the female. Juveniles are paler.

Has a short tail and a strong pointed bill. Climbs up tree-trunks where it moves in jerky hops, hunting for food, supported by the tail feathers which are held down against the trunk. Also feeds on the ground. Flight is very distinctive, with spells of undulating flight with folded wings alternating with every third or fourth wingbeat. It is not a very sociable species and lives alone except during the breeding season. During courtship the male pursues the female around a tree-trunk. When adopting a defensive attitude, the male sways its head from side to side, with its crest erect and its wings and tail spread. Unlike many other woodpeckers only exceptionally drums in spring.

CALL A loud, ringing peal of laughter.

REPRODUCTION From late April onwards. The nest is excavated in tree-trunks and the entrance is generally elliptical. It lays between five and seven oval white eggs per clutch. Incubation is carried out by both parents for eighteen or nineteen days and the young are reared by both parents. They are fed on regurgitated food.

FOOD Mainly the larvae of insects which live under bark. Also ants, berries and other plants.

DISTRIBUTION AND MOVEMENTS Breeds from southern Scandinavia, Britain and Iberia east across Europe to the Caspian Sea. Also breeds in northwest Africa and southern Iran. Mainly sedentary. Is a widespread resident breeder in England and Wales, less frequent in Scotland which it only colonised from 1951.

SUB-SPECIES *P.v. viridis:* Europe, except for the Iberian Peninsula, and Asia Minor. *P.v. sharpei* (pale grey cheeks): the Iberian Peninsula and the Pyrenees. Other sub-species are present in Asia and Africa.

(Left) Male Green Woodpecker
(top) and female. (Below)
Areas where the Green
Woodpecker may be seen all
year round (orange)

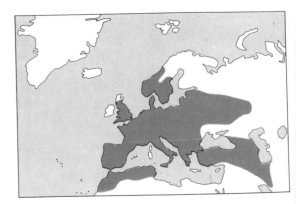

French: PIC CENDRÉ
Italian: PICCHIO CENERINO
Spanish: PITO CANO
German: GRAUSPECHT

Grey-headed Woodpecker
Picus canus

HABITAT Deciduous woods, parks and cultivated land. Also found in coniferous forests in mountainous regions.

IDENTIFICATION Length: 25 cm. Smaller than the Green Woodpecker but may easily be mistaken for it because of the similar green coloration. May be distinguished by its grey head and neck with a narrow black streak and the narrow black moustachial stripe. Sexes are alike but the male has a red forehead. Juveniles are browner with brown bars on their flanks. In behaviour is similar to the Green Woodpecker although it alights on the ground less frequently.

CALL Its call note is like the Green Woodpecker's but less sonorous. Its song is also similar but less harsh, and slows down towards the end. It often drums, especially in the spring.

REPRODUCTION March onwards (May in northern areas). It nests in holes in old or dead trees. Hole is excavated by both sexes. Lays between three and six glossy white eggs. Both sexes incubate the eggs for seventeen or eighteen days and both tend the young.

FOOD Insects and their larvae: very partial to ants.

DISTRIBUTION AND MOVEMENTS A predominantly Eurasian species which is found from central France and Scandinavia south to the Alps, the Balkans and east across Asia. It is generally sedentary. Many individuals come down to the plains in the winter, though some remain in the mountains, especially if there have not been heavy snow falls.

SUB-SPECIES Sub-species are present throughout Asia.

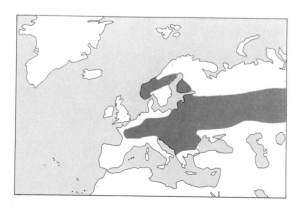

(Left) Areas where the Grey-headed Woodpecker may be seen all year round (orange)

103

French: PIC NOIR
Italian: PICCHIO NERO
Spanish: PITO NEGRO
German: SCHWARZSPECHT

Black Woodpecker
Dryocopuos martius

HABITAT Coniferous and mixed forests.

IDENTIFICATION Length: 45 cm. It is the largest European woodpecker and is easily identified by its completely black plumage which gives it a crow-like appearance. Roughly the same size as a crow but its flight is more undulating. The male's crown is bright red all over, while the female is only red on the nape. Its eyes are straw-coloured and its bill is pale ivory. Moves around constantly and draws attention to itself because of its distinctive call. It seems less agile on tree-trunks than many other woodpeckers, but it is nonetheless an expert climber. Has a distinctive angular way of holding its neck.

CALL A characteristic whistling 'clee-ee-aa' and a shrill, grating 'krree-krree-krree'. In flight it emits a brittle call note like the Green Woodpecker's but deeper, less piercing, and slower. It drums so energetically that it can be heard from far away, but it is not in the habit of drumming very often.

REPRODUCTION April to May. It bores large holes in trees, often in sound wood. Lays between three and six glossy white eggs which both birds incubate for twelve to fourteen days. Both parents also tend the young and, like many other woodpeckers, feed them on regurgitated food.

FOOD Wood-boring insects and their larvae; also ants and worms.

DISTRIBUTION AND MOVEMENTS A sedentary species distributed throughout the Palearctic region with sporadic, isolated pockets in the Pyrenees, central Spain, France and southern Italy. It occurs as far south as Greece: it is not present across the Mediterranean in North Africa although it is believed to have nested there when wooded areas were still extant. Some authors have strongly claimed that this species should be included on the British list, but these claims have so far been rejected.

SUB-SPECIES There is a sub-species in Asia.

(Below) Areas where the Black Woodpecker may be seen all year round (orange)

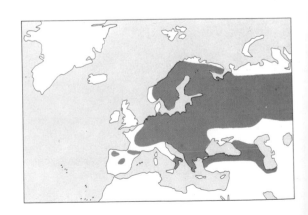

Great Spotted Woodpecker
Dendrocopos major

HABITAT It lives in woods, copses, parks and sometimes in gardens.

IDENTIFICATION Length: 23 cm. It is the most common black and white woodpecker in Europe. Differs from Lesser Spotted Woodpecker in being larger and has a black back with white markings on the shoulders and red under-tail coverts. Black crown (juveniles of both sexes have red crowns) and a red marking on the nape (found only in adult males). White underparts without streaks.

It rarely eats on the ground. Both male and female produce powerful, vibrant drumming notes rather like the sound of wind buffeting tree-tops. During courtship both sexes chase each other round and round branches. Flight is conspicuously bounding.

CALL A loud, sharp 'cheek-keek'.

REPRODUCTION From mid-May onwards. Its nest is a hole in a tree-trunk like the Green Woodpecker's. It lays from three to eight white eggs. Incubation takes sixteen days and is carried out mainly by the female, with some assistance from the male. Both parents rear the offspring.

FOOD Mainly the larvae of wood-eating insects: occasionally young birds and vegetable matter.

DISTRIBUTION AND MOVEMENTS Europe (except for the northernmost regions), Asia and northwest Africa. Mainly a resident species although some northern populations may migrate eruptively and some populations may be truly migrant. In Britain it is a widespread resident breeder, and also occurs as a winter and passage visitor. Large irruptions sometimes occur and individuals then spill over into Ireland.

SUB-SPECIES *D.m. major:* Scandinavia and the northern USSR. *D.m. pinetorum* (smaller): continental Europe (except for the Iberian Peninsula, Italy, Rumania and the southeastern USSR) and Asia Minor. *D.m. anglicus* (smaller and darker): England and Scotland. *D.m. italiae* (paler): southern France, the Pyrenees, Switzerland and Italy. *D.m. harterti* (darker): Corsica and Sardinia. *D.m. hispanus* (darker): the Iberian Peninsula. *D.m. candidus* (smaller and paler): Rumania and the southeastern USSR. *D.m. tenuirostris* (darker underparts): Crimea, the Caucasus and Transcaucasia. There are other sub-species present in Asia, Africa and the Canary Islands.

French: PIC ÉPEICHE
Italian: PICCHIO ROSSO MAGGIORE
Spanish: PICO PICAPINOS
German: BUNTSPECHT

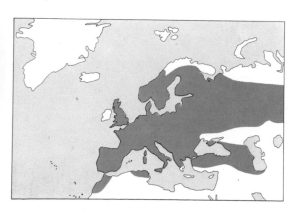

(Above) Adult Great Spotted Woodpecker (top) and juvenile. (Left) Areas where the Great Spotted Woodpecker may be seen all year round (orange)

French: PIC MAR
Italian: PICCHIO ROSSO MEZZANO
Spanish: PICO MEDIANO
German: MITTELSPECHT

Middle Spotted Woodpecker
Dendrocopos medius

HABITAT Mainly broad-leaved forests.

IDENTIFICATION Length: 21 cm. It can be identified by the light red crown without any black border and the sides of the head which are distinctly white with a narrow black moustachial stripe. Like the Great Spotted its back is boldly marked with two white ovals. Underparts are white; flanks densely covered with dark streaks and shade into reddish-pink on its belly and undertail.

CALL Like the Great Spotted Woodpecker's, but deeper.

REPRODUCTION April onwards. Lays four to eight glossy white eggs. Nest is an unlined cavity in a tree trunk. In some rare cases a natural cavity may be used. Lays four to eight smooth white eggs. Incubation period is not known.

FOOD Chiefly the larvae of insects.

DISTRIBUTION AND MOVEMENTS Sedentary but occasionally wanders. Present from central western Europe (but not Britain and Ireland) southern France and the Iberian Peninsula east to Asia Minor and Iran.

SUB-SPECIES Sub-species, which differ in the intensity of their coloration, are present in the Pyrenees, Turkey and Iran.

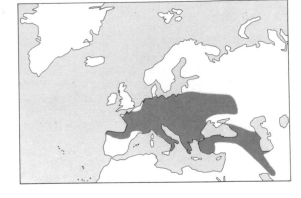

(Below) Middle Spotted Woodpecker. (Above right) Areas where the Middle Spotted Woodpecker may be seen all year round (orange)

Syrian Woodpecker
Dendrocopos syriacus

HABITAT Lives in the same environment as the Great Spotted Woodpecker.

IDENTIFICATION Length: 22 cm. Very similar to the Great Spotted Woodpecker both in size and general coloration. It has similar white shoulder patches and a black crown with a red patch on the nape of the male. However, it is fairly easy to distinguish because of its white cheeks which lack the black line that extends from chin to nape of the Great Spotted.

CALL Almost identical to the Great Spotted Woodpecker's.

REPRODUCTION The breeding season begins in mid-April. Five to seven glossy white eggs are laid which both sexes incubate for nine to fourteen days.

FOOD Insects and some fruit.

DISTRIBUTION AND MOVEMENTS A predominantly sedentary species found from Yugoslavia east to Iran, Syria and Iraq. It seems to have extended its distribution area to the northwest in recent years.

SUB-SPECIES Some authorities believe there is a Balkan sub-species *D.s. balcanicus* and a Transcaucasian sub-species *D.s. transcaucasicus*, but these classifications are not universally accepted.

(Facing page, bottom) Syrian Woodpecker. (Right) Areas where the Syrian Woodpecker may be seen all year round (orange)

White-backed Woodpecker
Dendrocopos leucotos

HABITAT Deciduous woods and less frequently found in coniferous woods.

IDENTIFICATION Length: 25 cm. Largest black and white woodpecker present in Europe. Back is a uniform black (without white 'epaulettes') and the rump is white—a feature which distinguishes if from most woodpeckers. Male has a white forehead and its crown is scarlet to the nape. The female has a black crown. The wings are heavily barred and lack any white patch.

CALL Like that of the Great Spotted Woodpecker but not as loud.

REPRODUCTION Late April onwards. It lays between three and six white eggs in a tree hole. Both sexes incubate the eggs for fourteen to sixteen days.

FOOD The larvae of wood-boring insects.

DISTRIBUTION AND MOVEMENTS Breeding distribution Eurasian, from central Europe and southern Scandinavia to Greece and Asia Minor and east to Japan and China. Populations are also resident in the region of the Spanish-French border.

SUB-SPECIES *D.l. lilfordi* is present in southeast Europe and Asia Minor. Other sub-species are found in Asia.

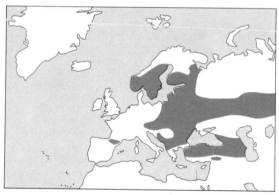

French: PIC À DOS BLANC
Italian: PICCHIO DORSOBIANCO
Spanish: PICO DORSIBLANCO
German: WEISSRÜCKENSPECHT

(Left) Areas where the White-backed Woodpecker may be seen all year round (orange)

French: PIC SYRIAQUE
Italian: PICCHIO ROSSO DI SIRIA
Spanish: PICO SIRIO
German: BLUTSPECHT

107

French: PIC MACULÉ
Italian: SUCCIALINFA COMUNE
Spanish: PICO SAPSUKER
German: GELBBAUCH-
SAFTSAUGERSPECHT

Lesser Spotted Woodpecker
Dendrocopos minor

French: PIC ÉPEICHETTE
Italian: PICCHIO ROSSO MINORE
Spanish: PICO MENOR
German: KLEINSPECHT

HABITAT Open woods, especially deciduous woods: also parkland and orchards.

IDENTIFICATION Length: 14 cm. The smallest woodpecker found in Europe—about the size of a Hedge Sparrow. Dirty white or slightly brown forehead. Crown red in the male and off-white in the female: juveniles of both sexes have little red on the heads. Underparts of adults white with some dark streaks on the flanks. Upper parts boldly barred to form a 'ladder-back' in black and white. Tends to spend more time in the canopy of trees than its larger cousins.

CALL A shrill repeated 'kee-kee-kee'.

REPRODUCTION From early May. Nest is a hole in a tree, usually in soft decayed wood: it may sometimes bore a hole in a side branch. Both adults bore the hole which consists of a tunnel about 3 cms in diameter which curves down to an elongated chamber. Eggs: four to six (sometimes three to eight) thin-shelled glossy white eggs are laid. Both sexes incubate, the male sitting at night, for fourteen days. Both tend the young, which hatch naked, feeding them with insects brought in the bill until they leave the nest after about three weeks.

FOOD Larvae of wood-boring insects and other inverte-

brates (especially spiders). On rare occasions eats fruit.

DISTRIBUTION AND MOVEMENTS Most of Europe and east across Asia as far as Japan. Also present in northern Africa and in the Azores. In Britain is a widespread although not numerous resident breeder, confined mainly to England and Wales.

SUB-SPECIES *D.m. minor:* northern continental Europe. *D.m. hortorum:* central and western Europe. *D.m. comminutus:* England and Wales. *D.m. buturlini:* Iberia, Italy and the Balkan peninsula.

(Above left) Male Lesser Spotted Woodpecker (right) and female. (Above right) Yellow-bellied Sapsucker. (Right) Areas where the Lesser Spotted Woodpecker may be seen all year round (orange)

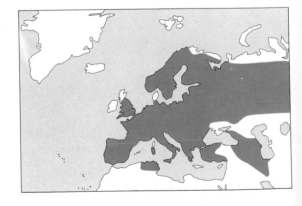

Yellow-bellied Sapsucker
Sphyrapicus varius

HABITAT Forests, orchards and plantations.

IDENTIFICATION Length: 24 cm. Varies greatly in coloration. Most commonly seen individuals have a red hood which is broken by a black streak running from the bill across the eye to the back of the head. Other black and white streaks run from the face to the neck and breast. Wings are strongly marked with white as is the back. White rump, black chin and red throat. Underparts off-white with V-shaped black markings. There are other varieties including one with a completely red head, neck, throat and breast.

CALL On the nest emits a 'you-ee-eek—you-ee-eek'; also a nasal 'hoy-hoy' and a muffled 'tak-tak'.

REPRODUCTION It excavates a hole in a dead tree or log and lays between four and seven white eggs. Incubation takes about fourteen days.

FOOD Mainly sap which it obtains by boring a series of parallel holes in trees with smooth bark.

DISTRIBUTION AND MOVEMENTS A North American species distributed from Alaska south to the Gulf of Mexico. It has occurred accidentally in the Antilles, the Bahamas, Greenland, Iceland and Britain.

Three-toed Woodpecker
Picoides tridactylus

HABITAT Mature coniferous forests and northern willow and birch forests.

IDENTIFICATION Length: 21 cm. Easily distinguished from all the other European species by the absence of red coloration, almost completely black wings and the broad white streak running from its nape to its rump. Cheeks are black. The centre of the crown is yellow in the male and black in the female. Only woodpecker, except for the White-backed, which has a white rump.

CALL Emits notes similar to those of the Great Spotted Woodpecker but softer.

REPRODUCTION Early May onwards. Nest is a hole usually bored in dead wood. Lays three to six white eggs. Both sexes incubate the eggs for fourteen days and both tend the young.

FOOD Wood-boring insects, seeds and fruit.

DISTRIBUTION AND MOVEMENTS A Holarctic species which nests from the Alps to Scandinavia east to eastern Siberia and Manchuria. In America it is distributed in arctic and alpine regions south to California. In winter it often travels south of its distribution area.

SUB-SPECIES A European sub-species *P.t. alpinus* is found in the Alps, the Carpathians and mountains in southeast Europe; there are other sub-species in Asia and America.

French: PIC TRIDACTYLE
Italian: PICCHIO TRIDATTILO
Spanish: PICO TRIDÁCTILO
German: DREIZEHENSPECHT

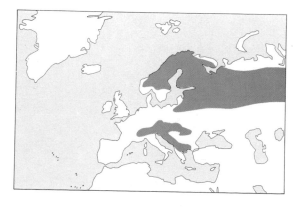

(Above) Female Three-toed Woodpecker (top) and male. (Left) Areas where the Three-toed Woodpecker may be seen all year round (orange)

ORDER **Passeriformes**

FAMILY **ALAUDIDAE: Larks**

F. V. Blackburn/Bruce Coleman

M. Boulton/Bruce Coleman

(Left) Red-capped Lark, a race of the Short-toed Lark *Calandrella cinerea* and (below) Skylark *Alauda arvensis*. (Facing page) Woodlark *Lullula arborea* with young

J. & S. Bottomley/Ardea

The order Passeriformes boasts more species than any other and, from the evolutionary point of view, is the most modern order of the class Aves (or birds). Within it, the lark family form a homogeneous, well-defined group. They are the first of the passerine or songbird families covered in the encyclopedia. Larks are predominantly ground-dwellers, generally found in open country. They walk or run but do not hop. Larks vary in length from twelve to twenty-three centimetres; the coloration is subdued, often cryptic, with grey-brown or sandy-buff upper parts and pale, usually speckled, underparts.

The Black Lark *Melanocorypha yeltoniensis* is entirely black in summer plumage: species of this genus, often known as calandra larks, are heavily built and have stout seed-eating bills. The most varied and colourful plumage is found in some races of the Shore Lark *Eremophila alpestris* and the so-called finch larks of the genus *Eremopterix*. The legs vary from short to medium in length; the tail is short or medium and the wings are in general fairly broad, but pointed, especially in the migrating species. The claw of the hind toe is often very long, straight and pointed. The shape of the bill may vary considerably, being adapted to the habits of the various species: short and cone-shaped in the genus *Calandrella*, cone-shaped and very strong in the calandra larks and *Ramphocoris* species, while in the genera *Alaemon* and *Chersophilus* the bill is long and curves downward.

The coloration of sub-species may vary greatly; indeed, this family offers excellent examples of the effect of natural selection on colour adaptation to the surroundings. In species of the genus *Ammomanes*, found in desert and semi-desert areas of northern Africa and of Asia, the different populations blend almost perfectly with their surroundings. The classic example is the Desert Lark *Ammomanes deserti* which is basically sandy in colour but varies greatly in shades of colour according to the dominant colour of its habitat. In Sudan the race *A.d. kollmanspergeri* lives among red sandstone and its plumage is uniform rufous-brown. The sub-species *A.d. azizi* is found in the chalky hills of eastern central Arabia, against which its drab sandy plumage renders it invisible. *A.d. annae*, found in black lava deserts in Jordan, is smoky-grey in colour while *A.d. phoenicuroides*, with light brownish-grey plumage, lives in arid, stony regions of northwestern India and Pakistan.

Other larks inhabit cultivated and less barren areas, so that their need to adapt their coloration to their surroundings is a more general one, related to the type of cultivation which geographically speaking varies little: a field of corn is much like any other field of corn anywhere. In such cases the plumage is spotted, as in the common Skylark *Alauda arvensis*. These species do display some

(Above) Fischer's Finch-Lark *Eremopterix leucopareia* from Africa. (Below) World distribution of the family Alaudidae

variation in colour, although less marked.

The Skylark is an excellent example of the concept of 'cline' or gradient of biological types. Its vast distribution area extends from Europe through Asia as far as Japan and from the Arctic Circle to Morocco. Starting from eastern Iran, the coloration of the various populations becomes stronger both to the east and to the west, while they gradually diminish in size from north to south, so that larks breeding in Italy are smaller than those of Britain and Ireland.

Although larks are generally birds of open country, whether arctic tundra or desert, nevertheless some species live in bushland. One species, the Woodlark *Lullula arborea*, freely perches and sings on trees.

The food of larks is predominantly vegetable, consisting mainly of seeds, although many insects are also taken especially in the breeding season. The larger species, with long, decurving bills, probe the ground in search of grubs.

The song of the lark is well-known: melodious and flute-like, often persistent, it is used both in courtship and for territorial defence. The best songsters of the family, such as the Skylark and the Calandra Lark *Melanocorypha calandra*, sing mostly on the wing, but there are species which sing perching on the ground, on a bush or even in trees like the already-mentioned Woodlark.

All larks build their nest on the ground, among grasses or in the open. It is usually a scrape lined with blades of dry grass, but many species of the genus *Mirafra* build a dome-shaped nest. Among species which nest in a hollow, the rim of the nest may be built up with small stones or other objects.

The family is mainly distributed in the Old World. Only the Shorelark is found also in North America, and there is also an isolated population in the Columbian Andes. There are about seventy-five species, grouped in about fifteen genera. The most numerous genus is *Mirafra* with twenty-one African species, one in Madagascar, two in Asia and one, the Singing Bush-lark *M. javanica*, whose range extends from northeastern Africa to Asia and parts of Australia. The monotypic genera include *Heteromirafra*, found in Africa, as are *Chersophilus* and *Pseudalaemon*, while the Thick-billed Lark *Ramphocoris clot-bey* occurs in North Africa and western Asia. *Certhilauda* contains three species, all South African; while the genus *Eremopterix*—the finch-larks—has seven species, of which five are confined to Africa: the Black-crowned Finch-lark *E. nigriceps* extends to the Cape Verde islands and the Ashy-crowned Finch-lark *E. grisea*, is found almost everywhere in India and Ceylon.

The Calandra larks of the genus *Melanocorypha*, numbering six species, are found from the Mediterranean to the deserts of Asia. The genus *Calandrella* contains eight species of much smaller larks in Africa and Eurasia. The genus *Galerida* numbers six species, of which two species are African and two Indian, while the common Crested Lark *G. cristata* and the Thekla Lark *G. theklae* overlap in southern Europe and northern Africa.

A. Christiansen

R. Richter/Ardea

(Above) Southern Singing
Bush-Lark *Mirafra cheniana*
from Africa and (left)
Crested Lark *Galerida cristata*
with young

113

French: ALOUETTE ISABELLINE
Italian: LODOLA DEL DESERTO
Spanish: TERRERA SAHARIANA
German: SANDLERCHE

French: ALOUETTE ÉLÉGANTE
Italian: LODOLA DEL DESERTO
CODABARRATA
Spanish: TERRERA COLINEGRA
German: BINDENSANDLERCHE

Bar-tailed Desert Lark
Ammomanes cincturus

HABITAT Sandy, stony or mixed desert terrain. More exclusively a desert species than the Desert Lark.

IDENTIFICATION Length: 13 cm. Uniformly pink-ish-beige, harmonising perfectly with its habitat. Less variable in coloration than Desert Lark. May be confused with the Desert Lark but differs in having a dark (almost black) sub-terminal band on the tail which is its main distinguishing feature. Another species with which it may be confused is Dunn's Lark (which has never been found in Europe) which, however, has all dark outer tail-feathers.
   Not a particularly shy species and may be approached with comparative ease, which helps identification. Often seen in small flocks.

CALL Song is weak and flute-like.

REPRODUCTION April and May. The nest, often built against a shelter such as a rock or a clump of grass, is surrounded by pebbles and usually contains two to four eggs (rarely five). The eggs differ from those of other larks in that the ground colour is white, with light black markings and deeper grey or lilac markings. Many eggs resemble those of the common Swallow. No information is available on incubation.

FOOD Mainly vegetable, but small invertebrates are also taken.

DISTRIBUTION AND MOVEMENTS North Africa and Asia. Both resident and migratory. In Europe the Bar-tailed Desert Lark has occurred as an accidental visitor.

SUB-SPECIES Sub-species are present in Asia and Africa.

Desert Lark
Ammomanes deserti

(Above left) Desert Lark and (right) Bar-tailed Desert Lark

HABITAT Deserts and semi-deserts; also rocky and stony ground sometimes with scattered trees.

IDENTIFICATION Length: 15 cm. Uniform sandy colour, but varying in shade in many of the sub-species according to habitat. Recognising it is largely a process of elimination: it has no crest, no special markings; the tail has no white or black upon it, thus distinguishing it from other species of the genus *Ammomanes*.

CALL A plaintive 'tweet'.

REPRODUCTION Begins in January in the south and as late as May in the north. The cup-shaped nest is built in a hollow in the ground, often in the shelter of a tuft of grass or of a rock, edged with pebbles around the exposed side. Eggs: lays three to five pink to greenish eggs with red-brown or purplish speckling. No information is available on incubation.

FOOD Plant material: also caterpillars.

DISTRIBUTION AND MOVEMENTS Mainly resident; found in North African deserts south to Ethiopia and Somalia. In Asia occurs from the Sinai peninsula and the Caspian east to Iraq and Iran. Accidental in Europe in Spain.

SUB-SPECIES As well as the nominate race, about twenty other sub-species are known.

French: SIRLI DES DÉSERTS
Italian: LODOLA BECCOCURVO
Spanish: ALONDRA IBIS
German: WÜSTENLÄUFERLERCHE

French: SIRLI DE DUPONT
Italian: LODOLA DI DUPONT
Spanish: ALONDRA DE DUPONT
German: DUPONT-LERCHE

Bifasciated Lark
Alaemon alaudipes

HABITAT Open, sandy terrain; also stony areas with very sparse vegetation.

IDENTIFICATION Length: 20 cm. One of the largest and most distinctive larks with very long, slightly decurved bill. The tail and legs are also long. Grey and beige coloration with streaked breast and white belly; striking black and white wing pattern. Pale back; outer tail-feathers show some white. Not very gregarious. At rest could be mistaken for a small courser. Sometimes known as the Hoopoe Lark as the wing pattern and bill resemble those of the Hoopoe.

CALL Emits a prolonged melodious whistling song which is uttered on the ground or in display flight.

REPRODUCTION April onwards. Like other larks, nests in hollows in the ground although sometimes in a clump of grass so that the nest is slightly raised. Eggs: two to four, white, with large greenish-brown or pink markings.

FOOD Mainly insect larvae which it digs out with its bill. Also seeds.

DISTRIBUTION AND MOVEMENTS A desert species, present from the Cape Verde islands through the Sahara and the Middle East and east through Syria and Iraq as far as western India. Accidental in Malta.

SUB-SPECIES Sub-species are present in Africa and southern Asia.

Dupont's Lark
Chersophilus duponti

HABITAT Dry areas both inland and on coasts; rocky desert or desert with low scrub.

IDENTIFICATION Length: 19 cm. Distinguished by rather erect gait and long, narrow, slightly decurved bill. Overall coloration varies from grey-brown to rufous-brown. Wings fairly uniform in colour, the breast streaked, the remaining underparts white, while the ground colour of the upper parts is covered with typically lark-like delicate spotting and streaking. Remarkably loath to fly and also shy: thus a very difficult species to observe. See also page 136.

CALL Emits a nasal 'dee-dee-dreee' with variations: also a double whistling note.

REPRODUCTION From March. Nest is a fairly deep cup-shaped hollow. Three to four smooth, white or pinkish eggs heavily spotted with a reddish or purple-brown colour are laid. No information is available on incubation.

FOOD Both vegetable and animal matter.

DISTRIBUTION AND MOVEMENTS Typical species of Algeria, Tunisia, Libya, Egypt and parts of Morocco: Dupont's Lark is one of the few species endemic to North Africa. May have nested in Portugal and is accidental in Spain, France and Italy.

SUB-SPECIES The sub-species *Ch.d. margaritae* occurs in the southern part of the range.

(Above left) Bifasciated Lark.
(Above) Dupont's Lark and
(right) the sub-species
C.d. margaritae

115

French: ALOUETTE CALANDRELLE
Italian: CALANDRELLA
Spanish: TERRERA COMÚN
German: KURZZEHENLERCHE

Short-toed Lark
Calandrella cinerea

HABITAT Uncultivated stony or sandy open areas.

IDENTIFICATION Length: 14 cm. Much smaller and paler than Skylark, lacks crest and has shorter bill. Upper parts buff with heavy dark streaking; underparts buff-white without streaking. Small blackish patch on sides of neck; sides of head brownish. Bill brownish, tinged yellow on lower mandible. Legs brownish. Complete moult between July and August. See also page 136.

CALL A short, twittering sparrow-like 'chi-chirp' and a 'ti-oo'.

REPRODUCTION Mid-April onwards. Nests in a hollow in the ground in the open, sometimes in a clump of grass. Nest is a cup of grasses or other vegetation and is lined—usually with feathers. Lays three to five smooth white or yellow eggs. Both sexes incubate, although mainly the female, for thirteen days. Double brooded.

FOOD Small seeds; also insects.

DISTRIBUTION AND MOVEMENTS Breeds in southern Europe including Iberia, southern France and other Mediterranean countries, northwest Africa and Asia. Winters in Africa, India and eastern China. Accidental in much of northern Europe including Britain and Ireland.

SUB-SPECIES *C.c brachydactyla*: southern Europe as far as the Crimea. *C.c. rubiginosa*: Malta and northern Africa. *C.c. artemisiana*: Caucasus, region between Caspian and Aral Seas, Transcaucasia, Asia Minor, Iran. Other sub-species are present in Asia.

Lesser Short-toed Lark
Calandrella rufescens

HABITAT Uncultivated stony or sandy open areas.

IDENTIFICATION Length: 14 cm. Very similar to Short-toed Lark but may be distinguished at close quarters by the fine streaking on the upper breast and absence of dark patches at the base of the neck. Coloration is more grey-brown and less rufous that the Short-toed Lark's. See also page 136.

CALL Like that of the Short-toed Lark.

REPRODUCTION From April onwards. Nest like that of the Short-toed Lark. Lays three to five white, yellow or buff eggs with grey-brown or reddish speckling—similar to those of the Short-toed. Further details are lacking.

DISTRIBUTION AND MOVEMENTS In Europe breeds in southern Spain and also in Russia from the northern shores of the Black Sea to the Caspian and the Urals and east as far as the Pacific seaboard of Siberia. Also breeds in the Middle East east to Afghanistan and in northern Africa. Is an accidental visitor northwards to Ireland where vagrant flocks have occurred.

SUB-SPECIES *C.r. apetzii* is present in Spain and *C.r. pispoletta* is found in Russia.

(Above) Short-toed Lark.
(Right) Breeding areas (yellow) and areas where the Short-toed Lark may be seen on passage (pink)

Sand Lark or Indian Sand Lark
Calandrella raytal

French: ALOUETTE DES SABLES
Italian: CALANDRELLA RAYTAL
Spanish: TERRERA RAYTAL
German: UFERLERCHE

HABITAT Sandy and shingle areas.

IDENTIFICATION Length: 14 cm. A small lark, typical of the genus *Calandrella,* with a relatively long and narrow bill, no crest and very short tail. Resembles a pale Short-toed Lark. The coloration, blending perfectly with its background, is silvery-sandy on the upper parts and grey-white on the underparts. The darker central part to the feathers of the crown, back, scapulars, wing coverts, secondaries and (less clearly) rump is typical of larks.

An agile bird that runs swiftly between rocks and on sand, occasionally undertaking short flights in search of insects or to gather seeds from the sparse grass.

CALL Similar to that of Short-toed Lark.

REPRODUCTION April to June. Lays three to four eggs, pale with various brown markings, in a simple scrape in the ground sheltered by a rock or, more rarely, by a bush.

FOOD Little data is available, but it appears that the diet often includes small invertebrates as well as seeds and other vegetable matter.

DISTRIBUTION AND MOVEMENTS A virtually sedentary species, although individuals nesting in higher altitudes may descend to the plains in winter. Found exclusively in India. Accidental in Europe, where it has been observed in southern Spain.

SUB-SPECIES Sub-species are present in India.

French: ALOUETTE PISPOLETTE
Italian: CALANDRINA, OR
PISPOLETTA
Spanish: TERRERA MARISMEÑA
German: STUMMELLERCHE

(Left) Lesser Short-toed Lark. (Facing page, bottom) Breeding areas (yellow) and areas where the Lesser Short-toed Lark may be seen all year round (orange)

French: ALOUETTE CALANDRE
Italian: CALANDRA
Spanish: CALANDRIA COMÚN
German: KALANDERLERCHE

Calandra Lark
Melanocorypha calandra

HABITAT Dry stony ground and grassy steppes. Also dry, open pastures and cultivated areas.

IDENTIFICATION Length: 20 cm. Distinguished by its large size, heavy build, stout horny yellow bill and wide black patch on either side of the neck. The buffish breast is lightly streaked brown. In flight the trailing white edge of the wing is conspicuous. See also page 136.

CALL A nasal 'kletka'. Also emits a Skylark-like song and notes mimicking those of other birds.

REPRODUCTION April onwards. Nest is a cup made of dry grasses and stems which is built in a hollow in the ground. Four to five eggs (rarely six or seven) are laid which are a dull white marked with brownish or purple-grey speckles. No information on incubation or nestlings is available.

FOOD Mainly seeds: also insects and their larvae.

DISTRIBUTION AND MOVEMENTS Breeds in southern Europe from Iberia east to Afghanistan: also northern Africa. Winters in the southern part of the breeding range. Accidental in Scandinavia and western and central Europe including Britain (twice).

SUB-SPECIES Sub-species are present in Asia.

Bimaculated Lark
Melanocorypha bimaculata

HABITAT Similar to that of the Calandra Lark, but more often found in barren, desert regions and at higher altitudes.

IDENTIFICATION Length: 16 cm. Very similar to Calandra Lark and considered by some authorities to be only a sub-species of that bird. However it is much smaller, with a conspicuous white eyestripe, less black at the base of the throat and generally paler background coloration. It may also be distinguished by the absence of a white edge to the tips of the secondaries and of white outer tail feathers. In flight, therefore, lacks the white trailing edge to the wing that· is a distinguishing feature in the Calandra Lark. The under-tail coverts are also lighter than the Calandra Lark's. See also page 136.

CALL The song, uttered mainly on the wing, is similar to that of Calandra Lark. It is also a good mimic of other birds' songs.

REPRODUCTION April to July. The nest is a cup in a hollow and is lined with soft vegetation. The three to six eggs which are laid vary in colour and shape but are usually greyish-white veined with brown or olive, with various buff, rufous, or lilac speckles.

FOOD Seeds and insects.

DISTRIBUTION AND MOVEMENTS Breeds from Asia Minor to Afghanistan and northwards to southern USSR. Migrates south to Egypt, Sudan, Ethiopia, Arabia and northwestern India. Accidental in Europe as far as Britain (twice in England).

SUB-SPECIES Sub-species are present in Asia.

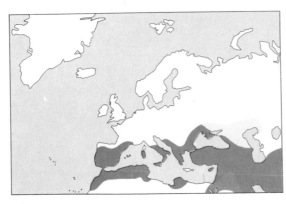

(Above) Calandra Lark. (Right) Breeding areas (yellow), wintering areas (magenta) and areas where the Calandra Lark may be seen all year round (orange)

White-winged Lark
Melanocorypha leucoptera

HABITAT Dry grassy steppes and semi-desert areas.

IDENTIFICATION Distinguished from other larks by large white wing-bar (hence its English name) which is very conspicuous in flight. Distinguishable from the Calandra Lark in particular by the absence of black on neck. Upper parts buff with dark streaks; crown, wing coverts and tail more rufous than those of other larks. Underparts whitish with throat and breast lightly spotted buff. See also page 136.

CALL The song is similar to the Skylark's.

REPRODUCTION April onwards. Nest is a cup of dried grass built in a hollow in the ground. The female lays four to eight creamy or greyish-white eggs which are speckled with grey, brown or olive. The female alone incubates for twelve days. Usually double-brooded.

FOOD Mainly seeds; also insects.

DISTRIBUTION AND MOVEMENTS Southern USSR, western Siberia and the Crimea. Migratory, winters south to Turkey, northern Iran and Transcaspia. May be regular in winter in Greece. Is an accidental visitor to Britain.

French: ALOUETTE LEUCOPTÈRE
Italian: CALANDRA SIBERIANA
Spanish: CALANDRIA ALIBLANCA
German: WEISSFLÜGELLERCHE

(Left) Breeding areas (yellow), wintering areas (magenta) and areas where the White-winged Lark may be seen all year round (orange)

French: ALOUETTE MONTICOLE
Italian: CALANDRA BIMACULATA
Spanish: CALANDRIA BIMACULADA
German: BERG-KALANDERLERCHE

(Left) Bimaculated Lark. (Facing page, bottom) Breeding areas (yellow), wintering areas (magenta) and areas where the Bimaculated Lark may be seen all year round (orange)

119

French: ALOUETTE NÈGRE
Italian: CALANDRA NERA
Spanish: CALANDRIA NEGRA
German: MOHRENLERCHE

Black Lark
Melanocorypha yeltoniensis

(Above) Black Lark in summer plumage (foreground) and winter plumage. (Below right) Areas where the Black Lark may be seen all year round (orange)

HABITAT Grassy and bushy steppes, also in desert. In winter may be found on cultivated land.

IDENTIFICATION Length: 20 cm. Male unmistakable: large and black with light sandy-coloured edges to the feathers which in winter partially obscure the black. Bill short and heavy, yellow with black tip. The female closely resembles a pale Calandra Lark, but may be distinguished by absence of black at base of neck and by blackish underwing. Neither male nor female has any white on wings or tail. Legs black.

On the ground runs to and fro, then rises on spread wings. At the end of the breeding season gathers in flocks. See also page 136.

CALL A clear chirping note. The song resembles the Skylark's song but is less melodious and is emitted in shorter bursts.

REPRODUCTION Begins late March to early May. Nests in hollows in the ground, building a cup lined with dry grass. Lays four or five eggs, occasionally six to eight, similar to those of Calandra Lark: greyish-white spotted with pale brown. Incubation period not known.

FOOD Mainly seeds; also insects.

DISTRIBUTION AND MOVEMENTS Southern USSR and western Siberia. In winter migrates towards Turkestan, the Caucasus, the Black Sea, northern Iran. It is accidental further west.

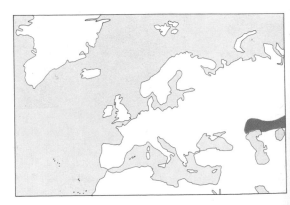

J. S. Wightman/Ardea

(Left) Young Skylarks
Alauda arvensis at the nest.
The long down on the back
and head acts as camouflage.
(Below) Red-capped Lark,
an African sub-species of
the Short-toed Lark
Calandrella cinerea

A. Christiansen

121

French: ALOUETTE HAUSSE-COL
Italian: ALLODOLA GOLAGIALLA
Spanish: ALONDRA CORNUDA
German: OHRENLERCHE

Shore Lark
Eremophila alpestris

HABITAT Breeds on arctic tundra and in rocky alpine areas. Winters on coasts.

IDENTIFICATION Length: 17 cm. Head and throat yellow; the pointed black 'horns' are joined by a black band across the forehead. Cheeks and base of neck black. This black and yellow pattern distinguishes it from other larks. Upper parts pink-brown, streaked dark brown on back. Underparts yellow-white; flanks rufous-grey; wings dark brown; tail brown with some white at sides. Bill grey and legs black. Complete moult in autumn. Juveniles have brown-black upper parts with reddish edges and whitish tips to the feathers; no black on head, brown cheeks, yellowish eyebrow. Underparts mottled brown on flanks and breast. Bill and legs yellowish.

An agile bird which runs and hops with equal facility on land or snow. Digs in snow to find food or a shelter for the night. Sociable. Flight swift and more undulating than that of the Skylark. See also page 136.

CALL Various notes: most common a shrill 'tsip' and 'tseep' similar to a Rock Pipit's; also a chirping 'tuup', 'tsueerrp' or a clear 'tsee-ee-tsee-tee-tee' with variations. Its short, high-pitched song resembles the Skylark's.

REPRODUCTION Mid-May onwards. Nests on the ground in the shelter of a tussock of grass or a rock, in dry, open areas. Lays four eggs (sometimes two to seven), greenish-white in colour, mottled yellowish-brown. The female alone incubates for ten to fourteen days. The young are tended by both parents and leave the nest after nine to twelve days. Usually double-brooded.

FOOD Small molluscs, crustaceans and insects: also seeds, buds and shoots of plants.

DISTRIBUTION AND MOVEMENTS Breeds in Europe in Scandinavia, northern USSR, Greece, southern Yugoslavia and Bulgaria. Also breeds through Asia Minor and Asia, North Africa and the Americas. Has bred recently in Scotland. Northern European populations winter on the east coasts of Britain, Germany, the Netherlands, Belgium and northern France. Accidental in Italy, Spain, Malta and Sicily.

SUB-SPECIES *E.a. flava*: northern Eurasia *E.a. balcanica*: Yugoslavia, Bulgaria, Greece. Many other sub-species in Asia, Africa and the Americas. The sub-species *E.a. alpestris* which breeds in eastern Canada has occurred as an accidental visitor to the Outer Hebrides.

(Right) Breeding areas (yellow), wintering areas (magenta) and areas where the Shore Lark may be seen all year round (orange)

Crested Lark
Galerida cristata

HABITAT Dry stony and sandy ground. Also frequents cultivated and urban areas: seen on roadsides, railway sidings and building sites.

IDENTIFICATION Length: 17 cm. Distinguished from Skylark by lighter coloration, longer erect crest, slightly curved, fairly long bill and tail which has dark centre and buff sides. Upper parts sandy brown, less streaked than in Skylark. Underparts buffish cream, streaked on breast. In flight has orange-buff patch on underwing, a further distinguishing feature from the Skylark. Legs brownish. Complete moult between August and November. Juveniles have more spotting on upper parts and fairly short crest.

Although basically terrestrial, will perch freely on bushes, walls, buildings and telephone wires. See also page 136.

CALL A liquid rising and falling 'whe-wheee-ooo': also a high-pitched double note.

REPRODUCTION Mid-April onwards. Nests on the ground in the shelter of a tussock of grass or among crops; also often on verges of quiet tracks. Both sexes build the cup-shaped nest of dry grass and small roots in the ground. Three to five grey-white or buff-white eggs (rarely six) are laid, speckled yellowish-brown and ashy. Female alone incubates the eggs for twelve to thirteen days. Both male and female feed the chicks which remain in the nest for nine to thirteen days. Two, sometimes three, broods per year.

FOOD Mainly cereals: also grass seeds and insects and their larvae.

DISTRIBUTION AND MOVEMENTS Breeds from southern Sweden, France and Iberia east across Eurasia to North Korea. Also breeds in northern and west Africa and Arabia. Mainly sedentary. Accidental in Britain.

SUB-SPECIES *G.c. cristata*: Europe except Iberia, Italy and the Balkans. *G.c. pallida* (paler): Spain and Portugal. *G.c. meridionalis* (browner): southern Italy. *G.c. caucasica* (paler): Balkans. Other sub-species are present in Asia and Africa.

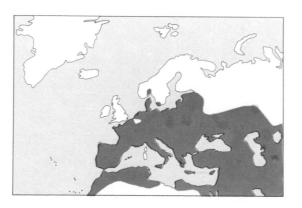

(Left) Areas where the Crested Lark may be seen all year round (orange)

Thekla Lark
Galerida theklae

HABITAT Similar to that of the Crested Lark, but prefers overgrown, more broken ground and avoids inhabited areas.

IDENTIFICATION Length: 16 cm. Practically indistinguishable from Crested Lark although the bill is shorter and the upper parts are greyer. Best distinguished by its song, which is like that of the Skylark, and is delivered in flight. See also page 136.

CALL Less liquid and melodious than that of the Crested Lark.

REPRODUCTION From April onwards. The nest is a shallow hollow in the ground lined with grasses. Three to six eggs are laid in each clutch and they are indistinguishable from those of the Crested Lark. The actual number appears to depend on weather conditions.

FOOD Seeds and small insects.

DISTRIBUTION AND MOVEMENTS Breeds in the southern Palearctic region from Spain and Portugal to southern France: also in northern Africa.

SUB-SPECIES Sub-species are present in Africa.

(Below) Areas where the Thekla Lark may be seen all year round (orange)

Woodlark
Lullula arborea

French: ALOUETTE LULU
Italian: TOTTAVILLA
Spanish: TOTOVÍA
German: HEIDELERCHE

HABITAT A wide variety of habitats including woodland, heaths, parkland, and cultivated land.

IDENTIFICATION Length: 15 cm. Crown and upper parts are rufous-brown, streaked brown-black; rump and under-tail coverts unmarked; underparts creamy white, blotched brown-black at sides of tail and on upper part of breast. In flight tail is noticeably shorter than the Skylark's. Whitish eyebrows meeting across the nape are an important field mark. Bill dark brown with paler lower mandible. Crest not always visible in the field. Legs pale. Complete moult at the end of autumn. Juveniles have creamy white barring on upper parts and smaller markings on breast.

Perches freely on bushes, trees, poles and telegraph wires. The male rises silently to a considerable height and begins to sing, circling and spiralling. During courtship both male and female raise the crest and open and close the tail, shaking the head from side to side. See also page 136.

CALL A soft 'tit-looiit'.

REPRODUCTION Late March onwards. Nest is a substantial cup built on the ground with dry grasses, lichens and small roots, and it is lined with finer materials. Sometimes exposed, but usually sheltered by vegetation. Three to five eggs are laid, rarely six, greyish-white, finely speckled with pinkish-brown, olive-brown and grey. Occasionally pure white. The female alone incubates for twelve to sixteen days. The young are fed by both parents and remain in the nest for about twelve days.

FOOD Mainly insects and their larvae, spiders and caterpillars. Also feeds on seeds and tender shoots of grasses.

DISTRIBUTION AND MOVEMENTS Europe, except for the far north, Asia Minor and northwest Africa. Winters in western Europe, the Mediterranean and sometimes also outside the breeding range. In Britain is a scarce and decreasing resident breeder in the south of England and parts of Wales.

SUB-SPECIES *L.a. pallida* (paler): southern Mediterranean peninsulas and northwest Africa.

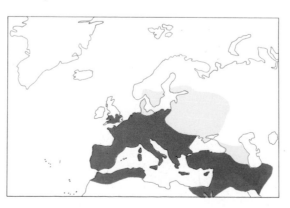

(Left) Breeding areas (yellow) wintering areas (magenta) and areas where the Woodlark may be seen all year round (orange)

125

French: ALOUETTE DES CHAMPS
Italian: ALLODOLA
Spanish: ALONDRA COMÚN
German: FELDLERCHE

Skylark
Alauda arvensis

HABITAT Open, grassy moorland, meadows, marshes and farmland.

IDENTIFICATION Length: 18 cm. Quite large, plain brown lark with inconspicuous crest. Upper parts brown, closely streaked black. Underparts buff-white with wide streaking on breast. Rather long tail with conspicuous white outer tail-feathers. Bill and legs dark brown. Complete moult between June and September. Juveniles have dark brown upper parts with buffish-brown margins and whitish tips to the feathers.

When disturbed crouches instead of running. Perches on tall plants and telephone wires when singing, or may rise to a height of several hundred metres. Then it plummets silently to the earth, only opening its wings when very close to the ground. Flight strong, slightly undulating, with several wingbeats alternating with periods when the wings are closed. In courtship the male erects the feathers on its head and breast and circles round the female with tail spread and one wing drooping: the female spreads her tail and vibrates her wings. See also page 136.

CALL A clear, liquid 'chirrup' or 'chee . . . r . . . ep' with variations.

REPRODUCTION From late April. Nests on the ground in a depression sheltered by tussocks of grass; the nest is a shallow cup made of dried grasses and is lined with finer grasses. Three or four eggs (sometimes five to seven), greenish-grey or creamy-grey, covered with dark greyish-brown mottling, are laid. The female alone incubates for about eleven days. The young are fed by both parents.

FOOD Seeds, leaves and sometimes grains. Also earthworms, beetles and some small ground animals.

DISTRIBUTION AND MOVEMENTS Breeds from Iberia, Britain and Ireland east across Eurasia to northern Japan. Mainly migratory: winters in the southern part of the breeding range, or just south of it. In Britain and Ireland is a widespread and numerous breeding bird, as well as a passage migrant and winter visitor in large numbers.

SUB-SPECIES *A.a. sierrae* (more rufous): Iberia. *A.a. cantarella* (greyer): southern Europe. Other sub-species are present in Asia and in Africa.

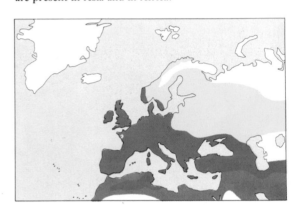

(Right) Breeding areas (yellow), wintering areas (magenta) and areas where the Skylark may be seen all year round (orange). (Facing page) Swallow *Hirundo rustica* at the nest

FAMILY HIRUNDINIDAE: Swallows and Martins

J. Carpenter/Bruce Coleman

(Below and right) The Sand Martin *Riparia riparia* is distinguished from the Crag Martin *Hirundo rupestris* by its white throat and brown breast-band. (Bottom) Red-rumped Swallow *Hirundo daurica;* its rufous-buff rump is distinctive

The family Hirundinidae which consists of swallows and martins is a well-defined group of small, long-winged aerial birds, numbering about seventy-eight species classified in nineteen genera.

The length of swallows and martins varies from nine to twenty-two centimetres (excluding the elongated, filiform outer tail-feathers). In many species the upper parts are black, brown, dark green or dark blue with a metallic lustre; some species have streaked underparts but most have white, chestnut or grey-brown underparts. A few have a white or rufous rump, and many have white patches on the tail, chiefly visible in flight and when the tail is spread. The bill is short and flat, with a wide gape; the head is fairly large but flattened and the neck is short. The wings are long and pointed although sometimes fairly broad; the tail may be very long, and it is usually forked. The legs are short, the tarsi (and sometimes toes) often feathered; the toes are small. Both swallows and martins often perch on wires or branches and even on the ground. The sexes are similar and there is one moult each year, after the breeding season.

The apparently superficial resemblance to swifts of the family Apodidae is probably due to the phenomenon of evolutionary convergence: swallows and martins are essentially aerial birds, catching their food (insects) in the air. Their flight is graceful and fast and they may often be seen feeding over fresh water. Unlike swifts, however, they regularly settle, do not mate in flight, and sleep perched close to one another in the nest, on telegraph wires, in reed beds and so forth. Martins and swifts are gregarious birds.

In temperate regions members of this family regularly migrate since in winter there is insufficient insect food available. In some exceptional cases, such as the Crag Martin *Hirundo rupestris*, individuals may spend the winter at the nesting grounds in a sort of lethargy, occasionally interrupted on sunny days when they fly out from their shelter (a crack in a tower or bell-tower, a cave, etc.) to catch any insects which have been tempted into activity by the sun.

They are colonial in their nesting habits. The nest, depending on the species, may be a tunnel or some other cavity. More usually it is an elaborate construction of mud glued together with saliva and fixed to rocks, walls or an overhang.

Some species excavate a tunnel in earthy or sandy river-banks or in banks some distance from water. Others build a cup-shaped nest of mud, more or less closed in, or sometimes with a tunnel entrance which may vary in shape and length. In some cases the structure of the nest is the best distinguishing feature of the species. The open cup-shaped nest of the common Swallow *Hirundo rustica* is well known: it is often built under rafters or bridges. The nest of the House Martin *Delichon urbica* is often seen stuck to cliffs or outcrops, but is more frequently built under the eaves or on the walls of buildings.

The family is virtually cosmopolitan in distribution: only in the most extreme latitudes and on some oceanic islands are swallows absent. Within the family, however, some genera are cosmopolitan and others have a more localised distribution. The Swallow nests from Eurasia to North America, as well as in parts of Africa, and migrates southwards as far as Argentina, southern Africa and Australia. The same genus *Hirundo* contains fourteen other species, mainly African, although one, the Pacific Swallow *H. tahitica*, is also widely distributed in Australia and the western Pacific. Of the four species of sand martin one, the common Sand Martin *Riparia riparia*, has a Holarctic distribution, while the species of the genus *Petrochelidon* are found in Africa, the Americas, Asia and the Australian region. The House Martin *Delichon urbica*, the Asiatic House Martin *D. dasypus* and Nepal House Martin *D. nipalensis* are found only in the Old World. The Crag Martin *Hirundo rupestris* and the Red-rumped Swallow *H. daurica* both build their nests on cliffs although the Red-rumped often frequents towns. A purely African genus is *Psalidoprocne*—the 'rough-winged swallows'—which consists of five to twelve species, depending

(Left) House Martins *Delichon urbica* rarely alight except to collect mud which they use to build their nests. (Below) Wire-tailed Swallow *Hirundo smithii* leaving its nest under a barn roof

J. Burton/Bruce Coleman

C. Loke/Photo Researchers

J. Van Wormer/Photo Researchers

on the authority consulted. They nest in natural cavities, as does the Grey-rumped Swallow *Pseudo-hirundo griseopyga*, which is unique in that it nests in the burrows of certain small rodents in plains: thus it must breed in the dry season to escape the danger of flooding.

The two species of the genus *Phedina*—the Mascarene Martin *P. borbonica* and the Congo Martin *P. brazzae*—are found respectively in the Malagasy region and in Africa. The White-backed Swallow *Cheramoeca leucosterna* is typical of some parts of Australia.

Some other genera are found exclusively in the Americas. Among the most common are species of the genus *Tachycineta* which includes the Tree Swallow *T. bicolor*, which resembles the House Martin of Europe. The Purple Martin *Progne subis* is widely distributed in North America. Its plumage is uniformly dark, and it often nests in purpose-built nesting-boxes. The Rough-winged Swallow *Stelgidopteryx ruficollis* is found throughout North America, while in South America the Blue and White Swallow *Notiochelidon cyanoleuca* nests in the abandoned nests of the Common Miner *Geositta cunicularia*, a passerine of the family Furnariidae which is typical of South America. The Golden Swallow *Kalochelidon euchrysea*, so named because of the metallic lustre of its upper parts, occurs exclusively in the islands of Hispaniola and Jamaica. Finally there is the African River Martin *Pseudochelidon eurystomina* whose classification with the family of swallows and martins is dubious. Not only is its bill heavier, the iris scarlet and the plumage glossy black, but it lacks the typical tracheal ring structure of the true swallows. It is found only in one part of the Congo.

(Above) House Martins *Delichon urbica* gather in large groups before migrating and (right) Swallow *Hirundo rustica* feeding young with food which is brought in the throat. (Left) World distribution of family Hirundinidae

H. Kinloch/Aquila

French: HIRONDELLE DE FENÊTRE
Italian: BALESTRUCCIO
Spanish: AVIÓN COMÚN
German: MEHLSCHWALBE

House Martin
Delichon urbica

HABITAT Breeds in or near inhabited areas; also on cliffs and bridges.

IDENTIFICATION Length: 12 cm. Distinguished from other hirundines by blue-black head, tail, back and wings; also by white rump and underparts. The tail is short and forked, without elongated streamers. In general the pure white rump together with the white underparts is the best way to identify this species. The white legs are feathered. Juveniles' upper parts are browner. See also page 142.

CALL A clear 'chirrp' or 'cheetirrip'; also a shrill 'tseep' of alarm.

REPRODUCTION End of May onwards. Nest is built by both sexes, on outer walls of buildings, under eaves and on cliffs. Nest is shaped like a rounded half-cup and at the top it has a small entrance hole. It is made of mud pellets strengthened with plant fibres. Eggs: four to five, white eggs, sometimes with fine red spots, are laid. Both sexes incubate the eggs for thirteen to nineteen days and both feed the young with food brought in their mouths.

FOOD Insects caught on the wing, especially flies and small beetles.

DISTRIBUTION AND MOVEMENTS Europe, Asia as far as northeastern Siberia and Japan and northwest Africa. Winters in Africa south of the Sahara. In Britain and Ireland is a widely distributed breeder, resident from mid-April to mid-October.

SUB-SPECIES Sub-species are present in Asia.

French: HIRONDELLE DE RIVAGE
Italian: TOPINO
Spanish: AVIÓN ZAPADOR
German: UFERSCHWALBE

Sand Martin
Riparia riparia

HABITAT Found in open country, near fresh water.

IDENTIFICATION Length: 12 cm. Smaller and more slender than the Swallow and House Martin: one of the smallest hirundines found in Europe. Uniform brown upper parts and white underparts with brown breast band. The tail is only slightly forked and has no white spots. Juveniles have a fringe of paler colour on the feathers of the upper parts. See also page 142.

CALL A sharp 'chreep' which is shriller than that of the House or Sand Martin.

REPRODUCTION Mid-May onwards. Nests in colonies in quarries, sand and gravel pits, river banks or on cliffs. Bores a tunnel which widens at the end, usually some metres up but in the extreme north of the range, where suitable sites are not available, it may nest at ground level. Both sexes excavate the nest, although occasionally existing holes may be used. Eggs: four or five white and moderately glossy eggs are laid. Both sexes incubate the eggs for twelve to sixteen days and both care for the young.

FOOD Mosquitoes and other small insects: usually catches them over water.

DISTRIBUTION AND MOVEMENTS Breeds from Britain and Ireland through Eurasia, except for the northernmost regions, to Japan. Also breeds in North America where it is known as the Bank Swallow. Winters south to tropical Africa, South America and Indo-China. In Britain and Ireland the Sand Martin is a widespread breeder although it is scarce in the north and west. Resident from March to October, and also occurs as a passage visitor.

SUB-SPECIES Sub-species found in Asia and Africa.

(Right) Breeding areas (yellow) and areas where the House Martin may be seen on passage (pink). (Far right) Breeding areas (yellow) and areas where the Sand Martin may be seen on passage (pink)

Franch: HIRONDELLE DES
ROCHERS
Italian: RONDINE MONTANA
Spanish: AVIÓN ROQUERO
German: FELSENSCHWALBE

Crag Martin
Hirundo rupestris

HABITAT Breeds on inland and sea cliffs and rocky islands. Also sometimes present in towns.

IDENTIFICATION Length: 14 cm. Plumage of underparts is light brown with characteristic white patches halfway down the tail, conspicuous when tail is spread. Unlike Sand Martin lacks a marked breast band. Juvenile more rufous than adult Crag Martin. Less gregarious than other martins and swallows. Its wings are broader than those of other martins, and it may be observed soaring by itself. See also page 142.

CALL Utters a weak 'chich' or 'chrrree'.

REPRODUCTION Late May onwards. Builds a cup-shaped nest, similar to that of the Swallow, but a little smaller. Nest is often fixed to a vertical rock face. Lays three to four white eggs with fine red and grey spots. The female alone incubates for about fourteen days.

FOOD Insects taken on the wing.

DISTRIBUTION AND MOVEMENTS Breeds from southern Europe eastwards across south and central Asia as far as China. Also breeds in the northern coastal belt of Algeria, Tunisia and part of Morocco. Is resident in parts of southwest Europe. Migrates southwards.

(Top) Sand Martin and (above) Crag Martin. (Left) Breeding areas (yellow), wintering areas (magenta), areas where the Crag Martin may be seen all year round (orange) and on passage (pink)

French: HIRONDELLE DE
CHEMINEE
Italian: RONDINE
Spanish: GOLONDRINA COMUN
German: RAUCHSCHWALBE

Swallow
Hirundo rustica

(Right) Breeding areas
(yellow), areas where the
Swallow may be seen all
year round (orange) and
on passage (pink)

HABITAT Open country and farms: generally breeds in buildings.

IDENTIFICATION Length: 19 cm. Most common hirundine in Europe. Easily distinguished by its elongated, tail streamers, metallic dark blue upper parts, chestnut forehead and throat. Underparts creamy-white with dark breast-band. Juveniles have shorter outer tail-feathers and are noticeably duller in colour.

Spends much time on the wing, but perches freely in groups on telegraph wires, buildings, bushes and branches; alights only rarely on the ground, where it moves with some difficulty. Sure, swift, very graceful flight. Hunts for insects over the surface of water, among vegetation, and sometimes high in the air. Gregarious, except during breeding season. See also page 142.

CALL A shrill 'tswit', often uttered in flight. Also a song consisting of twittering and bubbling notes.

REPRODUCTION Mid-May onwards. The cup-shaped nest, built by both sexes from mud and straw is generally constructed on rafters, sometimes under eaves and exceptionally in trees. Eggs: normally four to five, white with small rufous and grey markings. Female mainly incubates, for fourteen to sixteen days.

FOOD Insects.

DISTRIBUTION AND MOVEMENTS Breeds from Britain and Ireland east across Eurasia to Japan. Also breeds in northwest Africa, the Middle East and North America. Winters in tropical and southern Africa, India, the Philippines and South America. In Britain is a widely distributed breeder: most winter in South Africa. Also occurs on passage.

SUB-SPECIES Sub-species are present in Asia, Africa and North America.

Red-rumped Swallow
Hirundo daurica

French: HIRONDELLE ROUSSELINE
Italian: RONDINE ROSSICCI
Spanish: GOLONDRINA DAURICA
German: ROTELSCHWALBE

HABITAT Prefers rocky ground near the sea or near inland waters. In some regions it is also common on buildings and bridges.

IDENTIFICATION Length: 18 cm. It can be distinguished from the common Swallow by its reddish rump, chestnut-coloured nape, rufous throat and underparts and the absence of a dark collar. Dark blue crown and back with metallic highlights, forked tail and blackish wings. Unlike the common Swallow, it has no white markings on the margins of its tail. It differs from the House Martin in having a slimmer more elongated build. Sociable and often mixes with flocks of swallows and house martins. See also page 142.

CALL In flight it emits a thin, shrill 'quiitsch'. Alarm note: 'kee-eet'. Its song is chattering and resembles the Swallow's.

REPRODUCTION Late April onwards. Its feather-lined nest is made from mud and blades of grass and is situated on the underside of horizontal surfaces such as bridges, ceilings etc. Built by both sexes and has a tunnel entrance. The Red-rumped Swallow lays between three and five eggs (rarely six) which are white, sometimes with very fine reddish speckling. Both parents incubate the eggs and both also care for the young.

FOOD Insects caught on the wing.

DISTRIBUTION AND MOVEMENTS Breeds in northwest Africa, Iberia, southern France, sometimes in Italy and from the Balkans east across Asia Minor, through India to China. Winters in Africa and India. Is an accidental visitor to Britain.

SUB-SPECIES The sub-species which nests in Europe and northwest Africa is *H.d. rufula*. Other sub-species are present in Asia (including the nominate sub-species) and Africa.

(Left) Breeding areas (yellow) and areas where the Red-rumped Swallow may be seen on passage (pink)

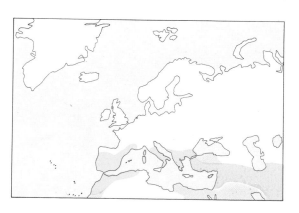

Larks in flight

1: SKYLARK (*Alauda arvensis*) Seen from above (a), it has pale borders to its wings and its outer tail feathers are white. Seen from below (b), the markings on its upper breast and the black and white coloration of its tail are visible. Small bill; fairly long wings. In flight often hovers, and emits a warbling song as it ascends and descends almost vertically.

2: CALANDRA LARK (*Melanocorypha calandra*) In comparison with the Skylark, the pale borders to its wings are more extensive when seen from above (a), and from below (b), it has a dark 'collar' and the black area on its tail is less extensive. Its bill is heavier and its tail shorter than the Skylark's. Emits its call while flying high in a circular motion (although also from lower down and even from the ground).

3. SHORT-TOED LARK (*Calandrella cinerea*) Seen from above (a), it lacks the pale wing border. Seen from below (b), it has small, dark markings on the sides of its breast which are, however, often hard to detect in the field. Often emits its song in aerial display flight when it bobs up and down.

4: LESSER SHORT-TOED LARK (*Calandrella rufescens*) Seen from above (a), it looks very like the Short-toed Lark. Seen from below (b), it has grey streaks on its upper breast. Song emitted in circling flight or as it rises in a spiral.

5: THEKLA LARK (*Galerida theklae*) Extremely difficult to distinguish from Crested Lark. Seen from above (a), its tail feathers—and often its lesser coverts—are orange. Seen from below (b), the forewing is greyish. In some individuals it is almost completely grey and lacks the narrow, buff trailing edge. Song is similar to that of the Skylark, and is emitted in circular display flight; it then plummets downward to the ground.

6: BIMACULATED LARK (*Melanocorypha bimaculata*) Seen from above (a), it can be identified by the white tip of its tail and the absence of white on the trailing edge of its wing. Seen from below (b), there is no white on its underwing. Smaller and more rufous than the similar Calandra Lark: also has smaller black neck patches.

7: CRESTED LARK (*Galerida cristata*) Seen from above (a), only its outer tail feathers are orange. Its wings are large and wide compared with the Skylark's and they lack the white trailing edge. Seen from below (b), its underwing is rufous. Long, erect crest is a conspicuous feature. Song sometimes emitted in flight, but does not soar like the Skylark.

8: WOODLARK (*Lullula arborea*) It has a short tail and wide wings (a). Seen from below (b), its black and white carpal patch is distinctive. It likes wooded areas and perches on trees where it sometimes sings: however, its song is usually emitted in circular flight.

9: DUPONT'S LARK (*Chersophilus duponti*) Seen from above (a), its tail is forked (in a V-shape), its wings are very wide and the long bill is curved. Seen from below (b), its pale underwing and the markings on its breast are distinctive features. It should be borne in mind, however, that grey individuals and others going through a distinctly reddish phase can be found together. Generally prefers to run rather than fly, unlike other larks.

10: BLACK LARK (*Melanocorypha yeltoniensis*) Male in winter plumage (a): as spring approaches, the brown turns to black. The female seen from above (b): the tail pattern and the white border on the secondaries and tertiaries are characteristic. Female seen from below (c): no white on underwing. Song is uttered in low circular flight which resembles that of an owl: also from the ground.

11: WHITE-WINGED LARK (*Melanocorypha leucoptera*) Seen from below (a), its wings are long and narrow; the pattern of its underwing is unique. Seen from above (b), the broad white trailing edge of the wing (it is slightly buff in the female) and the reddish coloration of the remaining plumage are distinctive. Song is either emitted in soaring flight like the Skylark's, or from the ground.

12: SHORE LARK (*Eremophila alpestris*) Seen from above (a), its forehead and tail are black, apart from the outer tail feathers, which are white. Seen from below (b), the black eye patch, the black 'collar' and the yellowish cheeks and throat are distinctive. Flight is more undulating than that of the Skylark, but its song is most frequently delivered from the ground.

Swifts in flight

1: WHITE-RUMPED SWIFT *(Apus caffer)* May be distinguished from other Swifts present in Europe—apart from the Little Swift—by its white rump (a). Unlike the Little Swift it has a distinctly forked tail and the coloration is uniformly darker. Also resembles the House Martin. *Delichon urbica* of the family Hirundinidae, but the White-rumped has much more extensive white coloration on the rump, a more deeply forked tail and underparts which are completely white except for the wings and the tail. Like almost all swifts it is aerial and only comes to land to breed.

2: ALPINE SWIFT *(Apus melba)* It can be distinguished from the Swift by its larger size, white belly and throat and brown breast band. The two species are sometimes found in the same area but rarely stay together for long as the Alpine Swift chases the Swift away. The flight of the Alpine Swift is even more powerful than that of the Swift.

3: LITTLE SWIFT *(Apus affinis)* The Little Swift is the smallest swift found in Europe. Its square tail distinguishes it from the White-rumped Swift although both have a white rump. The throat is also whitish, but the small size, short square tail and white rump are the best field marks.

4: WHITE-THROATED SPINETAIL SWIFT *(Chaetura caudacutus)* Seen from above (a), its back is paler than the rest of the plumage and the forehead is white. Seen from below (b), it has a distinctive white horseshoe-shaped marking from the tail to the flanks. The tail is very short and not forked, and the needle-shaped tips to the tail feathers have also given rise to the name Needle-tailed Swift for this species.

5: PALLID SWIFT *(Apus pallidus)* It is very difficult to distinguish from the Swift: the only appreciable difference is its paler coloration which varies from one subspecies to another. However, the white patch on its throat is usually more conspicuous and its forehead is paler than that of the Swift. Its slower wingbeats are also distinctive.

6: SWIFT *(Apus apus)* Very dark, smoke-grey plumage without the white coloration on the belly found in the Alpine Swift. Its upper parts are also a uniform colour. Forked tail and long, narrow, scyth-like wings like all swifts. Flight is vigorous and powerful: wheels and glides, and groups may be seen (and heard as they squeal loudly) chasing each other around buildings in inhabited areas.

(Right) Swifts *Apus apus* spend most of their life on the wing often wheeling and gliding as they search for food. (Following page) House Martin *Delichon urbica* looking out of the nest

S. Dalton/Bruce Coleman

Swallows in flight

1: **SAND MARTIN** *(Riparia riparia)* It is a small bird. Seen from below (a), its throat and breast are white and it has a distinctive brown breast band. Its upper parts (b) are a uniform brown and its tail is slightly forked. It holds its wings at a distinctive angle when gliding (c). Small size of the Sand Martin also helps to identify it.

2: **CRAG MARTIN** *(Hirundo rupestris)* From below (a), a dark area is visible around the base of the wing; its breast is paler than its remaining brownish underparts: unlike the Sand Martin has no dark breast band. Seen from above (b), its coloration is fairly uniform. The white markings on its tail are distinctive (c).

3: **SWALLOW** *(Hirundo rustica)* Seen from below (a), its throat and forehead are chestnut, the upper breast is blue, the belly is cream-coloured and it has a V-shaped marking on the tail. Upper parts (b) are blue-black. Its tail is very long and forked. Juveniles (c) have much shorter outer tail feathers than those of adults. Flies quickly and gracefully.

4: **RED-RUMPED SWALLOW** *(Hirundo daurica)* Seen from below (a), it can be distinguished from the Swallow by its rufous throat, breast and belly and by its completely dark undertail, and from above (b) by its reddish collar and rump. Flight slower than the Swallow's.

5: **HOUSE MARTIN** *(Delichon urbica)* Seen from below (a), the white coloration of its body contrasts with the black of its wings and tail. Seen from above (b), it is entirely black except for its white rump. It can be distinguished from the Sand Martin by its broader wings (c). White rump is, however, generally the best field mark.

(Right) Swallow *Hirundo rustica* approaching the nest and (preceding page) Swallow in flight. The chestnut throat and long tail streamers are distinctive

F. Blackburn/Bruce Coleman

Pipits and wagtails are small to medium-sized birds, generally with rather long tails and legs, and powerful toes: they often have greatly elongated claws, especially on the hind toes. They are insect-eating land birds, and in appearance and habits often resemble larks. Many species in the family have a curious habit of wagging their tails up and down more or less rhythmically. This has earned them the name wagtail in English as well as in other languages.

The family consists of about forty-eight species. Opinion varies as to the exact number of genera, but there are between four and six. Although the basic structure of the different species is similar, the family Motacillidae can be divided for convenience into two groups which differ in terms of coloration, although there are no absolutely clear distinctions between them and there are some species which display intermediate characteristics.

The first group—the wagtails—consists of species with contrasting coloration in which black, white, yellow and grey predominate. The outer tail feathers are white and, as already mentioned, they wag their tails up and down. Flight is quick and bounding, and wagtails run in a rather jerky fashion. Apart from the Forest Wagtail *Dendronanthus indicus* of the Indian forests, which is placed in a separate genus, the wagtails are all currently included in the single genus *Motacilla*. There are ten species in all and the distribution area lies almost entirely within the Old World, although none nest in Australia. The only one which has reached the Nearctic region is *Motacilla flava tschutchensis*—a sub-species of the Yellow Wagtail which nests in western Alaska.

The Yellow and Blue-headed Wagtails *Motacilla flava* has a vast distribution area covering much of the Palearctic region. It has branched out into a series of populations in which the coloration of the head feathers of males in nuptial plumage has become remarkably varied. Generally speaking, a certain type of coloration is predominant in certain areas, and most of the classifications into sub-species have been based on this feature. *Motacilla flava flava* is present in central Europe, *M. f. flavissima* in England, *M. f. thunbergi* is found in parts of Scandinavia, *M. f. feldegg* in Italy and southern Europe, and *M. f. iberiae* in the Iberian Peninsula. Numerous other sub-species, each with its own distinctive coloration are present throughout its range. However, within each sub-species and even within the same clutch, individuals may

(Above) White Wagtail *M. a. alba*, a sub-species of the Pied Wagtail *Motacilla alba*. (Right) Rock Pipit *A. s. petrosus* and (facing page) male Grey Wagtail *M. cinerea* at the nest

(Right) Richard's Pipit *Anthus novaeseelandiae* and (below) world distribution of the family Motacillidae

be found with the coloration of another sub-species (whose nesting area may be thousands of kilometres away) or with intermediate coloration. According to some authorities, this degree of variability can be attributed to the high incidence of local mutations which are also outwardly visible. Another theory is that the extremely high degree of variability, even on a local scale, is due to the fact that individuals from some populations stray from their normal migration routes, when returning from their winter quarters in the tropics, and infiltrate other populations. However, research carried out fairly recently in the wintering grounds in Africa has shown that as a rule, as far as different populations of Yellow Wagtails are concerned, the intruders are separated in terms of space and that some sub-species reach sexual maturity at different times and have different sexual cycles and therefore leave for their winter quarters on different dates. Consequently there would seem to be less chance of individuals associating with other populations.

Whatever the case may be, there is no doubt that this species shows exceptional genetic variability which can also be detected morphologically; it may well be that it is a species which has lived in unstable conditions over a long period with the result that a series of similar species have evolved. The variations in the coloration of males, though conspicuous, have surprisingly little effect on mating habits. In other words they do not lead to reproductive isolation, because the females appear to have no special preference for males of their own sub-species and vice versa. The females of the various races are difficult to distinguish and the juveniles are virtually impossible to distinguish from one another.

The other widely distributed species which has a similar, though less pronounced, degree of specific polymorphism is the White and Pied Wagtails *Motacilla alba*. The plumage of this small wagtail is black and white, and the tail is long. Several sub-species are known, but they are far more geographically distinct both at breeding and winter quarters. Because of this spatial separation, the Large Indian Pied Wagtail *Motacilla maderaspatensis* of India and the African Pied Wagtail *Motacilla aguimp* are often regarded as distinct species. Incidentally, this illustrates how difficult it is to give the exact number of species of the family as it varies according to different authorities. The sub-species present in Britain and Ireland is the Pied Wagtail *M. a. yarelli*. The White Wagtail *M. a. alba* breeds in continental Europe, Asia Minor, Iceland and Greenland.

Other species of wagtail which fortunately have fewer (and less confusing) sub-species are the Cape Wagtail *Motacilla capensis*, the Grey Wagtail *M. cinerea*, the Madagascar Wagtail *M. flaviventris* and the Citrine Wagtail *M. citreola*. The latter, like the Grey Wagtail, is distributed in the Palearctic region.

The second group of members of the family Motacillidae consists of the pipits. It includes species with mimetic coloration, similar to that of larks (although there is no connection between pipits and larks). They belong to three genera, the most numerous being *Anthus* which has thirteen known species in the Palearctic region, at least eleven in Africa and six in South America. The most widely distributed species with the largest number of sub-species are the Rock and Water Pipits *A. spinoletta*: there are three races which nest regularly in Europe. The species is divided into two distinct ecological groups: the Water Pipit *A. s. spinoletta* and the Rock Pipit *A. s. petrosus*. The Water Pipit breeds in mountainous areas of Spain and France east across Europe to the Balkans: in winter some occur in southern England. The Rock Pipit breeds on the coasts of Britain, Ireland and northwest France. Richard's Pipit *Anthus novaeseelandiae* occurs in western Europe as a vagrant from Siberia. The only exclusively North American species is Sprague's Pipit *A. spragueii*; the smallest species is the Short-tailed Pipit *A. brachyurus* from East Africa. The genus *Macronyx* includes eight species, all from Africa. The Golden Pipit *T meothylacus tenellus* is another African species. Its golden-yellow plumage and its behaviour make it appear to be the link between wagtails and pipits.

(Right) Yellow Wagtail *M.f. flavissima,* the British race of the Yellow Wagtail *Motacilla flava,* a species whose head colour varies throughout its range. (Below) African Pied Wagtail *M. aguimp* and (below right) Tree Pipit *Anthus trivialis*

L. R. Dawson

F. Blackburn/Bruce Coleman

J. Burton/Bruce Coleman

French: PIPIT DE RICHARD
Italian: CALANDRO MAGGIORE
Spanish: BISBITA DE RICHARD
German: SPORNPIEPER

Richard's Pipit
Anthus novaeseelandiae

HABITAT Damp meadowland and other marshy areas.

IDENTIFICATION Length: 18 cm. Is the largest and most long-legged pipit that occurs in Europe. Rufous upper parts heavily streaked with black-brown; rufous back, rump and supercilium; off-white throat; dark moustachial stripe; light rufous breast with brown streaks. Brown bill (slightly paler on the underside); yellowish-brown or pale pink legs; brown iris. Juveniles: brown upper parts with cream-coloured borders; reddish-white underparts, boldly streaked on the breast and flanks. Undulating flight. It runs fast on its long legs and has an erect carriage. See also page 164.

CALLS Emits a rather harsh and distinctive Sparrow-like 'rr-ree-eep'.

REPRODUCTION June–July. Nest is built of moss and fine grasses in a depression in the ground, sheltered by bushes or clumps of grass. It lays between four and six eggs ranging from greenish-grey to dirty pink. The eggs are either densely covered with olive speckles or with reddish-brown and grey markings. The duration of the incubation period is not known, but the female is chiefly responsible. There are two clutches.

FOOD Mainly insects: also worms and seeds.

DISTRIBUTION AND MOVEMENTS Asia, Australia, the Middle East and Africa. Palearctic populations winter in eastern and southern Asia. It is uncommon in western Europe. In Britain it is a regular autumn visitor in variable numbers, but in Ireland it is very rare. No doubt this species has been much overlooked in the past.

SUB-SPECIES The sub-species *A. n. richardi* occurs accidentally in Europe from western Siberia. There are other sub-species in Asia and in the Ethiopian and Australasian regions.

Tawny Pipit
Anthus campestris

French: PIPIT ROUSSELINE
Italian: CALANDRO
Spanish: BISBITA CAMPESTRE
German: BRACHPIEPER

HABITAT Dry open regions, often sandy, with bushy vegetation. Also present on steppes, stony ground and cultivated land during the winter.

IDENTIFICATION Length: 16 cm. Pale rufous upper parts, cream-coloured supercilium, brownish sides of the head and creamy-white throat. Breast and flanks pale with only a few dark streaks on the breast; Brown bill, pink at the base of the underside; yellow-pink legs; brown iris. Distinguished from Richard's Pipit by paler and less streaked plumage: legs also shorter. Juveniles: rufous upper parts with cream borders to the feathers; underparts streaked on the breast and flanks; clearly defined moustachial stripe. Flight is fast: emits a song in high display flight from which it plummets to the ground. See also page 164.

CALL Generally variations on a 'tsee-eep-tsee-ak', sometimes similar to that of the Yellow Wagtail. Its song is a repetitive metallic 'chee-vee-ee' heard chiefly in display flight. Also emits a hard 't-k-rr-t' or 't-rr-leet' when it is alarmed.

REPRODUCTION From mid-May onwards. Nest is made of stalks, dry grasses and roots. It is situated in a depression in the ground at the side of projecting rocks, among clumps of grass or in the shelter of bushes. The Tawny Pipit usually lays four or five eggs, though the clutch sometimes contains only two or three, and on rare occasions as many as six. The eggs are very shiny and have brown and violet markings on the off-white or greenish base colour: it is most unusual for them to be unmarked.

Incubation takes thirteen or fourteen days and is carried out by the female alone. The nestlings are fed either by the female or by both parents and leave the nest after twelve to fourteen days. There is normally only one clutch a year, although there may be a second in July.

FOOD Mainly insects and their larvae.

DISTRIBUTION AND MOVEMENTS Breeds from France and southern Sweden east to western Siberia. Also breeds in northwest Africa and the Middle East. Winters in Africa, Arabia and southern Asia. Accidental in northern Europe, but is a regular vagrant to Britain occuring annually in recent years. Also accidental in Ireland.

SUB-SPECIES A sub-species is present in Asia.

(Below) Breeding areas (yellow), wintering areas (magenta) and areas where the Tawny Pipit may be seen on passage (pink)

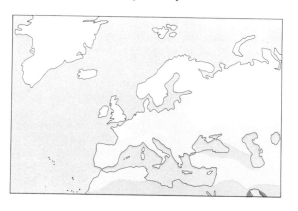

French: PIPIT DES ARBRES
Italian: PRISPOLONE
Spanish: BISBITA ARBÓREO
German: BAUMPIEPER

Tree Pipit
Anthus trivialis

(Below) Breeding areas (yellow) and areas where the Tree Pipit may be seen on passage (pink)

HABITAT Open woodland, heaths and hilly areas with thinly scattered trees and bushes.

IDENTIFICATION Length: 15 cm. Very similar to the Meadow Pipit, and different calls are the best way to distinguish the two. Adults: rufous and olive-brown upper parts with blackish streaks; yellowish supercilium, blackish-brown sides of the head and blackish moustachial stripe. Off-white throat; underparts varying from rufous to white on the belly, streaked with black at the sides of the throat and on the flanks. Bill is dark with a pale pink base; brownish-pink legs; brown iris. Juveniles: boldly streaked and redder upper parts. The Tree Pipit perches readily on tree-tops (hence its English name) and telephone wires, unlike many other species of the family. It is generally solitary. See also page 164.

CALL A harsh, shrill 'teez', which is louder than the Meadow Pipit's, when it is alarmed. Its song consists of several phrases, each of which is a repetition of a few syllables, ending in a distinctive 'see-ry-see-ry-see-ry'. Both the Tree and Meadow Pipits emit a song in aerial display, often as they fly upwards.

REPRODUCTION Mid-May onwards. The nest is a large cup of dry grasses and moss, with a soft lining of fine grasses and other plant material. The eggs, which number from four to six per clutch, with as many as eight on rare occasions, vary in shape and colour. They are usually reddish, violet, brown or grey, with varying amounts of speckles or dark streaks, which may be evenly distributed or may be concentrated round the blunt end.

Incubation is carried out by the female alone and takes twelve to fourteen days. The nestlings are fed by both parents and leave the nest after twelve or thirteen days. There are usually two clutches.

FOOD Mainly insects and their larvae: also millet and seeds.

DISTRIBUTION AND MOVEMENTS Breeds from Britain, Scandinavia, France and northern Spain east across Eurasia to eastern Siberia. Winters in tropical Africa and in India. In Britain it is a widespread breeder, resident from early April to September. Is also a numerous passage visitor. Has not been recorded breeding in Ireland.

SUB-SPECIES A sub-species is present in Asia.

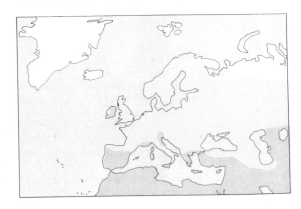

Petchora Pipit
Anthus gustavi

French: PIPIT DE LA PETCHORA
Italian: PISPOLA DELLA PECIORA
Spanish: BISBITA DEL PETCHORA
German: PETSCHORA-PIEPER

French: PIPIT INDIEN
Italian: PRISPOLONE INDIANO
Spanish: BISBITA DE HODGSON
German: INDISCHER BAUMPIEPER

Oriental Tree Pipit
Anthus hodgsoni

HABITAT Coniferous forests often in mountainous regions.

IDENTIFICATION Length: 14 cm. Its coloration is similar to that of the Tree Pipit, but its upper parts are olive-green rather than yellowish and its overall appearance is darker. The breast is more heavily marked than the Tree Pipit's with larger, coarser streaks: remaining underparts white. Conspicuous eye stripe is buff in front of the eye and paler behind. It has the characteristic habit of 'bobbing' its tail from the horizontal downwards as it walks. See also page 164.

CALL A loud 'tseee' like the Red-throated Pipit's.

REPRODUCTION Mid-June onwards. It builds its nest on the ground in forests, among heather or in clumps of long grass. There are four to six eggs per clutch and they vary considerably in colour and markings, although they are generally similar to those of the Tree Pipit they are not as heavily blotched. Both parents incubate the eggs and tend the young.

FOOD Probably insects and some seeds.

DISTRIBUTION AND MOVEMENTS It is a migrant species which nests from northeast Russia west to Mongolia, Kamchatka, Japan and western China, and south to the Himalayas. Winters in Indo-China. Is an accidental visitor to Europe where it has been recorded a number of times in Britain—at Fair Isle and less frequently on the mainland.

SUB-SPECIES The sub-species *A. h. yunnanensis* nests in Russia.

HABITAT Tundra and lightly wooded areas such as the edge of coniferous forests.

IDENTIFICATION Length: 14 cm. Adults: upper parts like those of the Red-throated Pipit in winter plumage but general coloration, especially on the crown and rump, is a deeper brown. Outer tail feathers buff, not white like the Red-throat's. Rufous-white underparts with conspicuous black-brown streaks on the breast and flanks. This species, like many other pipits and wagtails, is best distinguished by its call. See also page 164.

CALL Its song consists of trills like the Wood Warbler's followed by a deep, guttural warbling. It is emitted in flight.

REPRODUCTION Late June onwards. Nests in depressions in marshland or in clumps of grass by shrubs and willows. The nest is made of grass and other plants and lined with small leaves. Four or five pale grey eggs, sometimes tinged with pink, are laid. Usually the eggs have a fine grey speckling.

FOOD Insects.

DISTRIBUTION AND MOVEMENTS The northern USSR from the Petchora River to northeast Siberia. It winters in southeast Asia. Accidental in Britain at Fair Isle and occasionally elsewhere in Britain.

SUB-SPECIES Sub-species are present in the Commander Islands and southern Ussuriland.

(Above left) Oriental Tree Pipit and (above) Petchora Pipit

French: PIPIT FARLOUSE
Italian: PISPOLA
Spanish: BISBITA COMÚN
German: WIESENPIEPER

Meadow Pipit
Anthus pratensis

(Right) Breeding areas (yellow), wintering areas (magenta), areas where the Meadow Pipit may be seen all year round (orange) and on passage (pink)

HABITAT Hills, moors, meadows and peat-bogs. In winter frequents marshes, fresh-water margins, cultivated land and sea coasts.

IDENTIFICATION Length: 14 cm. Difficult to distinguish from the Tree Pipit: best told apart by their calls. The Tree Pipit also flies up into aerial display from a tree whereas the Meadow Pipit starts from the ground. Olive-brown upper parts with blackish streaks; greyish or yellowish supercilium; brown sides of the head; yellowish or whitish-grey underparts with bold blackish streaks on the breast, flanks and sides of the throat. Black tail feathers but with some white on the outer feathers. Brown bill with pale pink base; legs dark flesh-pink; brown iris. Complete moult: August to October. Juveniles: darker upper parts with narrower, pale borders; yellower underparts. See also page 164.

CALL A shrill 'pheet' which is similar to the Rock Pipit's call. Like the Tree Pipit emits a trilling song but it does not end in the same characteristic 'see-er' note.

REPRODUCTION Mid-April onwards. A well-concealed nest is built on the ground, under a tussock, using dry grass and sometimes moss. The nest is lined with fine plant material. It usually lays three to five eggs, occasionally as many as seven. Eggs are grey or green-grey with brown, chocolate-brown or ash-grey speckles and markings which are often concentrated at the blunt end: they are sometimes covered with fine dark streaks. Incubation takes eleven to fifteen days and is carried out

by the female alone. The nestlings are fed by both parents with insects carried in the bill, and leave the nest after thirteen or fourteen days. There are usually two clutches.

FOOD Mainly insects and their larvae; also earthworms, small molluscs and seeds.

DISTRIBUTION AND MOVEMENTS Breeds in the western Palearctic region: Greenland, Ireland, Scandinavia, Ireland and France east across Eurasia to the Balkans and northern Ukraine. In Britain and Ireland it is a numerous and widespread breeder as well as a passage migrant and winter visitor.

SUB-SPECIES The sub-species *A.p. theresae* breeds in western Ireland.

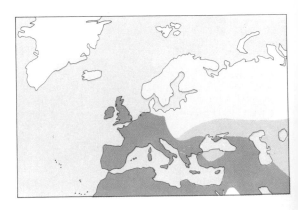

Red-throated Pipit
Anthus cervinus

French: PIPIT À GORGE ROUSSE
Italian: PISPOLA GOLAROSSA
Spanish: BISBITA GORGIRROJO
German: ROTKEHLPIEPER

HABITAT Coastal tundra areas, marshes and damp cultivated land.

IDENTIFICATION Length: 16 cm. Upper parts ranging from rufous to greyish-brown, boldly streaked with black-brown throughout most of the year. Plumage is darker than the similar Meadow Pipit's. Rufous supercilium, lores and throat (creamy-white in the female) with faint blackish moustachial stripe. Pale underparts and flanks: flanks and breast more strongly marked than the Meadow Pipit's.

Complete moult in July–August. In summer the male's breast and throat turn red and may not be streaked. Juveniles have yellower underparts than those of the female in winter plumage. See also page 164.

CALL A single, hard, sonorous and rather long drawn out 'tsee', chiefly emitted in flight. Its song is sharper, more prolonged and less melodious than that of the Meadow Pipit and is emitted at a greater height.

REPRODUCTION Mid-June onwards. Nests on the ground, often in damp sites, in the shelter of small bushes. The nest is made out of dry grasses lined with finer grass and occasionally hair. There are usually five or six eggs per clutch, though there may be four to seven. Eggs vary considerably in colour; grey, buff, olive or pinkish with grey, reddish or buff speckles. Incubation

is carried out by the female alone. Both parents care for the chicks which leave the nest after about twelve days.

FOOD Mainly insects and their larvae; also small worms. In winter it also eats molluscs and seeds.

DISTRIBUTION AND MOVEMENTS Breeds on tundra across Eurasia from northern Scandinavia to the Bering Straits. Winters in Africa and southern and southeast Asia. It is a passage visitor in central and eastern Europe, and a vagrant further west. In Britain and Ireland it is recorded more or less annually, mostly at Fair Isle.

(Above) Red-throated Pipit in winter plumage (foreground) and summer plumage. (Below) Breeding areas of the Red-throated Pipit (yellow) and wintering areas (magenta)

French: PIPIT SPIONCELLE
Italian: SPIONCELLO
Spanish: BISBITA RIBEREÑO
German: WASSERPIEPER

Rock and Water Pipits
Anthus spinoletta

(Above) Water Pipit *A.s. spinoletta* in summer plumage (foreground) and winter plumage. (Below) Breeding areas (yellow), wintering areas (magenta), areas where the Rock and Water Pipits may be seen all year round (orange) and on passage (pink). (Facing page, top) American Water Pipit *A.s. rubescens* and (bottom) British Rock Pipit *A.s. petrosus* (foreground) and Scandinavian Rock Pipit *A.s. littoralis*

HABITAT Mountainous regions and rocky coasts during the breeding season. In winter frequents marshy areas, water-courses, coasts and muddy ground.

IDENTIFICATION Length: 16 cm. Two quite distinct forms: the Water Pipit *A. s. spinoletta* which is an alpine bird breeding in mountainous districts; and the Rock Pipit *A. s. petrosus* which is confined to the coasts of northwest Europe including Britain. In winter the two are both dark grey with varying amounts of streaking, but in summer the Water Pipit becomes a lighter grey, unstreaked bird. At all seasons Rock Pipits are much darker and more heavily streaked than Water Pipits. See also page 164.

CALL Voices of all races similar: a sharp 'phest' when alarmed. Also emits a song in flight which resembles that of the Meadow Pipit.

REPRODUCTION April onwards. Nests in a recess or shallow depression in banks or cliffs and on the ground in a hole or under plants. The nest is made of dry stalks and moss, lined with fine vegetable fibres and a few hairs. It lays between four and six smooth, glossy eggs per clutch. The background colour is greyish or green-grey and they are heavily marked with brown and grey spots: markings may be concentrated around the larger end. Incubation is carried out by the female and takes about fourteen days. The chicks are reared by both parents and leave the nest after about sixteen days.

FOOD Mainly insects during the breeding season: in winter eats small molluscs, algae and seeds.

DISTRIBUTION AND MOVEMENTS Western Greenland, North America, Europe and Asia. Winters in its breeding areas and south to Africa. Rock and Water Pipits are widespread breeding birds in Europe and winter visitors to the British Isles. The Rock Pipit *A. s. petrosus* breeds on the coasts of northwest France and in Britain and Ireland. The sub-species *A. s. rubescens* has occurred as a vagrant in Britain and Ireland.

SUB-SPECIES *A. s. spinoletta* (Water Pipit): Spain, France, Switzerland, Germany, Poland, Italy, Austria, the Balkans and probably, Asia Minor. *A. s. kleinschmidti* (darker): Faeroes. *A. s. petrosus* (Rock Pipit): Britain and Ireland, coasts of northwest France and possibly the coasts of Norway. *A. s. littoralis*: Denmark, Sweden, Finland and the Kola Peninsula. Also coasts and islands of the Baltic. There are other sub-species in Asia, Greenland and North America.

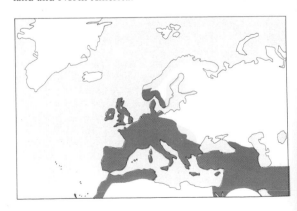

(Above) Richard's Pipit *Anthus novaeseelandiae* is the largest pipit to occur in Britain. (Right) Meadow Pipit *A. pratensis*

G. J. Broekhuysen/Ardea

Bruce Coleman

J. & S. Bottomley/Ardea

(Left) Red-throated Pipit *A. cervinus* is distinguished from the Meadow Pipit *A. pratensis* by its darker coloration and, in summer, its rufous throat. (Below left) Tree Pipit *A. trivialis* at the nest and (below right) Tawny Pipit *A. campestris*

S. Marsham/Bruce Coleman

P. S. Tacher/Photo Researchers

Yellow Wagtail
Motacilla flava

French: BERGERONNETTE
PRINTANIÈRE
Italian: CUTRETTOLA
Spanish: LAVANDERA BOYERA
German: SCHAFSTELZE

HABITAT Marshes, grassland and also cultivated land, usually close to water. Sometimes frequents salt-marshes.

IDENTIFICATION Length: 16 cm. Has many races and coloration varies considerably. Yellow Wagtail *M. f. flavissima* which breeds in Britain is described below. Adult male in breeding plumage: olive-green upper parts; white chin; bright yellow underparts; brown flight feathers with yellowish-white borders; brown tail feathers with borders ranging in colour from green to pale yellow. Blackish bill; black legs and brown iris. Head yellow: the colour of the head varies from yellow through blue to black according to sub-species. Complete moult: August–September.

In the autumn the head and mantle are greenish-brown; the rump and supercilium are yellowish-green; the underparts are yellow, tinged with rufous. The female has an off-white supercilium, a brown mantle and less of a rufous tinge on the underparts. Juveniles: black-brown upper parts; rufous supercilium, chin and throat; underparts ranging in colour from rufous to pale yellowish. However, females and especially juveniles of the various races are very similar and much more difficult to distinguish than the males.

The Yellow Wagtail's flight is notably bounding: it walks and runs in a lively fashion, wagging its tail and bobbing its head backwards and forwards.

CALL A shrill 'tsee-ay' or 'tseep' which is emitted in flight. Its song is a short and not very melodious Robin-like trilling which may be emitted in bounding flight or from a perch.

REPRODUCTION Mid-May onwards. The nest is situated in thick herbage or in a depression in the ground. It is small and cup-shaped and is made of grass, stalks and dry roots with an inner lining of hair, wool and sometimes feathers. There are five or six eggs, rarely seven, ranging in colour from yellowish-white to greenish, with grey-brown markings and, on rare occasions, black streaks and spots. Incubation takes thirteen or fourteen days and is carried out mainly by the female. The chicks

are tended by both parents and leave the nest after ten to thirteen days.

FOOD Insects and their larvae. Also worms and molluscs.

DISTRIBUTION AND MOVEMENTS It is distributed throughout much of the Palearctic region from Scandinavia, Britain and Iberia east to western Alaska. Also breeds south to Africa, Egypt and Manchuria. Winters in Africa (usually south of the Sahara) and southeast Asia. The Yellow Wagtail *M. f. flavissima* breeds in many counties in England and Wales: scarce in Scotland. Formerly bred in Ireland. The Blue-headed Wagtail *M. f. flava* breeds occasionally in Britain—almost annually—mainly in south and east England. It sometimes hybridises with the Yellow Wagtail. It also occurs on passage as does the Grey-headed Wagtail *M. f. thunbergi*.

SUB-SPECIES *M. f. flavissima* (greenish-yellow crown and yellow stripe over eye): breeds in Britain and locally on coasts of western Europe: rarely in Ireland. *M. f. flava*: southern Scandinavia east to the Urals and south to France, northern Italy and Rumania. *M. f. thunbergi* (dark ear coverts, yellow throat and breast): northern Scandinavia and USSR. Other sub-species are present throughout the range.

(Above) Male Blue-headed Wagtail *M.f. flava* (foreground) and female. (Right) Breeding areas (yellow), wintering areas (magenta), areas where the Yellow Wagtail may be seen all year round (orange) and on passage (pink). (Facing page, top) Ashy-headed Wagtail *M.f. cinereocapilla*, (centre right) Grey-headed Wagtail *M.f. thunbergi*, (centre left) Yellow Wagtail *M.f. flavissima* and (bottom) Black-headed Wagtail *M.f. feldegg*

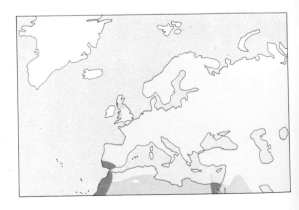

French: BERGERONNETTE CITRINE
Italian: CUTRETTOLA
TESTAGIALLA ORIENTALE
Spanish: LAVANDERA CITRINA
German: ZITRONENSTELZE

Citrine Wagtail
Motacilla citreola

HABITAT Breeds on meadows, tundra and moors. In winter frequents open country by fresh water.

IDENTIFICATION Length: 16 cm. Resembles a Yellow Wagtail, though its tail is slightly longer and the male's head is completely yellow in the summer, as are its underparts except for the flanks. There is a blackish marking at the base of its neck. Upper-parts grey. Blackish-brown flight feathers; broad white margins on the secondaries and wing coverts. Black tail with white outer tail feathers; off-white undertail. The female's head is olive green, and there are no black markings at the base of the neck. In winter the heads of both sexes are greenish-grey but their faces remain slightly yellow and there are dark streaks on their ear-coverts. Juveniles are very difficult to distinguish from juvenile Yellow Wagtails.

In nuptial flight the male flies upwards with rapid wingbeats, hovers, and then quickly descends at an oblique angle to alight on a branch or some other elevated perch. Wags its tail vigorously.

CALL Emits a sharp double 'tit'.

REPRODUCTION From late May. It nests on the ground, often in very damp places; in a hollow or bank or sheltered by an overhanging shrub or stone. The nest is made of dry grass and moss, often lined with hair and fur. Four or five pale grey or buff eggs are laid, finely speckled with grey-brown or light brown.

FOOD Little is known about its diet but it is thought to include insects and small crustaceans.

DISTRIBUTION AND MOVEMENTS It is partly migrant and nests from western Siberia to central Asia and in the easternmost part of European Russia north of the Caspian. It occurs south of the Caspian in Iran: also in the Himalayas. It winters as far south as India and occasionally Egypt. It is accidental in Europe. In Britain is a scarce visitor, recorded several times in Fair Isle and singly elsewhere. In 1976 a male was recorded feeding young in Essex.

SUB-SPECIES Sub-species are present in Asia.

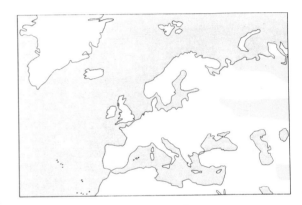

(Below) Male Citrine Wagtail (foreground) and female. (Right) Breeding areas of the Citrine Wagtail (yellow)

Grey Wagtail
Motacilla cinerea

HABITAT Mountain and hill streams; also lowlands near ponds, canals and cultivated areas.

IDENTIFICATION Length: 18 cm. In shape resembles the White Wagtail, but the Grey Wagtail has a longer tail. Upper parts blue-grey; rump and upper-tail coverts yellow-green; white eyestripe; sides of head grey with wide, white moustachial stripe. The chin and throat are black, a distinctive feature of this species. Remaining underparts bright yellow with some white on underwing; flight-feathers black, whitish at base. Bill greyish-black; legs brownish-pink; iris brown. Complete moult between July and October. In autumn and winter chin and throat become yellow-white, the eyebrow brownish and the sides of the head sprinkled with white; the breast is pale rufous-yellow. Female: as male, but 'bib' is white or freckled black and white; underparts paler. Juveniles: upper parts greenish-grey-brown; rump yellow-green; eyebrow, throat and breast yellowish. In all plumages the under-tail coverts are lemon yellow.

CALL A hard, metallic 'tseep' or 'tseetsett''. Also a 'tit', like the White Wagtail, but harsher. Song is a succession of twittering notes, and canary-like trills.

REPRODUCTION From the end of March onwards. The nest is built in a wide variety of places, but is often alongside a stream, and in mountainous areas up to 1,800 metres. Both male and female build the nest out of mosses, small twigs and dried leaves, and it is lined with hair and sometimes feathers. Eggs: four to six (sometimes only three and rarely seven), with buff or yellowish-white ground colour, finely freckled and spotted grey-brown or rufous-brown, often with dark streaks. The female incubates, sometimes with help from the male, for thirteen to fourteen days. The young are tended by both parents and leave the nest after twelve or thirteen days. Generally two broods.

FOOD Mainly insects and their larvae; also eats small crustaceans and molluscs and occasionally very small fish.

DISTRIBUTION AND MOVEMENTS Europe, except for the more northerly areas, and east to Japan; also northwest Africa. Partially migratory, wintering in its breeding-range or in northern tropical Africa, India and New Guinea. In Britain it breeds in all hilly districts and locally in the south and east.

SUB-SPECIES Sub-species are present in the Azores, the Canaries and in Asia.

French: BERGERONNETTE DES RUISSEAUX
Italian: BALLERINA GIALLA
Spanish: LAVANDERA CASCADENA
German: GEBIRGSTELZE

(Above) Female Grey Wagtail (foreground), male (centre) and juvenile. (Below) Breeding areas (yellow), wintering areas (magenta) and areas where the Grey Wagtail may be seen all year round (orange)

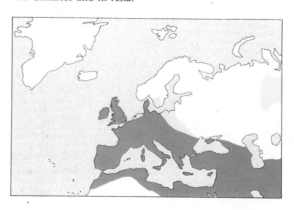

White and Pied Wagtails
Motacilla alba

HABITAT Farms, gardens, tundra, open country and inhabited areas. In winter is found more often on farm-land.

IDENTIFICATION Length: 18 cm. White Wagtail *M.a. alba*: adult male in nuptial plumage: crown, nape, chin and throat black; forehead and rest of head white; mantle and scapulars grey; underparts white; flanks greyish; flight-feathers greyish-black with white edges. Bill and legs black; iris brown-black. Complete moult between August and September. In winter crown is tinged grey, throat becomes white and upper breast blackish. Female has less black on head and throat and the white forehead is spotted black in summer, grey in winter. Pied Wagtail *M.a. yarrellii* differs only from above in having a black rather than grey back. Juveniles: upper parts brown-grey; underparts yellowish-white with greyer flanks and greyish throat; wing-feathers edged with buff.

Sociable, spends the night in communal roosts. Will often follow cattle and not infrequently perches on the backs of domestic stock.

CALL A distinctive high-pitched 'tschissik' or 'tschissip' also a 'tschik'. The song is a combination of repeated twittering call-notes uttered both in flight and when perched.

REPRODUCTION Nests from mid-April onwards in a wide variety of habitats, but prefers holes or crevices in buildings, rocks, cliffs, trees etc. Also nests on the ground and in old, abandoned nests. The nest consists of a mixture of dry grasses, lined with horsehair, wool, and feathers: it is built by the female alone. Eggs: five or six (occasionally three–seven) greyish to blue-white, speckled and streaked brownish and grey. The female incubates for a period of twelve to fourteen days. The young are tended by both parents and leave the nest after fourteen to fifteen days. Two or three broods in southerly areas; normally one brood in the northern regions.

FOOD Insects and their larvae; also small molluscs, worms and sometimes seeds.

DISTRIBUTION AND MOVEMENTS Europe, Asia, northwest Africa. Winters in the Mediterranean, in Africa, Asia Minor, and in western Europe. In Britain and Ireland the Pied Wagtail is a widespread and common breeding bird. The continental White Wagtail is a regular passage migrant.

SUB-SPECIES *M.a. alba*: South-central Europe. *M.a. yarrelli*: Britain and Ireland, southwestern Norway, Germany, Netherlands, Belgium and northwest France. *M.a. dulchunensis*: USSR. Other sub-species are present in Asia and Africa.

(Above) Pied Wagtail in summer plumage (foreground) and winter plumage. (Right) Breeding areas (yellow), wintering areas (magenta) and areas where the White and Pied Wagtails may be seen all year round (orange) and on passage (pink)

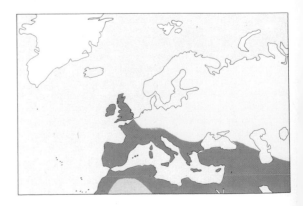

French: BERGERONNETTE GRISE
Italian: BALLERINA BIANCA
Spanish: LAVANDERA BLANCA
         COMÚN
German: BACHSTELZE

Passeriformes: Motacillidae

(Left) White Wagtail in
summer plumage (foreground)
and winter plumage. (Below)
Juvenile

163

Pipits in flight

1: WATER AND ROCK PIPITS *(Anthus spinoletta)*
A fairly large pipit with greyish plumage. The nominate
race *A.a. spinoletta* (the Water Pipit) has white outer tail
feathers (a); in the other sub-species they are greyish. In
spring and summer the underparts (b) are tinged pink.
Like many other members of the family flight is undulating and its song is often uttered in flight.

2: TAWNY PIPIT *(Anthus campestris)* Has a slender
silhouette like a wagtail's. Seen from above (a) the back is
lightly streaked. From below (b) has little or no streaking
on breast. Utters a song in high display flight.

3: RICHARD'S PIPIT *(Anthus novaeseelandiae)*
Largest and most long-tailed pipit occurring in Europe.
Upper parts (a) are strongly streaked. Bold streaking on
the breast (b).

4: TREE PIPIT *(Anthus trivialis)* From above (a) back
is less streaked than in Meadow Pipit and wing-coverts
are conspicuous; outer tail feathers are whitish. However,
best distinguished from very similar Meadow Pipit by its
voice. From below (b) flanks and upper breast are
yellowish with strongly marked, dark streaks.

5: ORIENTAL TREE PIPIT *(Anthus hodgsoni)* Seen
from above (a) has a conspicuous white eye-stripe
bordered with black; the back is uniform olive-green.
From below (b) the breast is strongly streaked.

6: RED-THROATED PIPIT *(Anthus cervinus)* In
summer plumage (a) throat is red. Back and rump are
always strongly streaked. Seen from below (b) in winter
plumage, the breast is heavily streaked.

7: MEADOW PIPIT *(Anthus pratensis)* Extremely
similar in appearance to the Tree Pipit. Seen from above
(a) back and rump are olive-brown with dark streaks.
From below (b) the breast is whitish with black streaks.

8: PETCHORA PIPIT *(Anthus gustavi)* Seen from
above (a) is similar to Red-throated Pipit, but coloration
is more buff. Has two pale streaks down its back. From
below (b): buffish-white with bold dark streaks.

(Right) Meadow Pipit *Anthus
pratensis*

FAMILY **PYCNONOTIDAE: Bulbuls**

C. A. W. Guiggisberg/Bruce Coleman

(Left) The Common Bulbul
P. barbatus which is frequently
seen in inhabited areas.
(Facing page) White-cheeked
Bulbul *P. leucogenys,*
sometimes called the White-
eared Bulbul

The family Pycnonotidae or bulbuls is found only in the Old World. Bulbuls are medium sized birds, although they vary, some being small, like sparrows and others larger and more like blackbirds. The wings are fairly short, while the tail is long. The bill, which is usually quite slender, is notched and surrounded at the base by stiff, well-developed bristles. The nostrils are elongated and oval. The tarsi and the toes are weak and sometimes very short. Bulbuls are not strong fliers.

The various species are not vividly coloured: they vary from olive-green to yellow and from grey to brown, with one almost completely black species. Often the only splash of colour is on the under-tail coverts, which may be crimson, yellow, white or rufous, although in some cases there are yellow or scarlet spots or streaks on the head and ear-coverts. The tail is also sometimes tawny or rufous in contrast with the uniform colour of the rest of the upper parts.

Many bulbuls live in dense forests or in wooded areas, including gardens and the edges of cultivated land. They are also found in mountainous country up to altitudes of over three thousand metres, in which case they generally descend to the plains in winter. Bulbuls are usually sedentary, but may perform short migrations. Some species are very tame and have no fear of man, but many live in bushes or scrub where observation may be

difficult. Except during the breeding season, they are noisy and gregarious birds, going about in parties in search of berries and fruits. Some species feed on buds and nectar, and almost all include some insects and spiders in their diet; indeed these constitute the basic food of several species. The song is often very rich and melodious and in some places bulbuls are even kept as caged songbirds.

The rather solid, cup-shaped nest is built of twigs, leaves and even lichens; the inside is often lined with blades of grass or small roots. It is built among bushes, occasionally at some height above the ground. The number of eggs laid varies from two to four, pink, creamy or white with strongly-marked, reddish-brown and purple spotting. Both sexes incubate the eggs and look after the young.

The distribution of the bulbuls ranges from Africa to Madagascar and the Mascarene Islands, and from southern Asia to Malaysia, the Philippines and the Moluccas. According to Rand and Deignan (the 1960 revision of the family) it consists of about one hundred and twenty species grouped in fifteen genera, ten of which are confined to Africa and Madagascar and two to southern Asia, while the genera *Pycnonotus* and *Criniger* are widespread in both Africa and Asia. The genus *Hypsipetes* is found from Madagascar

P. Steyn/Ardea

and the Mascarene Islands to eastern Asia. The typical genus *Pycnonotus* contains fifty species, the commonest being the Bulbul *P. barbatus* which is present in many parts of Africa; this is also the only species to have occurred accidentally in Europe. Several other similar species are found in both Africa and Asia, such as the White-cheeked Bulbul *P. leucogenys,* the Red-whiskered Bulbul *P. jocsa,* and the Red-vented Bulbul *P. cafer.* The Striated Bulbul *P. striatus,* olive with white streaks on the upper parts, is insectivorous and occurs in the mountain forests of southeast Asia. Two other bulbuls from southeast Asia, also olive-green in colour but with short, thick bills, are the Finch-billed Bulbul *Spizixos canifrons* and the Collared Finch-billed Bulbul *S. semitorques* which feed entirely on vegetable matter. Other African genera are *Chlorocichla* (five species) and *Phyllastrephus* (in which the males are larger than the females). The four African and the five southeast Asian species of the genus *Criniger* have well-developed crests. The vast range of the Black Bulbul *Hypsipetes madagascariensis* has resulted in the evolution of various local races. The Brown-eared Bulbul *H. amaurotis,* like other species of the same genus, has long, pointed feathers on the crown.

(Above) Red-eyed Bulbul *P. nigricans* is best distinguished by the colour of its eyes and under-tail coverts. (Left) World distribution of the family Pycnonotidae

Common Bulbul
Pycnonotus barbatus

French: BULBUL DES JARDINS
Italian: BULBUL AFRICANO
Spanish: BULBUL NARANJERO
German: GRAUBÜLBÜL

HABITAT Gardens and orchards in towns and villages, palm groves; also less cultivated and bushier areas and semi-desert.

IDENTIFICATION Length: 19 cm. Very sober plumage: head and throat black, upper parts dark grey-brown, underparts paler. Tail brown with bright yellow under-tail coverts in some sub-species. In the field appears dark above and light below.
Very active, lively bird. Does not fear man and its calls and song are often heard.

CALL The song is melodious and fairly loud, and the call is harsh.

REPRODUCTION From late May. Builds a thin, cup-shaped nest, generally in a tree or bush or occasionally on top of a low wall. It is made with plant material and lined with hair. The eggs are usually three in number (more rarely two or four), white or pink with much rufous or lilac spotting. Further information is not available.

FOOD A varied diet, consisting mainly of fruit, seeds and insects.

DISTRIBUTION AND MOVEMENTS Breeds in Africa, Asia Minor and Arabia. Resident. Accidental in Spain, doubtless from Morocco.

SUB-SPECIES Sub-species are present in Africa and Asia.

A. Christiansen

(Above) Grey-backed Fiscal Shrike *L. excubitoroides* has distinctive black wing and tail feathers

From the data currently available the family Laniidae or shrikes, appears to consist of a group of passerines whose main common attributes are their predatory habits, some general similarity of appearance, the shape of the bill—strong and hooked, often toothed as in the family Falconidae —and some similarities of behaviour which could easily be due to convergence.

According to recent authorities, this family, widely distributed especially in the Old World, consists of four sub-families: the true shrikes Laniinae; 'bush-shrikes' Malaconotinae; 'helmet-shrikes' Prionopinae; and finally the sub-family Pityriasinae, whose only member is the Bornean Bristlehead *Pityriasis gymnocephala*. It has still not been established whether the Malaconotinae or 'bush-shrikes' are really related to true shrikes. The Prionopinae are treated by some authorities as a separate family, but always placed next to the Laniidae. It is very doubtful whether the Bornean Bristlehead is really a shrike, but not enough is known about this species to classify it with

certainty. There is also disagreement on the number of species in the family, some authorities recognising from seventy-two (when 'helmet-shrikes' are classified as a separate family) to eighty-five. The shrike's bill is slightly hooked, and there is a notch on the lower mandible corresponding to the 'tooth' of the upper mandible. The 'rictal bristles' are well developed and the nostrils are round or oval. The legs are strong and the toes have sharp, hooked claws for holding prey. The wings are fairly broad, usually rounded in shape, with ten primaries, while the fairly long tail may be rounded or graduated.

The coloration and structure of the feathers varies considerably: some species (genera *Lanius*, *Laniarius* and *Dryoscopus*) are mainly black and white; some have touches of bright green, yellow or red (genera *Chlorophoneus*, *Telophorus* and *Malaconetus*) while some 'boubous' (genus *Laniarius*) are uniformly black. The young of many species are lightly barred, as are some adult females, or, very rarely, the adults of both sexes.

All shrikes are carnivorous and are bold and aggressive birds. They capture mostly insects but these are supplemented, especially in the larger species, by small reptiles, mammals and birds. Shrikes perch on a prominent lookout before swooping down on their prey and many species impale the prey on thorns, twigs, sticks, or even barbed wire. There are various suggestions to explain this behaviour: one is that it enables them to manipulate their prey more easily, another that it is a method of providing a stockpile of food against periods of shortage. Popular tradition has always inclined towards the latter theory, and the shrikes' reserves of food are known as 'larders'. This theory is also supported by the fact that in many cases the prey is impaled with care, often just by the point where the head joins the body, so that it remains alive although paralysed, thus avoiding, or, at least delaying, the effects of decomposition. Further support is forthcoming from the observation that during periods when food is plentiful, shrikes collect together all their prey without impaling them and eat only the innards.

Shrikes are generally solitary birds, usually found on the edges of woods, areas with scattered trees or even open ground as long as it provides bushes, dry branches, poles or other vantage points where they can perch, watchfully, waiting for their prey to come within reach. For many species telegraph wires have proved a marvellous invention and are favourite observation posts. Some shrikes, however, hunt their prey hopping from bough to bough in large trees or in thick undergrowth. Other species, like the Great Grey Shrike *Lanius excubitor* and the Lesser Grey Shrike

L. minor, occasionally hover in the same way as some falcons. Flight is usually dipping.

The call is generally somewhat discordant, although resonant, but several species have a relatively musical song and can mimic the songs of other birds. In some cases, for example, the Red-backed Shrike *L. collurio*, the plaintive notes seem to attract small birds which are promptly captured.

Shrikes build substantial cup-shaped nests, sometimes compact but often loosely-woven, in tall shrubs or trees. They lay from two to eight pink, brownish or bright green eggs, slightly glossy with irregular olive-brown or rufous markings. Both parents tend the young.

The sub-family Laniinae contains the true shrikes, which are widely distributed in the Palearctic region, Africa (except for Madagascar), Asia, and New Guinea (but not Australia or New Zealand). This sub-family includes only three genera: *Lanius, Corvinella* and *Urolestes;* the last is often included with *Corvinella*. Only two shrikes are found in North America, and even these are probably recent (in the geological sense) acquisitions to the Nearctic avifauna.

The species with a Holarctic distribution which is most widely found in the northern hemisphere is the Great Grey Shrike, which has been sub-divided into numerous races. It is the prototype of the 'grey shrikes', with pearl-grey upper parts, a contrasting black eye-stripe and black wings and tail. The wing also has a sort of white speculum, larger or smaller depending on the geographical sub-species, and the scapulars are paler, while the white underparts are sometimes lightly tinged pink.

(Below) Male Woodchat Shrike *Lanius senator* at the nest. The young are tended by both parents for about three weeks

M. D. England/Ardea

J. Burton/Bruce Coleman

The juveniles are barred and their coloration tends towards brown. Other species are similar to the Great Grey Shrike such as the Loggerhead Shrike *L. ludovicianus* (found only in North America) and the Lesser Grey Shrike (of southern Europe and neighbouring regions). Many other smaller species have somewhat brighter, more contrasting plumage, such as the Red-backed Shrike and a whole series of similar forms which are sometimes regarded as conspecific.

The Woodchat Shrike *L. senator* has a mainly Mediterranean distribution during the nesting season, but winters in tropical Africa. As is generally the case the species or sub-species nesting in more northerly regions tend to be migratory, while tropical species, or at any rate those with a southerly distribution, are usually sedentary.

Other members of the sub-family are found in Africa; still in the genus *Lanius*, some species, such as the Grey-backed Fiscal Shrike *L. excubitorius*, and the Long-tailed Fiscal Shrike *L. cabanisi*, have the habit, unusual in this family, of going about in groups which often perform spectacular displays.

The sub-family Malaconotinae is exclusively African, and its relationship to the tree shrikes is, as already mentioned, somewhat doubtful. Medium-sized birds (about the size of a blackbird), they are classified in thirty-nine species in nine genera. In some (genus *Malaconotus*) the bill is very strong while in others it is unusually weak for a shrike (genus *Telophonus*). Another genus is *Laniarius*, in which the coloration varies from mainly black to black and white or black upper parts with underparts variously coloured pink, rufous, red or yellow. The feathers of the rump are soft and 'frayed'. This feature is particularly evident in members of the genus *Dyrosocopus* in which the rump feathers form an erectile 'powder-puff', different in colour from the upper parts. Among the most handsome and strikingly coloured species are those of the genera *Chlorophoneus* and *Telophorus*. A characteristic of the genus *Malaconnotus* is that the tail is as long as the wings. This sub-family also includes the 'giants' among the shrikes: the Grey-headed Bush-Shrike *Malaconotus blanchoti* and the Pugnacious Bush-Shrike *M. gladiator*, species which may be up to twenty-nine centimetres long.

Another African sub-family, the Prionopinae, contains nine species. They are sociable species at all times including the breeding season, when several pairs will nest side by side and individuals will often unite to build a nest and care for the young. These 'helpers' are probably immature birds about one year old. Besides the genus *Prionops*, this sub-family includes the genera *Sigmodus* (both these genera have brightly-coloured caruncles beside the eyes) and *Eurocephalus*. They have been given the name 'helmet-shrikes' from the stiff, bristle-like feathers covering the forehead of many species.

The sole member of the sub-family *Pityriasinae* is the Bornean Bristlehead *P. gymnocephala*, characterised not only by its restricted distribution —it is found only in Borneo—but also by the bare, warty skin covering part of the head, the rest of which is covered with feathers modified to form a type of stiff bristle.

(Above) The Tropical Boubou *Laniarius aethiopicus* is seldom seen, but is easily identified by its very musical song (Left) World distribution of the family Laniidae

Red-backed Shrike
Lanius collurio

HABITAT Hedges, copses, heaths and other areas with tall, scattered bushes.

IDENTIFICATION Length: 18 cm. Male: black bands on top of head and light grey neck; upper back, wing-coverts and scapulars bright rust-red. Lower back and rump are blue-grey; under-parts whitish with pale pink on breast and flanks; flight-feathers black-brown bordered rust and whitish; tail black in the centre with white outer tail feathers broadening on the proximal half. Bill black, legs grey-black, iris brown. Female: upper parts and head brown, greyish neck, under-parts creamy-white, more or less barred brown except on belly; flight-feathers brown, edged pale; tail-feathers dark brown, the outer ones edged white. Bill brown, legs grey-brown. Juveniles: as female, but much more brown-black on upper parts. Moult between November and February. See also page 178.

CALL A harsh, grating 'shack-shack'. The song is quiet, musical and reminiscent of the Garden Warbler's.

REPRODUCTION From late May. The nest, is usually built a few metres from the ground, in young conifers or other shrubs. It is made of branches, twigs, roots and moss and lined with grass. Five or six (rarely seven) eggs are laid which are smooth and glossy and highly variable in colour: from pale green to pink, buff or almost white with brown, dark red, purple or grey blotches and speckles. The female incubates the eggs for fourteen to sixteen days although on very rare occasions the male will help incubate. Both tend the young.

DISTRIBUTION AND MOVEMENTS Breeds from Scandinavia, England and northern Iberia east across Eurasia. Winters in tropical and southern Africa, southern Iran and northern India. In Britain is a fast declining summer visitor to a few southern localities and a scarce passage migrant. An eastern sub-species has also occurred as a scarce visitor.

SUB-SPECIES *L.c. collurio*: Scandinavia, western USSR; southwards to Iberia and the Mediterranean and Asia Minor. *L.c. juxtus* (darker): central and southern England. *L.c. kobylini* (darker chestnut mantle): Crimea, the Caucasus and eastwards to Iran. Other sub-species are present in Asia.

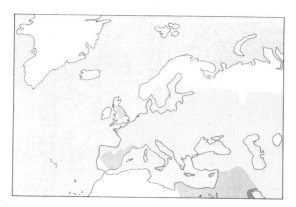

French: PIE-GRIÈCHE ÉCORCHEUR
Italian: AVERLA PICCOLA
Spanish: ALCAUDÓN DORSIRROJO
German: NEUNÖTER

(Below) Male Red-backed Shrike (foreground) and female. (Left) Breeding areas (yellow), wintering areas (magenta) and areas where the Red-backed Shrike may be seen on passage (pink)

French: PIE-GRIÈCHE À TÊTE
ROUSSE
Italian: AVERLA CAPIROSSA
Spanish: ALCAUDÓN COMÚN
German: ROTKOPFWÜRGER

Woodchat Shrike
Lanius senator

(Above) Woodchat Shrike (foreground) and the sub-species *L.s. badius.* (Below) Breeding areas (yellow) and areas where the Woodchat Shrike may be seen on passage (pink)

HABITAT Open, dry land, olive groves, gardens, thickets; rarely in forests. May be found up to a height of eight hundred metres.

IDENTIFICATION Length: 19 cm. Distinguished from Great Grey and Lesser Grey Shrikes by bright chestnut crown and nape. Wide black face-markings extend over forehead. Throat and underparts pure white; blackish wings and mantle contrasting with white shoulder-patches and conspicuous white wing-bar. Tail is black with white sides; rump white. Juvenile birds are mottled and barred buffs and browns, with traces of a whitish wing-bar.
Solitary and aggressive. Does not go more than a few hundred metres from the nest which it defends against any intruder. Lies in wait for its prey. During courtship the male stands in front of the female with fluffed-up feathers, offering her food. See also page 178.

CALL Besides the characteristic 'rretts' it may be identified by its alarm call 'skekskekskes'. Also emits a song which is more musical than that of most shrikes.

REPRODUCTION From late April. Nests in trees and exceptionally shrubs. The nest is a substantial cup, usually on an outer branch, made of roots and plant material and lined with feathers, wool and hair. Five or six (rarely seven) greenish-white (sometimes yellowish or pink), mottled grey-brown and ash-grey, eggs are laid. Incubation lasts about sixteen days; the female incubates almost exclusively and during this period she is fed by the male. Both tend the young who leave the nest after about nineteen or twenty days.

FOOD Chiefly insects; also snails and worms. The habit, common to many shrikes, of impaling prey makes it easy to dismember as well as being a method of storing food.

DISTRIBUTION AND MOVEMENTS Breeds from northwest Africa, Iberia and France east to Poland and through Asia Minor to Iran. Winters in tropical Africa. Is a vagrant to northern Europe and to Britain and Ireland in both spring and autumn.

SUB-SPECIES *L.s. senator:* continental Europe, northwest Africa and perhaps Asia Minor. *L.s. badius* (no white at base of primaries): Balearic Islands, Corsica and Sardinia.

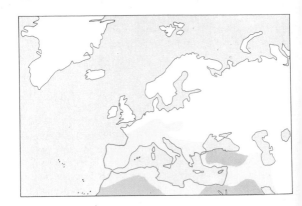

Masked Shrike
Lanius nubicus

HABITAT During breeding season is found in wooded areas including forest clearings, areas with large isolated trees or bushes, gardens and olive groves.

IDENTIFICATION Length: 17 cm. Adult male: forehead and broad eyestripe white; crown, nape, mantle, back and rump glossy black; scapulars white; upper-tail coverts black, tipped and edged white. Lores dark brown; ear-coverts brown-black; chin, throat, central belly and under-tail coverts white but with some orange on the flanks. Legs are black; iris dark brown. Complete moult in August-November. Females browner than males, and juveniles browner than the females. Tends to perch in less conspicuous positions than other shrikes. See also page 178.

CALL A characteristic, harsh 'keer-keer-keer'. The song is a pleasant warbling.

REPRODUCTION From April onwards. Generally nests in trees or shrubs at a height of three to ten metres on a lateral branch. The nest, is modest in size, made of roots, twigs and stems and is lined with roots and plant fibres. Eggs: four to six (sometimes seven),

yellowish-brown or buff, with dark brown and grey markings. Information on incubation and nestlings is lacking.

FOOD Chiefly insects: sometimes young birds.

DISTRIBUTION AND MOVEMENTS Southeastern Europe, including Greece, and Asia Minor. Winters in northwestern Africa. Accidental in southern Spain.

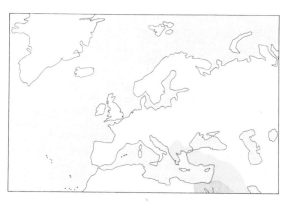

(Above) Male Masked Shrike (foreground) and juvenile. (Below) Breeding areas yellow) and areas where the Masked Shrike may be seen on passage (pink)

French: PIE-GRIÈCHE À POITRINE
ROSE
Italian: AVERLA CENERINA
Spanish: ALCAUDÓN CHICO
German: SCHWARZSTIRNWÜRGER

Lesser Grey Shrike
Lanius minor

HABITAT Open country with scattered trees and bushes: grassland, wasteland or cultivated areas. Also hedgerows and gardens.

IDENTIFICATION Length: 20 cm. Similar to Great Grey Shrike but smaller and wings proportionately longer. A distinctive black band covers forehead, eyes and lores and distinguishes it from the Great Grey Shrike. Lesser Grey Shrike's bill is also darker and it lacks the white eyestripe. Remaining upper parts light blue-grey; underparts white tinged mauve-pink; wings black with white patch at base of primaries. Outer tail-feathers mainly white, the others with increasing amounts of black at base; central tail-feathers black. Bill black; legs brown-black. Complete moult in autumn. Female: as male, but dingier grey and black; underparts less pinkish. Juveniles are pale yellowish-brown.

Flight is more direct and less undulating than that of the Great Grey Shrike. Also hovers more and appears more erect when perched. See also page 178.

CALL A characteristic 'shiek-shiek' or 'shek-ek-ek'. Also emits a light chattering and twittering song.

REPRODUCTION From mid-May. Nests at a height of three to ten metres in trees, although as low as one and a half metres in areas without higher trees. The nest is built on a horizontal branch or against the trunk and is made of twigs, stems and roots. It is lined with material such as hair, feathers, roots and fine grasses. Five to

seven smooth, glossy eggs are laid which are greenish-white with brown and violet-grey markings. Mainly the female incubates the eggs for about fifteen days.

FOOD Mainly insects: also small vertebrates, molluscs and fruit.

DISTRIBUTION AND MOVEMENTS Breeds from Spain and France east across Eurasia to Siberia and south to the Balkans and Asia Minor. Winters in Africa south of the equator. In northern Europe is a rare straggler, though is more or less identified annually in Britain. Has also occurred in Ireland.

SUB-SPECIES A sub-species is present in Asia.

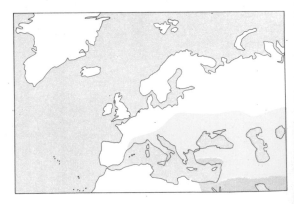

(Above) Adult Lesser Grey Shrike (foreground) and juvenile. (Right) Breeding areas (yellow) and areas where the Lesser Grey Shrike may be seen on passage (pink)

Great Grey Shrike
Lanius excubitor

French: PIE-GRIÈCHE GRISE
Italian: AVERLA MAGGIORE
Spanish: ALCAUDÓN REAL
German: RAUBWURGER

HABITAT Breeds in open forests and forest clearings, orchards, heathland, hedgerows and scrubland.

IDENTIFICATION Length: 25 cm. Is the largest shrike found in Europe, and its black, white and grey plumage is distinctive. Upper parts of head and neck light blue-grey, whitish towards rump; white eyestripe and black streak from bill through and beyond eye. Does not extend over forehead as in Lesser Grey Shrike. Underparts white, sometimes pinkish on breast; wings black with white patch which varies in size and white trailing edge; wing-coverts grey. Central tail-feathers black, tipped white, outer tail-feathers almost completely white. Bill and legs black. Complete moult between July and November. Female: as male, but often with greyish wavy lines on breast and flanks. Juveniles are more brownish. See also page 178.

CALL Emits a 'prri' or 'trru', often modified to a strident 'crriu' or a harsh 'kirr'. A characteristic 'shiek-shiek' is sometimes prolonged into a Magpie-like sound.

REPRODUCTION From April onwards. Nests at various heights from tall trees to thorn bushes. The nest is a bulky cup of dry grass, moss and twigs and is lined with roots, hair and feathers. The female lays five to seven smooth, glossy eggs (occasionally eight or nine) which are greenish-white and heavily marked with olive-brown and violet-grey markings. Incubation is carried out mainly by the female for an average of fifteen days. The young remain in the nest for nineteen to twenty days. Normally one brood, sometimes two.

FOOD Large insects and small vertebrates.

DISTRIBUTION AND MOVEMENTS Breeds from Scandinavia, Spain, France and Germany, east across Eurasia to the Pacific. Also breeds in northern Africa, Arabia and northern North America. Winters in its breeding range, except for birds from the extreme north which migrate just south of the breeding range. In Britain and Ireland is a passage migrant and winter visitor in small numbers.

SUB-SPECIES *L.e. excubitor:* from Scandinavia and USSR southwards to the Pyrenees and northern Italy and east to Siberia and Rumania. *L.e. homeyeri* (paler): from Bulgaria and Rumania eastwards to western Siberia. *L.e. meridionalis* (darker): southern France, Iberian peninsula. Other sub-species are present in Asia, Africa, North America and the Canary Islands.

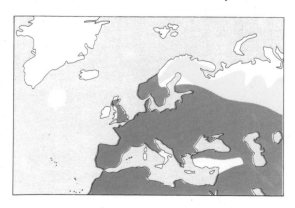

(Above) Male Great Grey Shrike (foreground) and female. (Left) Breeding areas (yellow), wintering areas (magenta) and areas where the Great Grey Shrike may be seen all year round (orange)

Shrikes in flight

1: GREAT GREY SHRIKE *(Lanius excubitor)* Black, white and grey plumage and large size are distinguishing features. The adult (a) differs from the juvenile (b) in having white scapulars. From beneath (c), throat and belly are white. Flight is more undulating than the Lesser Grey Shrike's and it hovers less.

2: RED-BACKED SHRIKE *(Lanius collurio)* The male (a) has chestnut back while the female (b) is uniformly brownish, lacking grey rump or white on tail. The combination of the chestnut back and blue-grey head is unique among shrikes in Europe. The male seen from below (c) has no white markings on underwing, but white on either side of the base of the tail may be seen in flight.

3: LESSER GREY SHRIKE *(Lanius minor)* Both male (a) and female (b) differ from Great Grey Shrike in that the grey of the upper parts does not extend to the wing-coverts; the tail-markings are also different. Underparts (c) darker than in Great Shrike, with contrasting markings on underwing. White wing-bar is a conspicuous feature in flight as are the proportionately longer wings and shorter tail.

4: MASKED SHRIKE *(Lanius nubicus)* Male (a) is black and white while female (b) has grey head, back and rump, the remaining plumage being lighter than the male's. Seen from below (c) the male has rufous-orange flanks.

5: WOODCHAT SHRIKE *(Lanius senator)* Adults (a) easily distinguished from all other shrikes by chestnut head. White wing-bars, shoulder patches and rump should also be noted. Juveniles (b) similar to adults but coloration is drabber. In flight when seen in profile (c) the chestnut head is the most distinctive and conspicuous feature.

(Right) Woodchat Shrike *L. senator* at the nest

H. Kinloch/Aquila

Passeriformes: Laniidae

(Above) Fiscal Shrike *Lanius collaris.* (Above right) Male Red-backed Shrike *L. collurio* feeding young. This species is rapidly declining in Britain. (Right) Grey-backed Fiscal Shrikes *L. excubitoroides*

180

ORDER Passeriformes
FAMILY BOMBYCILLIDAE: Waxwings

T. Suominen

Waxwings vary in length from sixteen to nineteen centimetres. Their plumage is soft and silky; all the species (three or four depending on which authority is followed) are tinged with a soft pastel grey or wine-colour. Some parts of the body are chestnut; the throat is black and there is a black eyestripe. The wings are greyish, and the secondaries are often tipped with a tiny, bright red or yellow waxy substance. The tail is also greyish, with a black sub-terminal band and a red or yellow tip.

The birds are all included in the one genus *Bombycilla* and breed in open coniferous and birch forests, especially in taiga. The Waxwing *B. garrulus* has a Holarctic distribution, (in North America it is called the Bohemian Waxwing) while the so-called Japanese Waxwing *B. japonica* is really a native of eastern Siberia. The Cedar Waxwing *B. cedrorum* is found only in North America. Waxwings undertake irregular migrations, more accurately known as irruptions, in winter as far south as central Europe, central China, Japan, and in the New World, as far as Central America. These movements appear at first sight to coincide with severe winters, but are, in fact, mainly linked with seasons when the waxwings' chief food, seeds and berries, are more or less abundant.

During these winter irruptions, waxwings seem tame and apparently without any fear of man. In winter they live in larger groups than in the breeding season, and frequently feed in gardens or along hedgerows.

A fourth species is sometimes included in this family: the Hypocolius *Hypocolius ampelinus*. This species could be classed as aberrant, mainly because so little is known about it; it is found only in parts of southwestern Asia.

The plumage is pale grey, with blue markings on the back, becoming light buff on the forehead and underparts. A black eyestripe extends from the bill to the nape. The primaries are black, tipped with white and the tail-feathers have a black terminal band: the tail is long, giving it a shrike-like shape. The females have no black on the head. The Hypocolius is smaller than the waxwings, but it resembles them in its soft plumage and delicate colouring, as well as in some structural features of the skeleton.

(Above) Waxwing *Bombycilla garrulus*. This species occurs erratically in Britain after mass eruptions from its breeding grounds in northern Europe. (Left) World distribution of the family Bombycillidae

S. Roberts/Ardea

Waxwing
Bombycilla garrulus

French: JASEUR BORÉAL
Italian: BECCOFRUSONE
Spanish: AMPELIS EUROPEO
German: SEIDENSCHWANZ

HABITAT Open coniferous or birch woods, especially in taiga. During its westward eruptions is seen among shrubs and in parks and gardens.

IDENTIFICATION Length: 18 cm. Unmistakable pink-brown crest and short, yellow-tipped tail. Black eye-stripe and black patch on throat. Upper parts chestnut with ash-grey rump. Underparts pinkish-brown, with chestnut under-tail coverts. The wings are dark, with characteristic yellow markings and scarlet wax-like tips to the secondaries (less conspicuous in the female). Bill and legs black; iris brown. Complete moult between October and November. The juveniles lack the black throat patch and have softly streaked underparts.

CALL The usual call-note is a weak, high-pitched, trilling 'zree', or a clear, firm piping: 'stirr'.

REPRODUCTION Late May onwards. Nests in a tree, usually a conifer, from a metre and a half to six metres up. Nest is a cup made of twigs, moss and lichens and is lined with hair and down. Eggs: four to six (rarely seven), pale blue or grey-blue and lightly marked with black and grey are laid. The female incubates for a period of fourteen days. Both parents tend the young who leave the nest after fifteen to seventeen days.

FOOD Chiefly berries: sometimes insects and seeds.

DISTRIBUTION AND MOVEMENTS Northern Europe, northern Asia and northwest North America. Migratory (usually irruptive) in some winters, when it may reach as far south as Asia Minor, Iran, China, Japan and the southwestern United States. Is a passage and winter visitor to Britain and Ireland in highly variable numbers. During invasions flocks may be sizeable and widespread.

SUB-SPECIES Sub-species are present in Asia and North America.

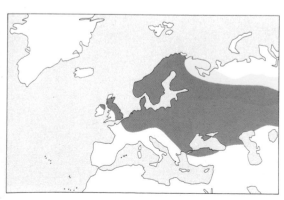

(Above) Female Waxwing (foreground), male (centre) and juvenile. (Left) Breeding areas (yellow), wintering areas (magenta) and areas where the Waxwing may be seen all year round (orange). (Facing page) Waxwing *B. garrulus*

ORDER Passeriformes
FAMILY CINCLIDAE:Dippers

J. B. & S. Bottomley/Ardea

184

This small family, which is distributed mainly in the Palearctic region and the New World, consists of only four species grouped in a single genus. These are birds of compact build and short compact tails which are commonly known as dippers or water-ouzels—names which aptly describe their appearance and behaviour.

The family Cinclidae demonstrates the great adaptability of birds of the order Passeriformes. The dippers have adapted to an aquatic environment without any radical modification to their basic structure, which is typical of songbirds. At first sight, dippers give no hint of their prowess in and under the water. The plumage is similar to that of all birds of the order, or perhaps slightly thicker; the legs are just like those of any Starling, sparrow or Blackbird; the bills are perfectly ordinary. Yet the Dipper *Cinclus cinclus*, which is common throughout Europe, is an expert swimmer, although it has to move its legs very fast because its toes are not webbed. It dives with unexpected skill, from a standstill, while walking or from the air. Dippers are among the few birds capable of swimming under water, even against the strong currents of the mountain streams, where the majority of species and sub-species live. They use their wings when swimming under water, but seem to have a certain amount of difficulty in staying at the bottom, so that their motion is undulating. Dippers catch fish, small invertebrates and larvae as they swim or walk in the turbulent waters. They manage to spot prey on the river bed without having to hunt under stones or debris.

(Below and facing page) Dipper *Cinclus cinclus*. Its white front is a distinctive feature

T. Suominen

(Right and far right) Dipper *C. cinclus* and (below) world distribution of the family Cinclidae

As if all these peculiarities were not enough, it has been shown that dippers can fly out of the water—although they often simply walk out. In the same way, they are capable of flying into the water and once they have re-surfaced, they sometimes swim around quietly. The only thing which makes their extraordinary feats slightly less impressive is that the water they dive into is fairly shallow—not more than one and a half metres deep—but even so their achievements are remarkable.

The adaptation to an aquatic environment is also demonstrated by the choice of nesting sites, which may be under the arch of a bridge, in the shelter of a rock, in the middle of a river, or, most frequently of all, under a waterfall. Dippers bear a slight resemblance to wrens, and this is not just a superficial similarity, since they have several characteristics in common, such as the type and quality of their song and the way they build their nests which are spherical, carefully constructed, covered with moss and softly lined.

The female lays four or five eggs per clutch (very occasionally three or six). Both parents tend the offspring which remain in the nest for fifteen to twenty days. Although their territorial instincts are normally well developed and the various pairs lay claim to their own share of the area where they live, so as not to quarrel over food, they sometimes form small groups in certain parts of their distribution area if they are forced to move off in search of prey, particularly during the winter.

The four species of the family are distributed between Eurasia, northern Africa and North, Central and South America. The European Dipper has, undoubtedly, the most extensive distribution area, since it is found in much of central Asia as well as Europe. It comes into contact with the most eastern Brown Dipper *C. pallasii* in Asia. The latter's plumage is a beautiful uniform chocolate-brown colour, not unlike that of the American Dipper *C. americanus* which occurs in the western part of North America from Panama to Alaska. Lastly, the various geographical races of the White-capped Dipper *C. leucocephalus* are found in many parts of the Andes.

French: CINCLE PLONGEUR
Italian: MERLO ACQUAIOLO
Spanish: MIRLO ACUÁTICO
German: WASSERAMSEL

Dipper
Cinclus cinclus

HABITAT Lives by swift-flowing streams and rivers in hills and mountains: in winter sometimes wanders to lowland streams.

IDENTIFICATION Length: 17 cm. Rather plump build with a distinctive short tail which is often cocked up. Very dark brown plumage with conspicuous white throat and breast. Chocolate-brown head and nape. The sexes are alike. Juveniles: dark grey upper parts, greyer white underparts with small dark grey markings. It lives alone or in pairs and always remains in the same territory. It likes perching on stones and rocks jutting over streams, and frequently dives into the water in search of food, swimming under water and on the surface. Its flight is low and direct.

CALL A brief 'zeet-zeet' and a metallic 'cleenk-cleenk'. Also emits a Wren-like song.

REPRODUCTION From February (rarely late March to April). The spherical nest is built by both sexes out of moss and dry grasses, and is lined with dead leaves. It is always close to fast-flowing water and is situated on rocks, under the piers of bridges or in cavities in trees and walls. The entrance of the nest points downwards towards the water. The Dipper lays four or five slightly ovate white eggs. Incubation takes sixteen days and is normally carried out by the female. Both tend the young who can dive and swim before they can fly.

FOOD Small fish and small invertebrates.

DISTRIBUTION AND MOVEMENTS Palearctic: breeds in Britain and Ireland and west of Europe: also southwest across Asia to Iran and China. Also breeds in northwest Africa.

SUB-SPECIES *C. c. hibernicus*: Ireland, the Isle of Man, the Hebrides and the west coast of Scotland. *C. c. gularis*: the Orkneys, Scotland, northern and western England and Wales. *C. c. cinclus*: Norway, Sweden, Finland and Russia, south to eastern Prussia and Brittany; also found in central France, the Pyrenees, north west Spain, northern Portugal, Corsica, Sardinia and northern Turkey. *C. c. aquaticus*: the rest of Europe.

(Above) The sub-species *C.c. aquaticus* (top left), adult Dipper (centre) and juvenile (right). (Left) Wintering areas (magenta) and areas where the Dipper may be seen all year round (orange)

187

ORDER **Passeriformes**

FAMILY **TROGLODYTIDAE: Wrens**

L. Gaggero

Wrens are small or medium-sized species of the order Passeriformes. They range in size from six and a half to twenty-five centimetres. Plumage is basically brown with lighter underparts and barred wings and tail. Some species have short tails, while others have normal or rather long tails, sometimes with white markings on the borders. The slender and often slightly curved bills also vary in length, but the basic shape is usually the same and reveals their insect-eating habits. These small, lively birds have strong legs; the wings are generally rounded. Most are sedentary, although some (or rather some populations of certain species), such as the Common Wren *Troglodytes troglodytes* of Europe, migrate for varying distances.

The Common Wren is one of the smallest European birds. It nests in mountains, in ravines in the hills or among bushes on Mediterranean islands, and in bushy areas. Such adaptability has naturally led to the development of numerous

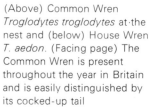

(Above) Common Wren *Troglodytes troglodytes* at·the nest and (below) House Wren *T. aedon*. (Facing page) The Common Wren is present throughout the year in Britain and is easily distinguished by its cocked-up tail

P. Katsaros/Photo Researchers

(Right) Common Wren *T. troglodytes* and (below) world distribution of the family Troglodytidae

R. Richter/Ardea

sub-species. The Common Wren has belonged to the avifauna of Europe since time immemorial and features in the legends and folklore of many countries. It is hard to believe that this popular small bird is actually an immigrant from North America, and that it probably originated in the tropical or sub-tropical parts of the New World where over sixty other species of wren now live. They are grouped in twelve to fourteen genera and form the entire family Troglodytidae.

Wrens' habitat is dense vegetation and sometimes cultivated land. They may live close to water. Some birds, such as certain northern European populations of the Wren, nest in man-made nest-boxes as does the House Wren *T. aedon* from North America. Provided there are bushes in the vicinity, wrens even live in desert regions. One species, the Cactus Wren *Campylorhynchus brunneicapillus*, frequents muddy, shingly riverside areas where it turns over stones and pebbles like a Turnstone *Arenaria interpres*. The Cactus Wren, as its name suggests, nests in a cactus or thorn-bearing tree, particularly in the so-called cholla cactus. The eggs and young are protected from predators by the sharp spines, yet the adult seems able to move with agility over the spines without coming to any harm. The Chestnut-breasted Wren *Cyphorrhinus thoracicus* lifts up dead leaves in search of insects and other small invertebrates. The Common Wren is also said to catch small fish, although only on rare occasions.

The family Troglodytidae includes numerous fine singers. Some species produce among the most beautiful and expressive songs of the bird world. Wrens' singing is not restricted to the breeding season, but may be heard all year round.

The more strictly tropical species are monogamous, but others like the Common Wren appear to be polygamous to varying degrees. Since the degree of polygamous behaviour often seems to be connected with the type of habitat—it is more common in populations inhabiting the most dense vegetation—the phenomenon is probably linked to the availability or ease of access to food supplies. Of course, polygamy is also allied to the gradual breakdown in close family ties—such as the building of several nests by a single pair and the male's comparative lack of interest in his offspring—and also to the way both males and females tend to feed the young of other wrens or even other species of bird.

The nest is often a complex spherical structure made by carefully weaving fine plant material with animal hair and wool. The male does most of the work among polygamous species and builds as many nests as he has 'wives'. Only females incubate the eggs, but the males of many species build separate nests for themselves and other males and females of the same species. The advantage of this is obvious as the smaller wrens lose body-heat rapidly. No less than sixty-three Common Wrens have been found huddled together for warmth in a single nest box in winter.

Common Wren
Troglodytes troglodytes

HABITAT A wide variety of habitats which provide low cover including hedgerows, cultivated land, reed beds, woody areas, rocky coasts and small islands.

IDENTIFICATION Length: 9 cm. Easily recognised by its small, round, plump shape and its distinctive small tail which is almost continuously cocked up. Its brown coloration is paler on the underparts. Dense dark bars on its wings, flanks and tail. Juveniles: like adults but with fewer bars.

It is very lively and constantly on the move. Hunts for insects among leaves on the ground, in cracks in the bark of trees—which it climbs like a small nuthatch—or among rocks; it sometimes flies for a short distance in pursuit of its prey. Its flight is direct and it launches itself with powerful wing-beats. Lives alone or in pairs during the nesting season. During courtship it fans out its wings and tail.

CALL A loud, slightly tremulous 'teet-teet-teet'; a repeated 'tee-tee-teech'. Its song is powerful considering its size, and consists of clear and vigorous trills which are often sustained.

REPRODUCTION Late April onwards. It nests in almost any type of hollow or cavity from ground level upwards, but prefers the side of a tree, steep bank or a wall up to a height of three metres. The nest is built by the male and, as he is often polygamous, he may build a number of nests and install females in them. The nest is a stout dome structure made of leaves, grass and other plant material which the female lines with feathers. Five to eight (occasionally up to sixteen) eggs are laid which are glossy white with very fine, dark spots. The female incubates for fourteen to seventeen days. Both tend the young.

FOOD Insects, spiders, seeds and larvae.

DISTRIBUTION AND MOVEMENTS Breeds in Iceland, Britain, Ireland east across Eurasia to Japan and south to India. Also breeds in northwest Africa and North America. Northernmost populations are partially migratory, sometimes wintering just south of the breeding range. Is a widespread and numerous resident breeder in Britain and Ireland, although there may be some local post-breeding wandering by some individuals.

SUB-SPECIES *T. t. troglodytes*: continental Europe. *T. t. islandicus* (large and dark with a long powerful bill): Iceland. *T. t. borealis* (paler than *T. t. islandicus*): Faeroes. *T. t. zetlandicus* (more reddish-brown than *T. t. islandicus*): the Shetland Islands. *T. t. fridariensis* (paler than the previous races): Fair Isle. *T. t. hebridensis* (similar coloration to *T. t. zetlandicus*): the Outer Hebrides. *T. t. hirtensis* (much paler and greyer than the previous races): St. Kilda Island. *T. t. indigenus* (darker, with duller upper parts): Ireland, the Inner Hebrides, Scotland and England. *T. t. koenigi* (darker, browner, less reddish): Corsica and Sardinia. *T. t. kabylorum* (paler upper parts and underparts): the Balearic Islands. *T. t. cypriotes* (more barred than the previous races): Crete, Rhodes, Cyprus and the Near East. *T. t. hyrcanus* (more greyish-brown upper parts): the Crimea, the Caucasus and Transcaucasia.

French: TROGLODYTE MIGNON
Italian: SCRICCIOLO
Spanish: CHOCHÍN
German: ZAUNKÖNIG

(Above) Common Wren (top), the sub-species *T.t. hirtensis* (centre), and *T.t. cypriotes* (bottom). (Left) Breeding areas (yellow), wintering areas (magenta) and areas where the Common Wren may be seen all year round (orange)

A. E. Staffan/Photo Researchers

H. Rice/Photo Researchers

Photo Researchers

(Left, far left and below) The Brown Thrasher *Toxostoma rufum* is a rare vagrant to Britain from North America. (Facing page) Catbird *Dumetella carolinensis* at the nest

The family Mimidae or mockingbirds consists of thirty-four species which are grouped in thirteen genera: nine of these are monotypic. Mockingbirds are about the size of thrushes but look larger because of their elongated tails; in some positions they are reminiscent of the larger species of wren. As they are mostly sedentary the wings are fairly short and rounded. The legs and bills are powerful, and the latter are rather long. The basic coloration of the mockingbirds is grey-brown or almost white, with varying amounts of speckles and streaks. In some species, such as the Catbird *Dumetella carolinensis*, the plumage is a uniform slate-grey which is almost black.

The Latin name Mimidae and the English name of the family is derived from the belief that many members of this family are capable of imitating the songs of other birds as well as reproducing series of sounds of various origins. However their skill at mimicry may have been overrated, since they are species with very varied songs which often include notes produced by other species with which they have never been in contact. Therefore, in such cases, mimicry is clearly out of the question. In other instances, however, they undoubtedly imitate certain noises and sounds. Mockingbirds also sing at night as well as in the day, and one species—the Sage Thrasher *Oreoscoptes montanus*—sings in flight.

They are basically arboreal in habits except when hunting for food, which consists mainly of ground-dwelling invertebrates and fruit. Mocking-

R. Kinne/Photo Researchers

R. Kinne/Photo Researchers

(Above) Pearly-eyed Thrasher
Margarops fuscatus and
(below) world distribution of
the family Mimidae

birds build their nests in bushes or in trees with dense foliage. The nests are cup-shaped and often quite large. There are between two and five eggs per clutch, the northernmost populations laying more eggs. The background colour of the eggs may be pale blue, cream or pale green and they may be plain or covered with markings. Incubation is usually carried out by the female for twelve to fifteen days, but the male sometimes takes part. Both parents feed the young.

Mockingbirds are aggressive and guard their territory courageously, even against such enemies as poisonous snakes. Like wrens, many mockingbirds defend their territory after the nesting season, either singly or in pairs. They do not appear to form social groups although several individuals may occasionally be seen feeding together.

The greatest variety of species is found in the arid regions of the western United States, but some are present as far south as Argentina and Chile. There are nine species of true mockingbird of the genus *Mimus*. One, the Galapogos Mockingbird *Mimus trifasciatus*, is exclusive to the Galapagos Islands. Species of the genus *Toxostoma* are gradually becoming more terresrial in their habits: their wings have grown shorter and less functional, while they have gradually developed powerful, scimitar-shaped bills which are ideal for digging in the ground. The Californian species, the Californian Thrasher *Toxostoma redivivum*, nests in the autumn as well as during the more normal spring-summer season. The Brown Thrasher *Toxostoma rufum* has strayed to Britain from North America. Species of the genus *Melanotis*—the Blue-and-White Mockingbird *M. hypoleucos* and the Blue Mockingbird *M. caerulescens*—have abnormal coloration; this is also true of the Catbird and the Black Catbird *Dumetella glabirostris* which has irridescent plumage.

Catbird
Dumetella carolinensis

French: OISEAU-CHAT
Italian: UCCELLO-GATTO
Spanish: PÁJARO GATO
German: KATZENVOGEL

HABITAT Forest undergrowth and bushy vegetation even in gardens and parks.

IDENTIFICATION Length: 23 cm, about the same size as a Blackbird. Black crown and nape; slate-grey back, rump, wings and tail; chestnut-coloured undertail. Its remaining underparts are a lighter grey, especially on the face and throat. Straight black bill. Black legs.

CALL Song is varied with a succession of staccato notes and musical phrases, but its call note is like a cat's miaow—hence its English name.

REPRODUCTION It builds its cup-shaped nest with great care, using sticks, twigs, grass and leaves and lining it with fur, moss and other soft material. The nest is usually situated among vegetation and contains between two and six shiny, pastel-green eggs. Incubation takes about fifteen days, and two weeks later the young birds leave the nest.

FOOD Mainly plants: berries and seeds. Also feeds on insects.

DISTRIBUTION AND MOVEMENTS A North American species which nests in the United States and southern Canada. It occasionally nests in the Antilles. Winters across eastern Mexico as far south as Panama and the islands in the Gulf of Mexico. It is accidental in Europe in Germany.

French: MOQUEUR ROUX
Italian: MIMO BRUNO
Spanish: TURDIDA
NORTEAMERICANO
German: ROTSICHELSPÖTTER

Brown Thrasher
Toxostoma rufum

HABITAT Hedges, fields with scattered bushes, the edges of woods and similar areas.

IDENTIFICATION Length: 28 cm. Light red-brown upper parts; creamy-white underparts with dense, black-brown markings. Grey cheeks and supercilium. Two narrow, off-white bars on its wing. Its long, curved bill is dark on the top and at the tip and pale on the lower mandible. Dark flesh-coloured legs; pale yellow iris.

(Facing page) Catbird *D. carolinensis:* this North American species is a rare vagrant to Europe

CALL Its song consists of a series of loud, melodious whistles, often repeated two or three times. Like all members of its family, it is a remarkable mimic. Its call note is a loud 'tee-oh-laa'.

REPRODUCTION The cup-shaped nest is made of twigs, dry leaves and other vegetation. Between four and six pale blue eggs, often with brown speckles and spots are laid. Incubation takes about fifteen days and is carried out by both male and female.

FOOD Mainly living creatures, especially insects and other small invertebrates. It also feeds on berries and seeds.

DISTRIBUTION AND MOVEMENTS Breeds from southern Canada south to the Gulf of Mexico and Florida. It is a partial migrant and northern populations winter south of the breeding range. Accidental in Britain in Dorset (once).

R. Kinne/Photo Researchers

ORDER Passeriformes
FAMILY PRUNELLIDAE: Accentors

R. Longo

The family Prunellidae consists of small, furtive birds with reddish or grey-brown upper parts, which are more often streaked than uniform. The underparts range in colour from grey to orange. Accentors resemble the family Turdidae in that the plumage of both sexes is similar and their habits, song and the coloration of their chicks are alike. However, they are close to the families Fringillidae and Ploceidae because they have crops and muscular gizzards which are adapted for grinding seeds.

From the zoogeographical point of view, the accentors are one of the few families which is exclusively Palearctic. The various species are so well adapted to cold climates and mountainous regions, that they do not necessarily migrate to warmer climates during the winter. The Dunnock or Hedge Sparrow *Prunella modularis*, whose distribution area is very large, is the only species which has ventured into a different environment. It has become a plain-dweller and above all a woodland bird, rather than a species of open, barren regions.

Wherever they live, accentors are rather solitary birds and even when a large number of them congregate in the same locality—as in the Mediterranean region during the winter—they are not truly gregarious.

(Above) Alpine Accentor *Prunella collaris* which closely resembles a Dunnock, although it is larger and more sturdily built

They feed primarily on the ground, making their way through the brushwood and brambles and emitting noises more like the cries of tiny mammals. They feed on small spiders, insects and seeds.

The stoutly built nest is shaped like a shallow cup and situated on the ground, among rocks or under a bush: it is usually well concealed. The vividness of the coloration of the eggs varies from one species to another, but they have a uniform blue background. There are between three and six eggs per clutch.

All twelve species are included in the single genus *Prunella*. The two largest species are the Alpine Accentor *P. collaris* and the Himalayan Accentor *P. himalayana*, which has been found at an altitude of over five thousand five hundred metres. Both species are Alpine and do not occur outside the rocky and often barren regions of the highest Eurasian mountains. Another species which lives at considerable altitudes, in the mountains of central Asia, is the Robin Accentor *P. rubecoilides*. However, its preferred habitat includes bushy vegetation (particularly rhododendrons and dwarf willows). The distribution area of the Siberian Accentor *P. montanella* appears to extend beyond the belt of taiga vegetation into tundra.

The Maroon-backed Accentor *P. immaculata*, a species with a chestnut-red back, lives from Nepal to southern China, in the heart of coniferous forests, near the ground, among decomposing vegetation. One of the species which undertakes limited migration is the Black-throated Accentor *P. atrogularis* from Asia: the sub-species *P. a. fagani* from the Yemen which lives at a height of two thousand metres travels south to lower altitudes during the winter.

The least alpine and most regular migrant of all the species is undoubtedly the Dunnock. Although it is found above the tree-line in the Caucasus, in the rest of its distribution area it prefers coniferous woods at medium or low altitudes, or even regions with bushy vegetation. It is also known as the Hedge Sparrow because its coloration is very like a sparrow's. In fact it frequently hunts for food on the ground—either seeds or insects, depending on the season—in the middle of dense, almost impenetrable bushes. However, its bill is much longer and narrower than a sparrow's.

(Above) The Dunnock *Prunella modularis* is easily distinguished by its grey head and underparts. (Left) World distribution of the family Prunellidae

Alpine Accentor
Prunella collaris

French: ACCENTEUR ALPIN
Italian: SORDONE
Spanish: ACENTOR ALPINO
German: ALPENBRAUNELLE

HABITAT Breeds on rocky and stony ground in mountain areas. Winters on barren, rocky ground at lower altitudes, usually in mountainous regions but sometimes on plains.

IDENTIFICATION Length: 17 cm. Similar in appearance to the Hedge Sparrow but more brightly coloured and more sturdily built. Whitish chin and throat with black markings and chestnut-coloured feathers which grow lighter towards the tip. This is easiest to see in flight. Streaked brown-grey upper parts. Juveniles lack throat markings.

CALL A clear, melodious 'cheer-cheep'; also a guttural 'chang'.

REPRODUCTION Late May onwards. The nest is built by both sexes, usually in cracks in rocks or among vegetation. It is a small, cup-shaped structure made out of roots, moss and lichen and lined with feathers and fur. Between three and five uniform pale blue and glossy eggs are laid. Incubation is carried out by both sexes and takes fifteen days. The offspring are cared for by both parents.

FOOD Insects and spiders; also seeds and berries.

DISTRIBUTION AND MOVEMENTS Palearctic: distributed discontinuously in mountainous regions of northwest Africa, central and southern Europe east through Asia to Japan. Sedentary, although some individuals wander to the south of the breeding range or just outside the southern limit. Is a vagrant to Britain most frequently occurring in southern England. About thirty individuals have been recorded, over half occurring from August to January.

SUB-SPECIES Sub-species are present in Asia.

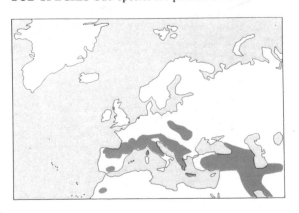

(Left) Wintering areas (magenta) and areas where the Alpine Accentor may be seen all year round (orange)

Dunnock
Prunella modularis

HABITAT Inhabits a wide variety of bushy areas including scrub, heaths, parks and gardens: also woodland.

IDENTIFICATION Length: 14 cm. Similar to a female House Sparrow, indeed it is often called the Hedge Sparrow, but grey head and underparts and the thin insect-eating bill distinguish it. The adult has black streaks on its upper parts, brown crown and ear-coverts and a narrow, dull yellow wing-bar. Juveniles are less reddish and more heavily speckled; their heads are browner.

The Dunnock hunts for food on the ground among dead leaves, either hopping about or dragging its body almost horizontally along the ground, with its legs bent and its belly almost brushing the earth. It perches on low branches among leaves and flies for short distances. Generally an inconspicuous bird, often remaining under cover.

CALL A high-pitched, whistling 'tseep'.

REPRODUCTION From early April (sometimes March). The nest is built by both sexes from twigs, moss, dry leaves and other plant material and is usually situated between a half to three metres above the ground in a tree or among shrubs and bushes. It is lined with moss and hair. The Dunnock lays four or five uniform bright blue (very rarely with small reddish markings), or plain white eggs. The female incubates the eggs for about twelve days although both sexes tend the young.

FOOD Insects, spiders and worms: also seeds.

DISTRIBUTION AND MOVEMENTS Breeds in Europe, Asia Minor, the Caucasus and Iran. The populations of western and southern Europe spend the winter in their nesting sites, but northern populations winter south to the Mediterranean islands and northern Africa. The Dunnock is a numerous and widely distributed resident breeder in Britain (except Shetland) and Ireland. British and Irish populations are essentially sedentary. Also occurs as a passage visitor from the continent.

SUB-SPECIES *P. m. modularis*: continental Europe. *P. m. hebridium* (the darkest race): Ireland, the Hebrides and part of the western Scottish mainland. *P. m. occidentalis* (paler): Scotland and England. *P. m. mabbotti* (darker and greyer): France, Portugal and Spain. *P. m. obscura* (browner): Crimea and the Caucasus.

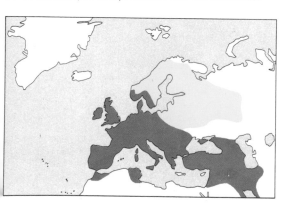

(Above) Adult Dunnock (bottom) and juvenile. (Left) Breeding areas (yellow), wintering areas (magenta) and areas where the Dunnock may be seen all year round (orange)

French: ACCENTEUR À GORGE
NOIRE
Italian: PASSERA SCOPAIOLA
GOLANERA
Spanish: ACENTOR DE GARGANTA
NEGRO
German: SCHWARZ-
KEHLBRAUNELLE

French: ACCENTEUR
MONTAGNARD
Italian: PASSERA SCOPAIOLA
ASIATICA
Spanish: ACENTOR DE PALLAS
German: BERGBRAUNELLE

Siberian Accentor
Prunella montanella

HABITAT Various types of dense bushes and under-growth, and taiga.

IDENTIFICATION Length: 16 cm. The main difference between this species and the Black-throated Accentor is the absence of black on its throat and its more reddish back; otherwise these species are very similar. Its underparts are also slightly yellower. Rather shy. Similar in behaviour to the Dunnock.

CALL Emits a loud, long song.

REPRODUCTION Begins early June. Well-built nest lined with fur and moss; it is sometimes as much as a metre above ground level. Five smooth and glossy bright blue eggs are usually laid. There may be two clutches, but no further information is available.

FOOD Mainly insects, although seeds and other plants have also been found in the stomachs of the few individuals which have been examined.

DISTRIBUTION AND MOVEMENTS Its distribution area has not been precisely defined, but it is found in mountainous regions in Siberia. It migrates across various parts of Siberia and Mongolia and winters from southern Manchuria to northern and central China and occasionally Japan. It is a vagrant in central and southern Europe.

SUB-SPECIES A sub-species is present in Asia.

(Above) Siberian Accentor

French: ACCENTEUR DE RADDE
Italian: PASSERA SCOPAIOLA
DI RADDE
Spanish: ACENTOR DE RADDE
German: BUNTBRAUNELLE

Black-throated Accentor
Prunella atrogularis

HABITAT Lives in thick undergrowth. May also inhabit areas with thinner vegetation.

IDENTIFICATION Length: 15 cm. Both sexes have black heads, lores, ear-coverts, cheeks and throats with a reddish sheen. A broad, light yellow-brown eyestripe and moustachial stripe are clearly visible. Back and the back of its neck are red (almost cinnamon-coloured) with black markings down the centre. Olive-brown rump and upper-tail coverts. Flanks are a pale, brown colour with a few reddish-brown streaks. Brown iris. Yellow-ochre legs. Juveniles are, in general, more speckled on the underparts.

CALL Emits a low, musical song.

REPRODUCTION From June onwards. Builds a nest in a thick bush near the ground. Nest is a cup made of grasses and other plant material. Lays three to six uniform bright blue eggs. No information is available on incubation.

FOOD Insects, spiders and seeds.

DISTRIBUTION AND MOVEMENTS Breeds in the northern Urals and central Asia: occurs on passage in western Siberia. Winters in southwest Asia.

SUB-SPECIES The nominate sub-species lives in the northern Urals. The sub-species *P. a. huttoni* is present in central Asia.

Radde's Accentor
Prunella ocularis

HABITAT Inhabits scrub, especially in mountainous regions.

IDENTIFICATION Length: 15 cm. Similar to Black-throated Accentor, but lacks the black throat markings. Dark, almost black, crown and sides of the head; ochre-grey back with dark centres to the feathers. Grey rump and upper-tail coverts which have a slightly olive-green tinge. Ochre white throat. The remaining underparts are a dirty greyish-white with tan markings. It also is a very secretive species and so is easiest to identify by its call.

CALL A short, melodious warbling consisting of three or four syllables.

REPRODUCTION From June onwards. Nest is built of twigs and roots and is thickly lined with plant material and hair. Lays three uniform blue eggs. No further information is available.

FOOD The diet of Radde's Accentor appears to consist mainly of insects.

DISTRIBUTION AND MOVEMENTS Southern Asia and Asia Minor including Armenia and Iran. Winters in central and southeast Iran.

(Facing page top) Black-throated Accentor. (Above) Radde's Accentor

ORDER Passeriformes
FAMILY **TURDIDAE: Thrushes and allies**

F. Blackburn/Bruce Coleman

204

Some ornithologists recommend the grouping of certain families of birds—which were classified separately according to earlier criteria—into a single family in order to simplify matters. In this way, thrushes and similar species together with other groups of birds, such as warblers and fly-catchers, have been classed in the huge family Muscicapidae. Although this is perfectly valid and justified in the context of the world's avifauna, the sub-division into separate families is equally valid on a regional scale, and the latter and more traditional method of classification has been followed here.

The family Turdidae or thrushes consists of about three hundred species which are grouped into a great many genera: many of them are mono-typic. They are generally rather slender, medium-sized passerines with fairly narrow bills and medium length tails. This family also contains some of the best songsters of Europe. As a rule, the plumage of juveniles differs considerably from that of adults, being speckled even in those species which have uniform adult coloration. Adults range in colour from grey to brown, from reddish to grey and from blue to green or black. Wheat-ears of the genus *Oenanthe* have a partial moult and a complete moult; this is also believed to be true of other species, including those of the genera *Monticola* and *Zoothera*.

Thrushes build their cup-shaped nests with care, lining them with vegetable fibres and rein-forcing them with a thin coat of mud. The nests are generally situated in a sheltered place among the branches of trees, but they may also be built

R. H. Bloomfield/Ardea

B. Bevan/Ardea

(Left) Male Stonechat *Saxicola torquata*: the male is distinctively black and chestnut. (Below) Female Whinchat *S. rubetra*: her plumage is similar to the male's but duller. (Bottom right) Male Redstart *Phoenicurus phoenicurus* in summer plumage and (bottom left) Rufous Bush Chat *Cercotrichas galactotes* feeding its young. (Facing page) Male Blackbird *Turdus merula*. The Blackbird is one of Europe's most common birds and the jet-black plumage and yellow-orange bill make it easily identifiable

R. T. Smith/Ardea

M. D. England/Ardea

J. Van Wormer/Photo Researchers

(Above) American Robin *Turdus migratorius*, one of the most frequent passerine vagrants from North America. (Right) The Song Thrush *T. philomelos* is often seen in urban areas in parkland and gardens. (Facing page left) Male Blue Rock Thrush *Monticola solitarius*: its blue coloration with black wings and tail is distinctive. (Facing page right) Female Wheatear *Oenanthe oenanthe* which, like other wheatears, feeds mainly on insects

in crevices in rocks on the ground.

Members of the family lay from three to six eggs per clutch. These are often pale blue with speckles which vary in density and size. In most species the female almost certainly incubates the eggs alone, but both parents take part in rearing the young. Incubation takes about thirteen or fourteen days.

Thrushes live in a variety of environments, but are generally terrestrial birds, although some species are strictly arboreal. Many also prefer to inhabit meadows or to be close to water-courses. The diet is also varied, including snails and plants (especially fruit). Some species are quite at home in the tropics while others prefer arctic tundra. The distribution of the family is almost world-wide: thrushes are only absent from the Antarctic and New Zealand, although European species (like the Blackbird *Turdus merula* and the Song Thrush *T. philomelos*) were successfully introduced into New Zealand in the nineteenth century.

The greatest number of species is found in the Old World and they are also the most evolved: in fact, it is thought that the origin of the family may have been Palearctic or even African. The populations of Australia, Papua, North, Central and South America must have been established in stages and at different periods—the degree of differentiation in races from islands or other restricted ecological pockets indicates this.

The family Turdidae can be roughly sub-divided into two groups. The first covers species such as wheatears, chats, rock thrushes, nightin-gales and redstarts: these smaller species, which are all fairly similar, are typified by the Wheatear

M. D. England/Ardea

A. Christiansen

I. Neufeldt/Ardea

Oenanthe oenanthe. It has comparatively thin legs and a remarkable variety of behaviour patterns, particularly as far as reproduction is concerned. One of the best known species of this family is the Robin *Erithacus rubecula* whose red face and breast are a familiar sight in cities and country. This group includes species whose characteristics are mid-way between those of Turdidae and other closely linked families like the Silviidae and the Muscicapidae. The Rufous Bush Chat *Cercotrichas galactotes* and other species are intermediate in appearance between warblers and thrushes.

The second group consists of 'true' thrushes. They are medium-sized song birds with a square tail and fairly thin bill. They are all fairly similar in structure to the Blackbird, which is one of the most common birds of Europe. Other well-known species of the genus *Turdus* are the Fieldfare *T. pilaris*, the Song Thrush and the Redwing *T. iliacus*. In this second group, the ecological counterparts of wheatears are chiefly the species of the genus *Monticola*. Two of the most beautiful European species belong to this genus: the Blue Rock Thrush *M. solitarius* and the Rock Thrush *M. saxatilis*.

(Above) Siberian Rubythroat *Luscinia calliope*: the male's bright red throat is conspicuous. (Left) World distribution of the family Turdidae

L. Gaggero

A. Lindau/Ardea

J. A. Hancock/Photo Researchers

(Above) Male Black Redstart
Phoenicurus ochruros feeding
its young. (Far left) Thrush
Nightingale *Luscinia luscinia*:
this species is very similar to
the Nightingale and also shares
its melodious song. (Left)
Robin *Erithacus rubecula*

French: TRAQUET TARIER
Italian: STIACCINO
Spanish: TARABILLA NORTEÑA
German: BRAUNKEHLCHEN

French: TRAQUET PÂTRE
Italian: SALTIMPALO
Spanish: TARABILLA COMÚN
German: SCHWARZKEHLCHEN

Stonechat
Saxicola torquata

HABITAT Inhabits moors, heaths, alpine meadows, cultivated land and scrub.

IDENTIFICATION Length: 12 cm. The male is distinctively black and chestnut: white half-collar, white wing-stripe and white rump. Upper parts mottled; reddish-brown underparts. Outside the breeding season the black becomes browner. Females and juveniles have darker streaks on the brown upper parts, although all show white wing-bars in flight.

CALL The usual note is a persistent 'sac-sac'. Also emits a short warble, sometimes in flight.

REPRODUCTION From late March. The cup-shaped nest is usually built on the ground among bushes. Normally lays five to six eggs (sometimes three to eight) which are pale blue or blue-green, finely marked with reddish-brown. The female incubates (the male rarely assists) for fourteen to fifteen days. Both tend the young which remain in the nest for about twelve days.

FOOD Chiefly insects.

DISTRIBUTION AND MOVEMENTS Breeds from Britain and Ireland east across Eurasia to Japan. Also breeds in northwest Africa and much of sub-Saharan Africa. Western populations are resident or partially migratory but eastern populations are highly migratory. In Britain and Ireland is a resident and migrant breeder in most maritime counties although it is scarce on the English east coast, restricted mainly to East Anglia and Northumberland. Formerly nested in most English counties but has been in decline since the 1940's.

SUB-SPECIES *S. t. rubicola*: Europe, except for Britain, Ireland, Portugal and the USSR. *S. t. hibernans*: Britain, Ireland and coastal areas of Portugal. *S. t. variegata*: Caucasus and regions north of the Caspian. *S. t. maura*: USSR. Other sub-species (including the nominate sub-species) are present in Asia and Africa.

(Above) The sub-species *S. t. hibernans* of the Stonechat which occurs in Britain and Ireland (top left) and the sub-species *S. t. rubicola* (centre). (Right) Breeding areas (yellow), areas where the Stonechat may be seen all year round (orange) and on passage (pink)

Whinchat
Saxicola rubetra

HABITAT Like that of the Stonechat, but also frequents riverside meadows and waste ground.

IDENTIFICATION Length: 12 cm. Very like Stonechat, but male may be distinguished by very conspicuous white supercilium and less upright stance. Female is similar to the female Stonechat, but is browner and has pale supercilium.

CALL A short and harsh 'tic-tic-tyoo'.

REPRODUCTION From late May. Nest is a cup built of dead grass and moss on the ground, usually sheltered by vegetation. Four to seven light blue eggs finely speckled with brown are laid. The female alone incubates for thirteen or fourteen days. Both tend the young.

FOOD Insects.

DISTRIBUTION AND MOVEMENTS Breeds in Britain, Ireland, Scandinavia, and the USSR southward to France, northern Portugal, northern Spain, north Africa, Italy, and the Balkans and east across the Caucasus and Asia Minor to Iran. Migratory, wintering in both eastern and western tropical and equatorial Africa. In Britain is widely distributed in the west and north—sparse elsewhere. Also breeds in Ireland and occurs in both countries on passage to inland and coastal areas where it is not found breeding. British and Irish populations are resident from April to September: they winter south to Africa.

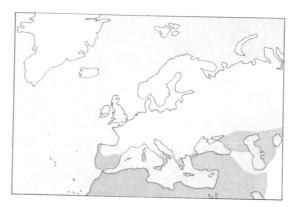

(Facing page, top right) Whinchat. (Below left) Breeding areas (yellow) and areas where the Whinchat may be seen on passage (pink)

Wheatear
Oenanthe oenanthe

HABITAT Tundra, moorland, desert and other open countryside.

IDENTIFICATION Length: 14 cm. Main distinguishing feature in both sexes is the pure white rump and sides of tail, contrasting with black tip and central tail-feathers. May be distinguished from other wheatears by its head pattern, which consists of a grey crown, black cheeks and white eyestripe. The male in winter plumage resembles the female, but with browner coloration. Juveniles are spotted, with tail and wings like those of female. Black bill and legs. See also page 254.

CALL A hard 'chack-chack' or 'weet-chack-chack': song is a squeaking warble.

REPRODUCTION From late March. Nest is a loose heap of plant material in a hole in a rock or wall, in rodents' ground burrows, or in hollow objects like pipes and boxes. Eggs: generally six, pale blue, unmarked eggs are laid. Incubation lasts for fourteen days and is carried out mainly by the female. Both tend the young.

FOOD Chiefly insects.

DISTRIBUTION AND MOVEMENTS Holarctic breeding distribution, including much of Europe and Asia, arctic regions of North America: also northwest Africa. Winters mainly in Africa. Is a widely distributed migrant breeder in Britain and Ireland, although only locally in southern England. Also occurs on passage in Britain and Ireland, mainly to coastal areas.

SUB-SPECIES *O. o. oenanthe*: Continental Europe, North America, Asia. *O. o. leucorrhoa*: northeastern Canada, Ellesmere Island, Jan Mayen, Faeroes and Iceland. *O. o. seebohmi*: northwest Africa.

French: TRAQUET MOTTEUX
Italian: CULBIANCO
Spanish: COLLALBA GRIS
German: STEINSCHMÄTZER

(Above) Male Wheatear (left) and female. (Left) Breeding areas (yellow), wintering areas (magenta) and areas where the Wheatear may be seen on passage (pink)

211

Red-rumped Wheatear
Oenanthe moesta

French: TRAQUET À TÊTE GRISE
Italian: MONACHELLA TESTA-
GRIGIA
Spanish: COLLALBA A OPISPILLO
ROJO
German: ROTBÜRZELSTEIN-
SCHMÄTZER

HABITAT Open semi-desert country.

IDENTIFICATION Length: 16 cm. One of the largest wheatears. The male has a grey head; back is black and rump is rufous like the Red-tailed Wheatear's, but may be distinguished from the latter by black mantle and white on wings. Also resembles Mourning Wheater but has more white on wings. Female has a rufous instead of grey-brown head. See also page 252.

CALL The Red-rumped Wheater emits a distinctive whirring and ascending song.

REPRODUCTION From February. Nests in a hole in the ground, usually a small mammal's burrow. Lays four or five smooth, pale blue eggs with few, very small speckles. No further information on reproduction is available.

FOOD Mainly insects.

DISTRIBUTION AND MOVEMENTS Breeds throughout northern Africa and east to Egypt and the Middle East. Fairly sedentary species: the more northerly populations sometimes move south in winter.

SUB-SPECIES A sub-species is present in Asia.

Pied Wheatear
Oenanthe pleschanka

HABITAT Open, stony country; also cultivated land and even gardens.

IDENTIFICATION Length: 14 cm. Similar to Mourning Wheatear but male has buff-tinged underparts. Crown and nape white and under-tail coverts white. Similar to the black-throated form of the Black-eared Wheatear but black mantle distinguishes it. However, the female is very similar to the female Black-eared Wheatear although her back and wings are more earth-brown. See also page 254.

CALL A harsh 'zak-zak': song is rasping like the Black-eared Wheatear's.

REPRODUCTION From late April. Nest is a cup of grasses in a hole, a crevice, a bank or rocky outcrop, under a stone on the ground or in a hole in a wall. Lays four to six blue or green-blue eggs with red-brown splotches. Incubation period not known.

DISTRIBUTION AND MOVEMENTS Breeds from Rumania, Bulgaria and the USSR across central Asia. Winters in southern Arabia and eastern Africa. Is a rare vagrant to Britain.

SUB-SPECIES A sub-species is present in Cyprus.

(Above) Male Red-rumped Wheatear (left) and female. (Right) Areas where the Red-rumped Wheatear may be seen all year round (orange)

French: TRAQUET PIE
Italian: MONACHELLA
DORSONERO
Spanish: COLLALBA PÍA
German: NONNENSTEIN-
SCHMÄTZER

(Above) Female Pied
Wheatear (left) and male.
(Facing page below) Breeding
areas (yellow) and areas
where the Pied Wheatear
may be seen on passage (pink)

Finsch's Wheatear
Oenanthe finschii

HABITAT Stony desert and areas with low scrub.

IDENTIFICATION Length: 13 cm. Male has more white on the upper parts except for the light phase of the Black-eared Wheatear. Underparts also white, except for black throat. Wings black. The females are duller and the throat may be black or pale. Upper parts are brown, like the wings, which are darker with pale borders. However, most female wheatears are similar. Finsch's Wheatear is a shy species. See also page 252.

CALL Unrecorded.

REPRODUCTION From mid-April. Like many other wheatears is double-brooded. Nest is a cup made of stems and grasses and is constructed in a crevice among rocks or in sandy banks. Lays four or five light blue eggs which are speckled and blotched with varying amounts of reddish brown. No further information is available.

FOOD Insects.

DISTRIBUTION AND MOVEMENTS Breeds in Asia Minor, the Middle East, and regions to the south of the Caspian Sea east to Iran and Afghanistan. Partly migratory.

SUB-SPECIES The sub-species *O. f. barnesi* is found in Asia.

French: TRAQUET DE FINSCH
Italian: MONACHELLA DI FINSCH
Spanish: COLLALBA DE FINSCH
German: FINSCH-TRAUERSTEIN-
SCHMÄTZER

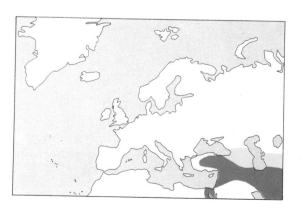

(Above) Male Finsch's
Wheatear (left) and female.
(Left) Breeding areas (yellow),
wintering areas (magenta)
and areas where Finsch's
Wheatear may be seen all
year round (orange)

French: TRAQUET DU DÉSERT
Italian: MONACHELLA DEL DESERTO
Spanish: COLLALBA DESÉRTICA
German: WÜSTENSTEIN-SCHMÄTZER

Desert Wheatear
Oenanthe deserti

HABITAT Desert and semi-desert regions: sometimes cultivated land.

IDENTIFICATION Length: 14 cm. Chief characteristics are the almost completely black tail and strongly marked white edges to the wing coverts. Male is distinguished by black throat; the only species with which it could be confused is the Black-eared Wheatear in the black-throated phase, but the Desert Wheatear may be distinguished by more white on wings and the black of the wings which joins the black of the throat. Rump and upper parts are lightly tinged rufous, especially in the female; underparts buff. Female has whitish throat: wings browner than those of male. See also page 252.

CALL The call-note is a soft, plaintive whistle. Short, chattering song.

REPRODUCTION Mid-April onwards. Nest is built among stones, in holes or burrows and in crevices in walls. It is made from dried grasses and lined with hair and feathers. Eggs: four to five, pale blue with reddish-brown markings. The female alone probably incubates the eggs.

FOOD Insects.

DISTRIBUTION AND MOVEMENTS Breeds from northern Africa east through the Middle East and Iran into China. Sedentary and migratory: Asian populations migrate south. Accidental in western Europe and Britain.

SUB-SPECIES Sub-species are present in Africa and Asia.

(Above) Female Desert Wheatear (left), male (centre) and the sub-species *O. d. atrogularis* (right). (Right) Breeding areas (yellow), wintering areas (magenta) and areas where the Desert Wheatear may be seen all year round (orange)

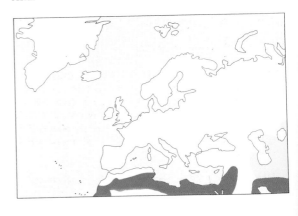

Isabelline Wheatear
Oenanthe isabellina

HABITAT Desert areas and steppes: also plains with little vegetation.

IDENTIFICATION Length: 16 cm. Sexes are similar. Distinguishing features are the fairly large size and the uniform pale sandy-grey coloration. Rather upright stance and long legs. Similar to the female Greenland Wheatear but underwing is whiter. Differs from Wheatear in having sandy upper parts and pale underparts; head and bill are larger. See also page 252.

CALL A loud 'cheep' or a whistling 'weet-weet'. Song is loud and mimetic.

REPRODUCTION From March onwards. Nests in a crack or hole in a bank, or in a rodent's burrow: is also said to dig its own hole. Nest is made of roots and dried grasses and is lined with hair and wool. Eggs: four to six, pale blue, usually unmarked. The female alone incubates for fifteen days. Both parents tend the young.

FOOD Probably insects.

DISTRIBUTION AND MOVEMENTS Breeds from southern Greece (although very locally) east through the southeastern USSR, Caucasus, Asia Minor, Middle East and central and southwestern Asia. Winters in, and beyond, the southern parts of the range. Very rare vagrant to Britain.

French: TRAQUET ISABELLE
Italian: CULBIANCO ISABELLINO
Spanish: COLLALBA ISABEL
German: ISABELLSTEIN-
SCHMÄTZER

(Left) Breeding areas (yellow) and areas where the Isabelline Wheatear may be seen on passage (pink). (Below) Male Red-tailed Wheatear (left) and female

Red-tailed Wheatear
Oenanthe xanthoprymna

HABITAT Semi-desert regions and rocky hillsides.

IDENTIFICATION Length: 14 cm. Resembles black-throated form of the Black-eared Wheatear, but may be distinguished by rufous-ochre rump and base of tail-feathers, brown not black mantle and no white on wings. Greyish head with brownish ear coverts; light eye-stripe; rufous-buff flanks and under-tail coverts. The females have more uniform coloration but are still marked with the red on the tail. See also page 252.

CALL Call-note and song similar to those of Wheatear.

REPRODUCTION From late March. The cup-shaped nest is built in rock crevices among fallen rocks and screes. It is lined with grasses, hair etc. Eggs: four to five, white, lightly tinged pale blue with sparse red-brown markings. No further information is available.

FOOD Ants and other insects.

DISTRIBUTION AND MOVEMENTS Breeds from the Middle East and Asia Minor east to Iran, the USSR and southern Asia. Migratory, wintering from north-western India through southern Iran to North Africa. It is not known for certain whether all populations migrate: some may only move to lower altitudes within the breeding range.

SUB-SPECIES The sub-species *O. x. chrysopigia* is found in southwestern Asia.

French: TRAQUET À QUEUE
ROUSSE
Italian: MONACHELLA
CODAROSSA
German: ROTSCHWANZSTEIN-
SCHMÄTZER

(Above) Male Rock Thrush *Monticola saxatilis* (top),
Female Redstart *P. phoenicurus* (centre) and male
Wheatear *O. oenanthe*. (Above left) Female Rock Thrush
and (left) Robin *Erithacus rubecula*. (Facing page,
far right) Male Redstart *Phoenicurus phoenicurus*.
(Facing page left) Blue-headed Rock Thrush *M. gularis*
(top), Isabelline Wheatear *O. isabellina* (centre) and
Red-spotted Bluethroat *Luscinia svecica svecica*

I. Neufeldt/Ardea

W. Curth/Ardea

R. Richter/Ardea

A. J. Deane/Bruce Coleman

French: TRAQUET RIEUR
Italian: MONACHELLA NERA
Spanish: COLLALBA NEGRA
German: TRAUERSTEINSCHMÄTZER

Black Wheatear
Oenanthe leucura

HABITAT Cliffs, rocky slopes and other rocky areas.

IDENTIFICATION Length: 18 cm. Unmistakable, due to large size and all black plumage except for white rump and under-tail coverts. Females and juveniles are browner. See also page 254.

CALL Short, staccato and warbling song, beginning and ending with chattering. Call is a 'pee-pee-pee'.

REPRODUCTION March onwards. Nests in a hole or crevice which has a parapet of small stones at the entrance. The nest is a bulky cup of plant material. Eggs: four to six, bluish-white with rust-coloured markings. Incubated mainly by the female for about sixteen days.

FOOD Insects.

DISTRIBUTION AND MOVEMENTS Breeds in France, Spain, Italy and northwest Africa. Mainly resident although some may wander eastwards in the Mediterranean area. Vagrant to Britain and Ireland.

SUB-SPECIES A sub-species is present in Africa.

(Above) Male Black Wheatear (left) and female. (Right) Areas where the Black Wheatear may be seen all year round (orange)

White-crowned Black Wheatear

Oenanthe leucopyga

Passeriformes: Turdidae

French: TRAQUET À TÊTE
BLANCHE
Italian: MONACHELLA
TESTABIANCA
Spanish: COLLALBA NEGRA DE
BREHM
German: WEISSBÜRZELSTEIN-
SCHMÄTZER

HABITAT Desert country, but also found in inhabited areas.

IDENTIFICATION Length: 15 cm. Unmistakable due to its white rump, tail and white cap: remaining plumage, including belly, black. Female and juveniles have black heads and are distinguishable from male and juvenile Black Wheatears only by the outer tail feathers which are white at the tip. Also resembles Hooded Wheatear but has a black, not white, belly.

CALL The song consists of a short, quiet, musical phrase.

REPRODUCTION From February: nests in the Sahara and other arid regions. The nest is made in holes or crevices or among rocks: occasionally in holes or cracks in walls. The nest is a cup made of grass and twigs lined with wool and hair. From two to five (usually three or four) very pale blue (sometimes white) eggs are laid. They are speckled with light reddish-brown. No information is available on incubation or nestlings.

FOOD Mainly insects: sometimes also lizards.

DISTRIBUTION AND MOVEMENTS Nests across northern Africa and the Sahara east into Arabia. Winters in the breeding range. Accidental in Malta.

SUB-SPECIES *O. l. ernesti*: Sinai desert.

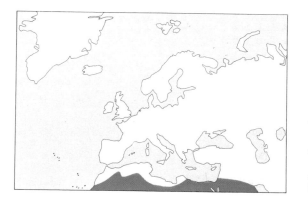

(Above) Adult White-crowned Black Wheatear (foreground) and juvenile. (Left) Areas where the White-crowned Black Wheatear may be seen all year round (orange). (Overleaf) Nightingale *Luscinia megarhynchos* feeding its young at the nest

L. Gaggero

J. Markham

E. Burgess/Ardea

(Above) Nightingale *Luscinia megarhynchos* at the nest. The long rufous tail is a distinctive feature. (Left) The Thrush Nightingale *L. luscinia* is similar to the Nightingale but when seen at close range can be distinguished by its darker brown plumage and speckled breast

French: TRAQUET OREILLARD
Italian: MONACHELLA
Spanish: COLLALBA RUBIA
German: MITTELMEERSTEIN-
SCHMÄTZER

Black-eared Wheatear

Oenanthe hispanica

HABITAT Dry, rocky areas, mountain slopes and vineyards.

IDENTIFICATION Length: 14 cm. Male: black patch at eye and cheek with whitish throat: also a form with black throat and face. Upper parts variable from light golden-buff to pure white. Tail white with black central feathers and tip; much whiter than Common Wheatear. Female resembles female Wheatear but has darker wings and cheeks. See also page 254.

CALL A grating call: its song is similar to that of the Wheatear.

REPRODUCTION May onwards: Nest is a shallow cup of grass and moss usually situated at ground level in grass or bush or in a hollow under a stone. Usually lays four or five light blue eggs, lightly speckled with reddish-brown. The female alone incubates the eggs although both tend the young. Double-brooded.

DISTRIBUTION AND MOVEMENTS Southwest Palearctic: breeds in southern Europe, Africa, Asia Minor and the Middle East. Migratory, wintering south of the Sahara. Accidental in Britain.

SUB-SPECIES *O.h. hispanica*: Spain, Portugal, France, Italy, Sicily, Yugoslavia and Africa. *O.h. melanoleuca*: Balkan peninsula, Asia Minor and the Middle East.

(Above left) Male Black-eared Wheatear, (centre) male of the sub-species *O.h. melanoleuca* and female. (Right) Breeding areas (yellow) and areas where the Black-eared Wheatear may be seen on passage (pink)

Blue Rock Thrush
Monticola solitarius

French: MERLE BLEU
Italian: PASSERO SOLITARIO
Spanish: ROQUERO SOLITARIO
German: BLAUMERLE

HABITAT Mainly rocky, mountainous and desert regions, including those near coasts. Often found in towns in southeast Europe.

IDENTIFICATION Length: 20 cm. Slightly larger than Rock Thrush. Male has unmistakable blue plumage, with dark wings and tail. In winter loses the blue gloss and appears blackish. Female has blue-brown upper parts and almost grey underparts, both barred black and brown: distinguishable from female Rock Thrush by lack of rufous in tail. Often found by itself perching on a rock, wings drooping and tail spread, uttering its loud, melodious song.

CALL Fluting, Blackbird-like song, heard particularly in the morning and at sunset. Also emits a high-pitched 'tseee'.

REPRODUCTION From May onwards: single-brooded. Nests in crevices in rocks or in old buildings: occasionally in a hole in a tree. The cup-shaped nest is built by the female and is lined with soft materials. The eggs are blue-green like those of the Rock Thrush but somewhat paler and are only sometimes marked with reddish-brown speckles. Four to six eggs are laid, and incubated by the female alone for about fifteen days.

FOOD Insects and their larvae.

DISTRIBUTION AND MOVEMENTS A predominantly migratory species in the eastern part of its range, but resident in southern Europe and in North Africa. Found from the western coasts of southern Europe and North Africa to Japan, through southeast Europe, Turkey, Iran, the USSR and China. Winters to the south of this zone, mainly around the Sahara, in southern Arabia, East Africa, Indo-China, the Malaysian archipelago and the Philippines.

SUB-SPECIES Apart from the nominate sub-species, four other sub-species are recognised which occur from the southern part of the Caspian east to Japan.

(Right) Male Blue Rock Thrush (foreground) and female. (Below) Breeding areas (yellow), wintering areas (magenta), areas where the Blue Rock Thrush may be seen all year round (orange) and on passage (pink)

223

Rock Thrush
Monticola saxatilis

French: MERLE DE ROCHE
Italian: CODIROSSONE
Spanish: ROQUERO ROJO
German: STEINRÖTEL

HABITAT Nests in open rocky areas and in mountains in the west of its range. Winters in savannah.

IDENTIFICATION Length: 19 cm. A compact, plump bird, like the Song Thrush in shape; tail shorter and characteristically orange in colour with brown central tail feathers in all plumages. In the breeding season the male is unmistakable, with slate-blue head, neck and mantle, white rump and back, orange-buff underparts and dark wings. Female has brown upper parts mottled with darker brown. Bill dark brown, legs brown. Juveniles resemble females.

Moves on the ground in long hops. Is timid and shy; gregarious only on migration. Perches on rocks, trees, buildings and occasionally telegraph wires.

CALL Usual note: a 'chack-chack', softer than that of the Blackbird. Also a high-pitched 'feed'. Loud, fluting and warbling song, uttered from a perch or during the brief courtship flight.

REPRODUCTION May onwards. The nest is built by the female in shallow cavities or in buildings. Eggs: four or five, pale blue, often unmarked, sometimes spotted reddish-brown. Incubation is carried out by the female for fourteen or fifteen days. The young are tended by both sexes.

FOOD Insects: also worms, small molluscs and various kinds of berries.

DISTRIBUTION AND MOVEMENTS Breeds in northwest Africa and Iberia through southern and central Europe east across Asia to China. Winters in Africa south of the Sahara. Is a rare vagrant to Britain.

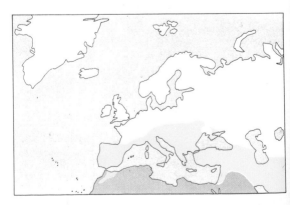

(Above) Male Rock Thrush (foreground) and female. (Right) Breeding areas (yellow) and areas where the Rock Thrush may be seen on passage (pink)

French: ROUGEQUEUE DE
         MOUSSIER
Italian: CODIROSSO ALGERINO
Spanish: COLIRROJO DIADEMADO
German: DIADEMROTSCHWANZ

Moussier's Redstart
Phoenicurus moussieri

HABITAT Forests and hills: also mountain slopes.

IDENTIFICATION Length: 12 cm. Male has strongly contrasting plumage: red underparts, rump and tail and black head, back and wings. Wide white eyestripe extends from the forehead to the neck; also a large white wing-patch. Female closely resembles female Redstart with grey-brown back and head, light rufous-buff underparts and chestnut rump.

CALL A harsh 'wheet'.

REPRODUCTION From mid-April. Normally lays four eggs, white or pale blue in colour. Nest is a loose cup made of plant material which is usually concealed in a bush or sometimes in a tree hole. Further information is not available.

FOOD Mainly insects.

DISTRIBUTION AND MOVEMENTS One of the few species endemic to North Africa, it is widespread in Morocco, Algeria and Tunisia. In winter moves southward and eastward. Accidental in Italy.

Güldenstadt's Redstart
Phoenicurus erythrogaster

HABITAT High rocky mountain slopes. Descends to tree level in winter.

IDENTIFICATION Length: 18 cm. Largest European redstart, and easily distinguished by red upper-tail coverts, black back, white head.. Throat and upper breast are black, remaining underparts dark rusty-red. Females' coloration much more subdued, but tail and upper-tail coverts are same colour as in male: juveniles more like females.

CALL Its call and song are said to resemble the Black Redstart's, but this has not been definitely established.

REPRODUCTION From middle of May. Eggs: four white, speckled with brown. Nest is concealed under a bush. Incubation lasts for about thirteen days. Further information is lacking.

FOOD Mainly insects.

DISTRIBUTION AND MOVEMENTS The range is discontinuous, with nesting populations in the Caucasus, the mountains of Iran, around the Caspian, in central Asia and in a limited area of east central Siberia.

SUB-SPECIES *P.e. grandis:* Turkestan and Kashmir.

French: ROUGEQUEUE DE
         GÜLDENSTADT
Italian: CODIROSSO DI
         GÜLDENSTADT
Spanish: COLIRROJO DE
         GÜLDENSTADT
German: GÜLDENSTADTS
         ROTSCHWANZ

(Top) Male Moussier's Redstart (foreground) and female. (Above) Male Güldenstadt's Redstart (foreground) and female

French: ROUGEQUEUE NOIR
Italian: CODIROSSO
SPAZZACAMINO
Spanish: COLIRROJO TIZÓN
German: HAUSROTSCHWANZ

Black Redstart
Phoenicurus ochruros

(Above) Male Black Redstart
(foreground) and female.
(Right) Breeding areas
(yellow), wintering areas
(magenta) and areas where
the Black Redstart may be
seen all year round (orange)

HABITAT Rocky hills and mountains: also towns.

IDENTIFICATION Length: 14 cm. Darker than Redstart, with no chestnut or buff on underparts. Adult male: sooty black, with breast and throat black, whitish wing-patch; no white on forehead; plumage paler in winter. Female and juveniles darker than female and juvenile Redstart, particularly on underparts.

CALL Emits a 'tseep'. Song is a staccato warble.

REPRODUCTION From early April. Eggs: four to six, white or light blue. The female builds a cup-shaped nest of plant material in a variety of areas including cliffs, ruined buildings and hollow trees. The female alone incubates for about fifteen days: both tend the young.

FOOD Chiefly insects.

DISTRIBUTION AND MOVEMENTS Eastern-central Europe, southern Europe, Morocco, Asia Minor and central Asia. Winters in northern Africa, western and southern Europe including Britain, Iraq, Arabia and Iran. Colonised Britain from 1923, during the war it took to breeding on bombed sites in central London. Now re-established on industrial wasteland and construction sites.

SUB-SPECIES *P.o. ochruros:* Caucasus, Iran. *P.o. gibraltariensis:* Norway, Sweden, Poland, USSR, Italy, Sardinia, Sicily, Balkan peninsula. *P.o. aterrimus:* Portugal and Spain.

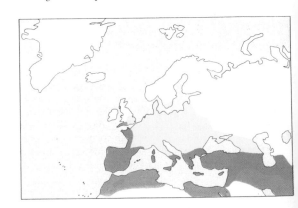

French: ROUGEQUEUE À FRONT
BLANC
Italian: CODIROSSO
Spanish: COLIRROJO REAL
German: GARTENROTSCHWANZ

Redstart
Phoenicurus phoenicurus

HABITAT Nests in deciduous woods, gardens and parkland. In winter is present in bushy regions and gardens.

IDENTIFICATION Length: 14 cm. Both male and female have rusty-red tail. Adult male: face and throat black with white patch at base of upper mandible. Breast, flanks and rump rust-coloured. In winter male's plumage is duller. Female: upper parts greyish-brown, underparts pale buff. Juveniles: breast mottled, like juvenile Robin, but with the characteristic red tail.

CALL A call-note 'weet'. Also a chat-like 'twee-tuc'.

REPRODUCTION Usually from mid-May onwards. Breeds in a wide variety of habitats, usually constructing a cup of dried grasses in a tree-hole. May also nest in an old building. Lays six or seven glossy light blue eggs. The female alone builds the nest and incubates the eggs for eleven to fourteen days.

FOOD Insects.

DISTRIBUTION AND MOVEMENTS Western and central Europe, North Africa, Siberia, Asia Minor and Near East. Winters in Africa and in Arabia. In Britain is a widespread summer visitor more numerous in the north and west.

SUB-SPECIES *P.p. samamisicus:* the Caucasus.

(Above) Male Redstart (foreground) and female. (Left) Breeding areas (yellow) and areas where the Redstart may be seen on passage (pink)

French: ROUGEGORGE
Italian: PETTIROSSO
Spanish: PETIRROJO
German: ROTKEHLCHEN

Robin
Erithacus rubecula

HABITAT Generally nests in forests with dense undergrowth; also in scrub, gardens, hedgerows and town parks. In the western part of its breeding range it is a common suburban bird.

IDENTIFICATION Length: 14 cm. One of the easiest European birds to identify: the red face distinguishes it from other red-breasted birds. Adults have a red-orange breast, throat and forehead, olive-brown upper parts. In the British sub-species the orange is a deeper shade and is edged with a grey band. Juveniles lack the orange on the breast and have dark-brown and buff mottling. Trusting with humans, especially the British sub-species. Although generally lives in dense vegetation, likes to feed in the open, especially in summer: it flies to the ground, seizes food, and returns to its perch; the whole sequence is then repeated. On the ground moves in a rapid succession of long hops, in an almost hunched position for a step or two, then stops and assumes an upright posture.

Flight is usually short: shows pale under-tail coverts as it flies. Aggressive towards its own kind and birds of other species. Both sexes defend their territory. In attitude of defence, head is held erect to display orange breast and body is rapidly swayed sideways.

CALL A repeated, persistent 'tic' is the most common call. Song is thin and warbling and may be heard almost throughout the year.

REPRODUCTION Late March onwards. The nest is built in holes in banks, in cavities in trees or in hedges; the female builds it out of leaves and moss and lines it with fine roots and hair. In Britain and Ireland also breeds in walls or on buildings. Eggs: five to six, normally white and non-glossy, with small sandy or reddish markings which vary in intensity. The female alone incubates for twelve to fifteen days. The young are tended by both sexes: double or occasionally treble brooded.

FOOD Chiefly insects.

DISTRIBUTION AND MOVEMENTS Breeds in Azores, Madeira, Canaries, Siberia, northwest Africa, Britain and Ireland and throughout continental Europe, Asia Minor and northern Iran. Northern populations are migratory and some birds move south to winter in the Sahara, Egypt, Iran and Iraq. In Britain and Ireland is a numerous and widely distributed resident and migrant breeder, although absent from the Shetlands.

SUB-SPECIES *E.r. rubecula*: Europe (except for Britain and Ireland), Crimea and Caucasus, Mediterranean, Asia Minor, Canaries, Azores, northwest Africa. Winters from Germany to the Near East and to Egypt. *E.r. melophilus*: Britain and Ireland. Other sub-species are present in Africa and Asia, including *E.r. caucasicus*.

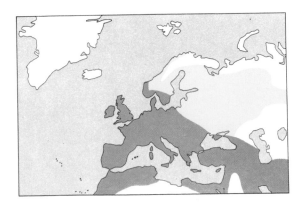

(Above) Adult Robin (foreground) and the sub-species *E.r. melophilus*. (Left) Breeding areas (yellow), wintering areas (magenta) and areas where the Robin may be seen all year round (orange)

Nightingale

Luscinia megarhynchos

HABITAT Nests in deciduous glades and copses with dense undergrowth. Also frequents bushy areas including hedgerows and large gardens.

IDENTIFICATION Length: 16 cm. Resembles a large all-brown Robin. The characteristic song is its best identifying feature. Adult: upper parts uniform warm brown, tail rufous, underparts light grey-brown, tending towards whitish on throat and abdomen. Juveniles have mottling and spotting like young Robins, from which they are best distinguished by the chestnut-brown tail and larger size.

A solitary bird which skulks among foliage although, in Mediterranean Europe, it will sing from an open perch. When perched, holds the wings slightly drooping. Often feeds on the ground and in undergrowth. Flight like that of Robin. During courtship, the spread tail is moved up and down and the wings and head are drooped.

CALL A light 'weet' is the call-note; there is also a loud 'tec', a short, soft 'tac', and a 'kerr' of alarm. The song is rich, highly varied and melodious; some notes are rapidly repeated. The range includes a bubbling 'chuk-chuk' and a slow 'piu-piu-piu' rising to a crescendo. The Nightingale sings all year round, both by day and night.

REPRODUCTION From May onwards. The nest is a loose cup made of dead grasses and leaves and lined with grass or hair; it is built by the female on or near the ground in herbage or under shrubs. Eggs: four to five,

background colour varying from dull blue-green to grey-green with fine reddish markings that may appear as an almost uniform tint or mottling. The female alone incubates for thirteen to fourteen days. The young are tended by both parents and are able to leave the nest eleven or twelve days after hatching.

FOOD Worms, insects and their larvae, fruit and berries.

DISTRIBUTION AND MOVEMENTS Western and central Europe, Mediterranean, northwest Africa, Asia Minor and south central Asia. Winters in tropical Africa. Is a migrant breeder in southeast England and distinctly scarce further north: vagrant in Ireland.

SUB-SPECIES *L.m. hafizi* (larger and paler) occurs from the Volga delta east as far as western Sinkiang and south to northeastern Afghanistan. *L.m. africana* is found in the Crimea, the Caucasus, Syria, Iran, Iraq and northwest Afghanistan.

French: ROSSIGNOL PHILOMÈLE
Italian: USIGNOLO
Spanish: RUISEÑOR COMÚN
German: NACHTIGALL

(Left) Breeding areas (yellow) and areas where the Nightingale may be seen on passage (pink)

French: ' ROSSIGNOL PROGNÉ
Italian: USIGNOLO MAGGIORE
Spanish: RUISEÑOR RUSO
German: SPROSSER

Thrush Nightingale
Luscinia luscinia

HABITAT Nests in marshy undergrowth, thickets, scrub and among crops.

IDENTIFICATION Length: 16 cm. Very similar to the Nightingale, but distinguished by darker brown coloration, less rufous tail and especially by light brown mottling on breast. Juveniles are less rufous than juvenile Nightingales. Generally more confined to damp thickets.

CALL The call-note is a 'weett' which is more high-pitched than that of Nightingale. The song is louder and even more melodious than Nightingale's although equally variable. However it lacks a crescendo.

REPRODUCTION Beginning of May or June, depending on the latitude. Nests on the ground among herbage or under shrubs, among roots or fallen branches. Nest is built in a hollow in vegetation litter by the female. Eggs: four to six, similar to Nightingale's eggs. The female incubates for thirteen days: both tend the young.

FOOD Worms, insects and their larvae: also berries.

DISTRIBUTION AND MOVEMENTS Breeds in southern Scandinavia, Germany, eastern Europe, Caucasus and the USSR. Winters in east Africa. Accidental in Britain.

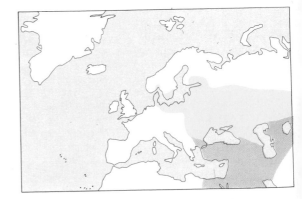

(Right) Breeding areas (yellow) and areas where the Thrush Nightingale may be seen on passage (pink). (Preceding page) Nightingale *Luscinia megarhynchos*

Siberian Rubythroat
Luscinia calliope

French: CALLIOPE SIBÉRIENNE
Italian: CALLIOPE
Spanish: RUISEÑOR CALÍOPE
German: RUBINKEHLCHEN

HABITAT Breeds in forests, in scrub, at forest edges and amongst undergrowth.

IDENTIFICATION Length: 14 cm. Male in summer plumage is easily distinguished by his vermilion throat, while the female has a whitish throat, sometimes with a few red spots. Larger than the Bluethroat, and distinguished from the Robin by the two white eye-stripes and the confinement of the red to the throat—not onto the forehead or breast. The long legs are also characteristic. Juveniles closely resemble juvenile Robins, but have a faint supercilium and moustachial stripe.

CALL A loud whistling 'tuiut'.

REPRODUCTION From late May. Nest is a loosely built cup of plant material tucked into a grass tussock, under a shrub or occasionally slightly off the ground. Four to six eggs are laid, light blue mottled with reddish-brown. The female alone incubates for about fourteen days.

FOOD Insects and their larvae.

DISTRIBUTION AND MOVEMENTS Breeds in a vast zone from the western Urals to the Pacific coast of Asia. An isolated population nests in China (Kansu and northern Szechwan). Migratory over much of its range, wintering mainly in India, Burma, and Thailand. Accidental on Fair Isle.

(Above) Male Siberian Rubythroat (foreground) and female

French: GORGEBLEUE
Italian: PETTAZZURRO
Spanish: PECHIAZUL
German: BLAUKEHLCHEN

Bluethroat
Luscinia svecica

HABITAT Inhabits thickets usually by fresh water: also tundra. On migration in cover.

IDENTIFICATION Length: 14 cm. Similar in shape to a Robin, but may be distinguished by rufous base of tail, pale eyestripe and black band on chest. In summer the male has a bright blue throat-patch. The Scandinavian sub-species *L.s. svecica* is distinguished by the presence of a reddish spot in the middle of the blue throat, while the central and southern European form *L.s. cyanecula* has a whitish patch on the throat, not very much blue, a black border and a dark pectoral band. The sub-species *L.s. magna* from Asia Minor either has a small white spot or no spot.

The female's plumage is brownish with a whitish throat-patch with black streaks at the sides, forming a sort of irregular pectoral band, often with traces of blue or chestnut. Juveniles resemble young Robins, but are distinguished by the chestnut base to the tail. They lack the adults' spot on the throat.

CALL A characteristic 'tac'. Song is varied and melodious, similar to songs of the Nightingale and Woodlark, but more high-pitched and less rich.

REPRODUCTION May onwards. The nest, made of dried grasses and roots and lined with hair, is built in well-hidden holes in banks or in hummocks in marshy ground. Eggs: five to seven, varying in colour from pale green to blue. Finely speckled or tinted with reddish-brown. The female alone incubates for about fifteen days although both tend the young.

FOOD Insects and their larvae, worms, seeds and berries.

DISTRIBUTION AND MOVEMENTS From Scandinavia east across northern Eurasia to western Alaska; south to western France and central Europe, including central Spain. Also breeds east to Iran, Turkestan and central Asia. Winters in northern Africa, the Mediterranean region, the Middle East and southeast Asia. In Britain and Ireland is a scarce passage migrant which is most numerous in autumn.

SUB-SPECIES *L.s. cyanecula* is present in eastern and central Europe, central and western France, and central Spain; *L.s. volgae:* central USSR. *L.s. pallidogularis* (upper parts paler and greyer): USSR. *L.s. magna:* northeastern Caucasus. Other sub-species are present in Asia.

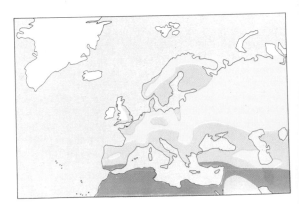

(Left) Male Bluethroat (bottom), female (centre) and the sub-species *L.s. cyanecula* (top). (Right) Breeding areas (yellow), wintering areas (magenta) and areas where the Bluethroat may be seen on passage (pink)

Red-flanked Bluetail
Tarsiger cyanurus

French: ROSSIGNOL À FLANCS
ROUX
Italian: CODAZZURRO
Spanish: COLIAZUL CEJIBLANCO
German: BLAUSCHWANZ

HABITAT In the breeding season frequents densely wooded areas, both coniferous and mixed, often with damp or wet undergrowth. On migration often seen in gardens, parks and orchards.

IDENTIFICATION Length: 14 cm. Similar in size to a Redstart. Adult male unmistakable with blue upper parts, glossy orange-yellow flanks, and remaining underparts creamy-white tinged buff on the breast. Tail, rump and eyestripe blue. Female is much more subdued olive-brown in colour except for tail which is blue but much paler. Underparts white except for flanks which are orange like the male's. Juveniles: brownish upper parts with light mottling. Blue upper tail distinguishes them from juvenile Robins.

CALL Generally sings from an elevated perch such as a branch or fallen tree. The song is short and resonant, reminiscent of that of the Song Thrush. Call like that of Robin: 'tic-tic'

REPRODUCTION From late May. The nest consists of a cup of dead grasses, roots and moss which may be situated up to a metre off the ground or on the ground, in natural hollows in fallen trees, in banks, or among the roots of large trees. It is lined with needles or with lichens and mosses and contains four to seven white eggs which are sometimes spotted at the larger end. The female alone incubates; the period is not known.

FOOD Chiefly insects and their larvae.

DISTRIBUTION AND MOVEMENTS Present in the taiga zone from Finland and northern Russia east through Siberia, and southwards to the Himalayas, northwest India and China. Also found in Japan except for the more southerly areas. The northern populations migrate, moving south to winter in southeast Asia. In Britain is a very rare vagrant.

SUB-SPECIES *T.c. rufilatus* (brighter blue in colour) Himalayan region and China. *T.c. ussuriensis* and *T.c. pacificus* have also been described by some authorities as isolated Indian and Chinese races.

(Right) Male Red-flanked Bluetail (bottom), juvenile (centre) and female. (Below) Breeding areas (yellow)

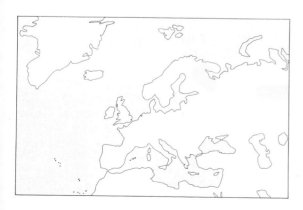

Passeriformes: Turdidae

French: IRANIE À GORGE BLANCHE
Italian: PETTIROSSO GOLABIANCA
German: WEISSKEHLSÄNGER

White-throated Robin
Irania gutturalis

HABITAT Scrub, particularly in mountainous and stony regions.

IDENTIFICATION Length: 17 cm. Sides of head black, throat and eyestripe white: this head pattern makes it easily identifiable. Upper parts grey, underparts rust-coloured. Tail and upper tail coverts black, flight-feathers brown-black. Female more brownish and lacks white eyestripe and any black on head; throat is whitish, upper breast greyish and flanks tinged with a touch of orange. Juveniles are mottled with upper parts spotted ochre bordered dark. Often skulks in bushes like the Nightingale but sometimes seen perching in the open on stones.

CALL The song is a succession of loud bell-like notes.

REPRODUCTION Late April to May. The nest is built close to the ground, among bushes or the lower branches of trees. It consists of a cup of dry grass lined with plant material. Four to five eggs are laid, light green-blue with rust-coloured markings. Further information is unavailable.

FOOD Mainly insects.

DISTRIBUTION AND MOVEMENTS Asia Minor, northern Iran, Afghanistan and central Asia. Most individuals migrate in winter to southern Arabia and eastern Africa. Accidental in Greece and Sweden.

French: GRIVETTE SOLITAIRE
Italian: TORDO EREMITA
Spanish: ZORZAL HERMIT
German: EINSIEDLERDROSSEL

(Top) Male White-throated Robin (foreground) and female. (Above right) Breeding areas (yellow) and areas where the White-throated Robin may be seen on passage (pink). (Above) Hermit Thrush

Hermit Thrush
Catharus guttatus

HABITAT Nests chiefly in mixed or coniferous woods.

IDENTIFICATION Length: 18 cm. Upper parts grey-brown shading to red-brown on rump and tail. Underparts white with small black spots arranged in stripes at sides of throat, on breast and flanks. Short brownish bill. Legs flesh-brown and iris dark brown.

CALL A 'quoit' or 'chack'. The song is melodious and reminiscent of the Nightingale's.

REPRODUCTION The nest is a compact structure made of interlaced bark fibres, grass stems and ferns, clad externally with moss and lined inside with pine needles, small roots, etc. Eggs: three to six, very pale blue, usually unmarked. Incubated for twelve days.

FOOD Mainly animal (such as insects, spiders and small slugs). Also vegetable substances such as berries and fruit.

DISTRIBUTION AND MOVEMENTS Migratory, nesting from central Alaska over most of Canada, southwards to the mountains of California and New Mexico and east to Connecticut and Massachusetts. Winters from British Columbia to Guatemala and along the coast of the Gulf of Mexico as far as Florida. Accidental in western Europe, in Iceland, Germany and Fair Isle.

Grey-cheeked Thrush
Catharus minimus

HABITAT Breeds mainly in broad-leaved woods.

IDENTIFICATION Length: 20 cm. It is a small thrush with a grey-brown back. Very like Swainson's Thrush *C. ustulatus*. Almost the only differences between these two species are that the Grey-cheeked Thrush has, as its English name indicates, grey cheeks, an inconspicuous eye-ring, less warm coloration on the throat and breast and a greyer back.

CALL A long and low, nasal 'kwee-ah'.

REPRODUCTION The nest is made of grass and twigs, lined with a smooth coat of mud. There are between three and six speckled, pale blue-green eggs per clutch.

FOOD Mainly insects and other invertebrates. Also berries and fruit.

DISTRIBUTION AND MOVEMENTS Breeds in northeast Siberia and across Alaska and Canada as far as Newfoundland and throughout the northeastern United States. Like many of the vagrant thrushes to Europe it occurs mainly in the autumn. *C.m. bicknelli* and the nominate sub-species have both occurred as accidentals in Britain.

SUB-SPECIES *C.m. bicknelli:* southeast Canada and northeast United States.

(Above right) Grey-cheeked Thrush and (right) Swainson's Thrush

French: GRIVE À JOUES GRISES
Italian: TORDO MINIMO
German: GRAUWANGENDROSSEL

Swainson's Thrush
Catharus ustulatus

HABITAT Breeds in coniferous and broad-leaved forests.

IDENTIFICATION Length: 18 cm. This small North American thrush, also sometimes called the Olive-backed Thrush, has uniform brown or olive-grey plumage, with pale underparts and black markings on its throat and breast. It resembles a small Song Thrush. Its throat, upper breast and the sides of its head are washed with buff coloration. It also has a fairly conspicuous buff eye-ring. The careful observation of these characteristics enables one to distinguish this species from the similar Grey-cheeked Thrush even from some distance.

CALL An alarm note consisting of a weak 'weet'. Its song is a series of musical notes.

REPRODUCTION The construction of its nest is rather elaborate but it is not usually coated with mud. Between three and five pale-blue eggs with brown speckles are laid.

FOOD Insects and other small invertebrates: also fruit, berries, and other plant matter.

DISTRIBUTION AND MOVEMENTS Breeds in Alaska, eastern Newfoundland and the northeast United States, and south to California and West Virginia. It is migrant and winters from Central America south to Peru. It is accidental in Europe in Italy and Britain.

SUB-SPECIES There are several sub-species present in North America.

French: GRIVE PETITE
Italian: TORDO DI SWAINSON
German: ZWERGDROSSEL

French: GRIVE MUSICIENNE
Italian: TORDO BOTTACCIO
Spanish: ZORZAL COMÚN
German: SINGDROSSEL

Song Thrush
Turdus philomelos

HABITAT Gardens, thickets, hedges, copses and woods. Frequently present in suburban areas.

IDENTIFICATION Length: 23 cm. Distinguishable from the Mistle Thrush and the Fieldfare by its smaller size, warmer coloration of the uniform brown upper parts and by its buff-orange breast and flanks which have smaller and narrower black markings. In flight: golden-brown axillaries and underwings. Uniform warm brown tail: lacks white in tail unlike Mistle Thrush. Dark brown (almost black) primaries and secondaries. Rufous tips to its wing coverts which form two wing-bars. Juveniles have streaked upper parts. Distinguishable from the Redwing by lack of chestnut coloration on the flanks and underwing: also has no eyestripe.

CALL Its normal note which is emitted chiefly in flight is a thin 'seep' or 'teek' like the Redwing's, but less penetrating and prolonged. Also emits a loud, clear song consisting of a series of simple but musical phrases which are repeated three or four times from the tops of trees or bushes.

REPRODUCTION Generally from April onwards, although the nest may sometimes be built in March. The nest consists of a cup made of grasses and other plant materials smoothly lined with mud. It is built by the female and contains four or five bright blue eggs which are lightly speckled with black or reddish-brown markings. Incubation is carried out by the female for eleven to fifteen days. Both parents tend the young which remain in the nest for twelve to sixteen days.

FOOD Worms, molluscs, insects, fruit and larvae.

DISTRIBUTION AND MOVEMENTS Breeds from Scandinavia (except for the northernmost regions), Britain and Ireland eastwards across Europe to western Siberia. Also breeds in Asia Minor east to Iraq and in northern Africa. Is a widespread and numerous breeder in Britain and Ireland with the exception of Shetland, where it only occasionally nests. Also occurs as a passage and winter visitor.

SUB-SPECIES *T.p. philomelos:* Scandinavia, central Germany, southern Czechoslovakia, the Urals and central western Siberia. *T.p. hebridensis:* the Outer Hebrides and the Isle of Skye. *T.p. clarkei:* Britain and Ireland (apart from the areas inhabited by *T.p. hebridensis*), southern Netherlands, northwest France.

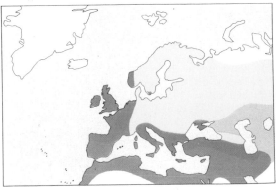

(Right) Breeding areas (yellow), wintering areas (magenta), areas where the Song Thrush may be seen all year round (orange) and on passage (pink)

238

Eye-browed Thrush
Turdus obscurus

French: GRIVE OBSCURE
Italian: TORDO OSCURO
German: WEISSBRAUENDROSSEL

HABITAT Dense coniferous or mixed forests.

IDENTIFICATION Length: 22 cm. Male resembles a small Redwing, but rufous coloration extends to the sides of the unstreaked breast. Male has olive-brown upper parts, a narrow pale eyestripe, ash-grey throat and sides of the head and neck, rust-coloured flanks and white belly and under-tail coverts. The upper part of the female's crown is brown and lacks any grey tinge and her throat is white with brown markings.

CALL A low 'chuck'.

REPRODUCTION Mid June onwards. The nest is a cup of grasses, roots, twigs and bark: it may be reinforced with mud and is situated one to five metres above the ground in the fork of a tree. Lays five to six eggs which resemble those of a Fieldfare. May be double brooded. Further details are not known.

FOOD Not yet determined.

DISTRIBUTION AND MOVEMENTS Accidental in Europe. Breeds in Siberia and eastern Asia. Migratory: winters in Burma and southern China south to Indonesia.

239

French: GRIVE À GORGE NOIRE
Italian: TORDO GOLANERA
Spanish: ZORZAL PAPINEGRO
German: SCHWARZKEHLDROSSEL

Black-throated Thrush
Turdus ruficollis

HABITAT Taiga and sub-alpine scrub.

IDENTIFICATION Length: 22 cm. Male may be distinguished by its uniform grey-black upper parts and contrasting white underparts. Black throat and upper breast (red in the sub-species *T.r. ruficollis*) and dull white breast and abdomen, sometimes slightly streaked with brown. Grey streaks on the flanks; white-tipped under-tail feathers. Female: black streaks on the throat; black markings on part of the breast. Both male and female show rufous coloration under the wings when seen in flight. See also page 256.

CALL Emits a Blackbird-like chuckling call.

REPRODUCTION From May onwards. Nest is a cup of grass, moss and twigs and is lined with mud. It is built low in a tree or in a log or stump, or on the ground. Lays four to seven smooth, light blue eggs similar to those of the Blackbird. The female alone incubates although both parents tend the young.

FOOD Probably like that of other thrushes.

DISTRIBUTION AND MOVEMENTS Breeds in central Asia: winters in Iran through Afghanistan and India. Is accidental in western Europe including Britain.

SUB-SPECIES *T.r. atrogularis* breeds in the west and north of the range and is known as the Black-throated Thrush. *T.r. ruficollis* breeds in the remainder of the range and is known as the Red-throated Thrush.

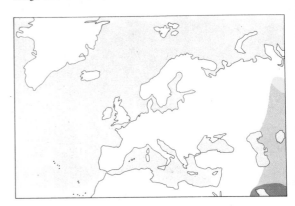

(Below) Red-throated Thrush *T.r. ruficollis* and (below right) male Black-throated Thrush (foreground) and female. (Right) Breeding areas (yellow), wintering areas (magenta) and areas where the Black-throated Thrush may be seen on passage (pink)

Blackbird
Turdus merula

French: MERLE NOIR
Italian: MERLO
Spanish: MIRLO COMÚN
German: AMSEL

HABITAT Gardens, thickets, hedges and broad-leaved and coniferous forests. Also cultivated land, parks and gardens: common in towns in western Europe.

IDENTIFICATION Length: 25 cm. One of the most common birds in Europe. The male is unmistakable, with its glossy, uniform, completely black plumage and bright orange-yellow bill and eye-ring. Female: uniform dark brown upper parts; rufous-brown underparts with variable dark streaks; paler, off-white throat: its bill is brown with very little yellow coloration (rarely yellow like the male's). Juveniles: paler and more rufous than the female, with more noticeable streaks on the underparts. Juvenile male: blackish bill and browner mantle. Dark brown legs. Partial albinos are quite common and can be distinguished from the Ring Ouzel by the absence of a grey marking on the wing and by the voice.

It runs on the ground and hops quickly, with brief pauses: often seen standing with head to one side listening for worms. When it alights on the ground, holds its tail open and raised while the wings are almost drooping. Flight is usually low and brief and although it may be seen in flocks, it is only truly gregarious on migration. See also page 256.

CALL Its usual note is a low 'chook-chook-chook' which develops into a strident chattering when alarmed. Also emits an insistent 'cheek-cheek-cheek'. Its warbling and musical song is emitted when it perches on trees or buildings, or occasionally from the ground or bushes.

REPRODUCTION From February in the south, from March or April in the north. Nests in hedges, bushes, or trees. Also nests on buildings or in crevices in walls. The female builds the nest: it consists of a solid cup of plant materials mixed with mud, and is lined with finer grasses and other materials such as pine needles. Four or five (sometimes three to nine) eggs are laid which are light blue in colour with reddish-brown and grey speckles. Incubation is carried out by the female (occasionally the male may sit on the eggs but he does not incubate) for eleven to seventeen days. The offspring are tended by both parents. Frequently double brooded.

FOOD Plants and animals, including fruit, seeds, insects and small molluscs.

DISTRIBUTION AND MOVEMENTS Europe (except for the most northerly regions), Asia Minor, southeast Asia and northwest Africa. The populations of northern and eastern Europe migrate to the Mediterranean region. In Britain and Ireland the Blackbird is a widespread and numerous resident and migrant breeder. Its breeding range is spreading and now includes more marginal habitats such as city centres and small islands. Breeding populations of Britain are mostly sedentary although some move long distances within the country.

SUB-SPECIES *T.m. merula*: western and northeast Europe. *T.m. aterrimus* (duller) the Balkans, southern USSR and Asia Minor east to northern Iran. Other sub-species are present in Asia and Africa.

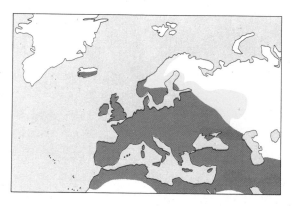

(Above) Male Blackbird (foreground) and female. (Left) Breeding areas (yellow), wintering areas (magenta) and areas where the Blackbird may be seen all year round (orange)

French: MERLE À PLASTRON
Italian: MERLO DAL COLLARE
Spanish: MIRLO CAPIBLANCO
German: RINGDROSSEL

Ring Ouzel
Turdus torquatus

HABITAT Moorland, bushy or rocky hills and mountainsides.

IDENTIFICATION Length: 24 cm. The adult male is unmistakable because of its dull, uniform black plumage with a white, crescent-shaped breast band: this white band distinguishes it from the male Blackbird. After the autumn moult its feathers are edged with white, particularly on the underparts. It may be mistaken for a partially albino Blackbird but it can be identified by the presence of a greyish marking on its flight feathers (which can be seen when it is perching) and by its call. Yellowish bill with a blackish tip; brown legs. The female is browner, with more conspicuous pale margins to the feathers; narrower collar, tinged with brown. Juveniles lack collars and are like young Blackbirds, but less reddish and more greyish and brown; their underparts are heavily streaked and marked with whitish and dark brown coloration. See also page 256.

CALL A clear, chirping call note: 'pee-ee-oo'; a harsh, loud 'tak-tak-tak' often tailing off into a vibrant chattering, and a 'cheek-cheek' like the Blackbird's. Its song is a simple succession of three or four clear whistles.

REPRODUCTION From mid-April. The nest is built by both male and female in a hollow or under an overhang of a stream bank or cliff. Also builds its cup-shaped nest (which has no mud lining) in trees or bushes. There are usually four or five blue-green eggs with reddish-brown markings. Incubation is carried out by both sexes and takes thirteen or fourteen days. The offspring are tended by both parents.

FOOD Worms, insects, small molluscs and fruit.

DISTRIBUTION AND MOVEMENTS Breeds in Britain, Ireland and northwest Europe: also mountainous areas of central and southern Europe, the Caucasus and northern Iran. Migratory, wintering at lower levels in the south of the range or beyond, but also sedentary. In Britain breeds in the north and west on upland moors: also breeds in Ireland. Although it has decreased in some areas it is still fairly widely distributed. British birds winter in southern France, northeast Spain and northwest Africa.

SUB-SPECIES *T.t. torquatus:* northwest Europe, Britain and Ireland. *T.t. alpestris:* central and southern Europe. *T.t. amicorum:* the Caucasus, the Caspian region and Iran.

(Above) Male Ring Ouzel (top), juvenile (centre) and the sub-species *T.t. alpestris* (bottom). (Right) Breeding areas (yellow), wintering areas (magenta), areas where the Ring Ouzel may be seen all year round (orange) and on passage (pink)

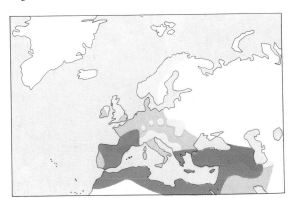

Mistle Thrush
Turdus viscivorus

Passeriformes: Turdidae

French: GRIVE DRAINE
Italian: TORDELA
Spanish: ZORZAL CHARLO
German: MISTELDROSSEL

HABITAT Coniferous and broad-leaved forests, also parks and gardens. In the south of its range frequents mainly mountains: elsewhere often found in suburban areas. Also found in moorland and mountains outside the breeding season.

IDENTIFICATION Length: 26 cm. Differs from the Song Thrush and the Redwing by larger size, greyer upper parts, more densely spotted underparts with larger markings, and a more upright stance with its head raised. Grey-brown upper parts with yellowish borders to the feathers on its back. Buff-white underparts with brown spots; chestnut undertail; white axillaries and underwing. Greyish-chestnut tail. In flight it may be mistaken for the Fieldfare because of its white underwing, but its upper parts and tail are not so dark and it is more solidly built than the Fieldfare. Male and female are similar. Juveniles are heavily spotted with off-white coloration on the head, coverts and mantle. See also page 256.

CALL A dry, vibrant chattering with cawing notes, particularly when it is excited. Also a rapid 'tak-tak-tak' and a soft 'see-ee-ee' like that of the Redwing. Song is repetitive in character but has the fluting tone of the Blackbird.

REPRODUCTION From February onwards in the south to late May in the north. The female builds the nest of plant material mixed with mud. The nest is situated in the fork of a tree or in a bush a metre and a half to nine metres up. May also be built in holes in walls, in low shrubs or hedgerows. There are four eggs ranging from creamy-bronze to bluish-green in colour; they are marked with brown and lilac blotches and speckles. Incubation is carried out by the female and takes twelve to fifteen days. Both parents tend the young.

FOOD Fruit, berries and seeds: also worms, insects, larvae, molluscs and spiders. May kill the young of other birds to feed its own chicks.

DISTRIBUTION AND MOVEMENTS Breeds from Britain, Ireland, Scandinavia and Iberia east across Europe to central Siberia and south to the Middle East and Afghanistan. Also breeds in northwest Africa. It is a resident or partial migrant to the south (although sometimes beyond) of its breeding areas. It is a numerous breeding species in Britain and Ireland except in Shetland and the Outer Hebrides.

SUB-SPECIES *T.v. tauricus*: restricted to the forests of southern Crimea. *T.v. deichleri*: Corsica, Sardinia and northern Africa. Another sub-species is present in Asia.

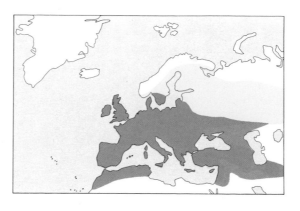

(Left) Breeding areas (yellow), wintering areas (magenta) and areas where the Mistle Thrush may be seen all year round (orange)

French: GRIVE MAUVIS
Italian: TORDO SASSELLO
Spanish: ZORZAL MALVÍS
German: ROTDROSSEL

Redwing
Turdus iliacus

HABITAT Forests: also gardens and parks in some areas. In winter frequents open meadowland and hedgerows.

IDENTIFICATION Length: 21 cm. It is the smallest of the common thrushes of Europe. Differs from the larger Song Thrush in having a conspicuous cream-white supercilium, warm chestnut flanks (not rufous), chestnut axillaries (not rufous) and streaked (not spotted) buff-white breast and flanks. Brown upper parts; dark brown tail with buff-white coloration on the tips of the feathers: dark brown primaries and secondaries. See also page 256.

CALL Emits a high 'seeii': also a harsher 'chitick'. Song is repetitive, brief and flutier than the Song Thrush's.

REPRODUCTION From late April onwards. Builds its nest in a tree, shrub, in a cavity in a bank, on a stump or on broken ground. The female alone builds the nest which is a thick cup of grasses, usually lined with mud and a layer of fine grasses. Lays four or five (rarely two to eight) smooth and glossy light blue or green-blue eggs which are abundantly marked with red-brown speckles. The female alone incubates for eleven to fifteen days.

FOOD Worms, molluscs, insects and sometimes berries.

DISTRIBUTION AND MOVEMENTS Breeds from Iceland, the Faeroes and northern Europe east across Europe to Siberia as far as Lake Baikal. Mainly migratory: winters in Britain and Ireland, central and southern Europe, north Africa, Egypt and apparently northwest India. In Britain it is a very scarce breeder although it now probably nests every year, chiefly in the north. However, the Redwing is a common and widespread winter and passage visitor.

SUB-SPECIES *T.i. coburni*: breeds in Iceland and the Faeroes.

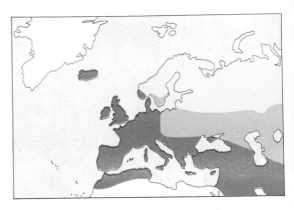

(Right) Breeding areas (yellow), wintering areas (magenta), areas where the Redwing may be seen all year round (orange) and on passage (pink)

American Robin
Turdus migratorius

Passeriformes: Turdidae

French: MERLE MIGRATEUR
Italian: TORDO MIGRATORE
Spanish: ROBÍN AMERICANO
German: WANDERDROSSEL

HABITAT During the breeding season is often associated with urban areas. Otherwise frequents wooded areas.

IDENTIFICATION Length: 24 cm. Apart from its unique coloration, in behaviour and characteristics it resembles the Blackbird. The most striking feature of its plumage is the red breast. This coloration extends over the remaining underparts (except for its throat which is off-white with black streaks). Dark, slate-grey upper parts with even darker wings and tail: tail has white markings on the tip. Also has a prominent 'broken' white eye-ring. Female's coloration is a duller version of the male's. Juveniles have dark markings on their breasts and streaked backs. Albinos and partial albinos are not uncommon in this species—another characteristic it shares with the Blackbird. See also page 256.

CALL Similar to the Blackbird's but more raucous: a 'kwik, kuuik, kwik'. Also emits a soft 'pit, pit'.

REPRODUCTION Its cup-shaped nest is made out of plants and mud and is usually situated on a bush or tree (at variable distances from the ground) but rarely on the ground. There are between three and six plain, pastel blue eggs per clutch. Incubation takes about thirteen days and is carried out mainly by the female.

FOOD Mainly earth-worms. Also feeds on insects and fruit.

DISTRIBUTION AND MOVEMENTS A North American species which nests in most of the continent from Alaska, Mackenzie and Quebec south to southern Mexico. It is a partial migrant and winters from southern Canada to Guatemala. It is accidental in Europe, and is one of the most common transatlantic passerine vagrants although it still does not occur annually in Britain.

SUB-SPECIES There are numerous sub-species in North America.

245

(Right) The Redwing *Turdus iliacus* is easily distinguished from other thrushes by its white eyestripe and reddish-brown flanks. (Below) Blackbirds *Turdus merula* feeding with thrushes

A. Visage/Jacana

J. Burton/Bruce Coleman

(Left) American Robin *Turdus migratorius* feeding its young at the nest and (bottom left) Song Thrush *T. philomelos*. (Below and bottom right) Two species of Whistling Thrush of the genus *Myiophoneus* from southeast Asia

E. Burgess/Ardea

R. K. Mustern/Bruce Coleman

H. Chaumeton/Jacana

P. Jackson/Bruce Coleman

French: GRIVE LITORNE
Italian: CESENA
Spanish: ZORZAL REAL
German: WACHOLDERDROSSEL

Fieldfare
Turdus pilaris

(Below right) Breeding areas (yellow), wintering areas (magenta), areas where the Fieldfare may be seen all year round (orange) and on passage (pink)

HABITAT During the breeding season it inhabits both coniferous and broad-leaved forests: also parks, orchards, gardens and cultivated land. Winters in open country and farmland.

IDENTIFICATION Length: 25 cm. Smaller than the Mistle Thrush but much larger than the Song Thrush and the Redwing. It can be identified by its blue-grey head and rump, chestnut back and blackish tail. In flight shows very conspicuous white axillaries and underwing: this may lead to confusion with the Mistle Thrush and it is then best distinguished by its call note. Black streaks on its crown; whitish supercilium; golden-brown throat and breast with black streaks; its remaining underparts are white, heavily spotted with black on the flanks; blackish-brown wings. Male and female are alike. The coloration of juveniles is duller than that of adults after moulting.

The Fieldfare is noisy during the breeding season but

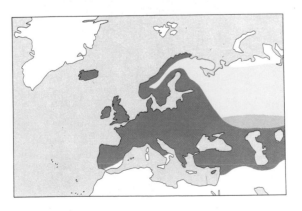

is otherwise shy and wary. Extremely sociable. It is nomadic during the winter, often travelling in conspicuous groups. It behaves like the Mistle Thrush on the ground and the flight of the two species is similar. See also page 256.

CALL Its characteristic note, especially in flight, is a hard, chuckling 'cha-cha-cha-chak'. Also a soft, long drawn out 'see-ee'. It emits other harsh notes when excited or in danger. Its song is a mixture of shrill, rapid notes: sings mainly in flight.

REPRODUCTION From April onwards. Nests in colonies in trees, on posts or stumps or on the ground. The female alone builds the nest, which is a cup of plant material, lined with mud and, in turn, lined with finer grasses. It lays five or six eggs similar to those of the Blackbird or Ring Ouzel. However, the coloration of its eggs is highly variable. Incubation takes eleven to fourteen days and is carried out by the female alone. The offspring are tended by both parents.

FOOD Molluscs, worms, insects, spiders, fruit and seeds.

DISTRIBUTION AND MOVEMENTS Breeds in northern and central Europe and northern Asia. Migrant and resident: winters in western and southern Europe or sometimes at the nesting ground. Northern populations migrate well south into southwest Asia, Asia Minor, Iran and sometimes Iberia. In Britain it has nested on several occasions. It is a widespread and numerous winter and passage visitor to Britain and Ireland from October to April.

Dusky Thrush and Naumann's Thrush
Turdus naumanni

French: GRIVE À AILES ROUSSES
Italian: CESENA FOSCA
Spanish: ZORZAL EUNOMO
German: ROSTFLÜGELDROSSEL

(Left) Naumann's Thrush *T.n. naumanni* and (below) Dusky Thrush *T.n. eunomus*

HABITAT Breeds on the edges of forests and in sparsely wooded countryside. Winters in open fields.

IDENTIFICATION Length: 23 cm. The Dusky Thrush *T.n. eunomus* is distinguished by its conspicuous whitish supercilium from the quite distinct nominate sub-species Naumann's Thrush *T.n. naumanni*. Blackish-brown upper parts are streaked with chestnut, particularly on the back; additionally the lesser coverts are blacker. Pale throat with crescent-shaped markings on the sides which are blackish in winter: streaked blackish-brown and grey-brown breast; white abdomen and central part of the breast; blackish undertail feathers with brown streaks and white tips; chestnut underwing and blackish-brown tail feathers with chestnut margins. Naumann's Thrush may be distinguished from the Dusky Thrush by its rufous tail and breast. See also page 256.

CALL Resembles that of the Song Thrush.

REPRODUCTION From May onwards. It lays four or five eggs: further information is lacking.

FOOD Worms, insects, seeds and berries.

DISTRIBUTION AND MOVEMENTS Breeds in Siberia. Winters in eastern and southeast Asia. It is accidental in Europe (Norway, Britain, the Netherlands, Belgium, France and Italy).

SUB-SPECIES Dusky Thrush *T.n. eunomus* (described above). Naumann's Thrush *T.n. naumanni:* speckled with chestnut coloration on the breast and flanks.

French: MERLE SIBÉRIEN
Italian: TORDO SIBERIANO
Spanish: ZORZAL SIBERIANO
German: SIBIRISCHE DROSSEL

Siberian Thrush
Turdus sibiricus

(Right) Male Siberian Thrush
(foreground) and female

HABITAT It prefers dense woods and forests with abundant bushy vegetation either on plains or in the mountains.

IDENTIFICATION Length: 20 cm. Adult male: its basic colour is an almost uniform slate-black with a very conspicuous white supercilium. White markings on the outer tail feathers which are not always clearly visible when at rest. White crescent-shaped markings on the undertail. In flight its most conspicuous characteristic is a white band on the underwing and another smaller band on its wing coverts. The female resembles the female Song Thrush: olive-brown upper parts, speckles on the sides and front of its neck and crescent-shaped dark markings on its underparts. Juveniles are much more heavily spotted. See also page 256.

CALL A fluty whistle.

REPRODUCTION It usually builds its cup-shaped nest in bushes or on the branches of leafy trees. The nest is lined with twigs and fine' blades of grass and partly coated with mud. The Siberian Thrush lays four or five eggs similar to those of the Fieldfare.

FOOD Mainly earthworms and other invertebrates.

DISTRIBUTION AND MOVEMENTS It nests from central Siberia east to Japan and winters in southeast Asia. It is accidental in western Europe including Britain.

SUB-SPECIES *T.s. davidsoni:* Japan.

French: AGROBATE ROUX
Italian: USIGNOLO D'AFRICA
Spanish: ALZACOLA
German: HECKENSÄNGER

White's Thrush
Zoothera dauma

French: GRIVE DORÉE
Italian: TORDO DORATO
Spanish: ZORZAL DORADO
German: ERDDROSSEL

HABITAT Dense forests with thick undergrowth.

IDENTIFICATION Length: 27 cm. Larger than the other breeding thrushes of Europe. Adults: olive-brown upper parts tinged with yellowish coloration. Easily distinguished by black crescent shaped markings on upper and underparts. A wide black band and white bar on the underwing are visible in flight. Brown central tail feathers; the outer tail feathers are darker and have whitish margins. Flight is markedly undulating. See also page 256.

CALL Emits musical 'chirrup' like the Mistle Thrush.

REPRODUCTION From mid-May onwards. It lays four or five bluish-green eggs. See also page 256.

FOOD Insects and fruit.

DISTRIBUTION AND MOVEMENTS Breeds in Siberia, Japan, China, India, Ceylon and Australia. Palearctic populations winter in northern India, Indo-China and the Philippines. Accidental in Europe including Britain.

SUB-SPECIES There are numerous sub-species in Asia.

(Above right) Adult White's Thrush

Rufous Bush Chat
Cercotrichas galactotes

HABITAT Dry bushy environments including gardens, vineyards, olive groves and other types of cultivated land.

IDENTIFICATION Length: 15 cm. Also known as the Rufous Bush Robin. Has slender build with exceptionally long legs. Unmistakable rusty-chestnut coloration of the upper parts. The long, fan-shaped tail with brightly coloured rusty-chestnut central feathers ending in a large, white, black-barred tip is also conspicuous, especially in flight. Dark chestnut wings; pale underwing. Brown underparts; prominent whitish supercilium and dark border round the eye. Male and female are very similar; juveniles are almost identical to adults, but their upper parts are paler.
The Rufous Bush Chat hops about on the ground without attempting to conceal itself, with its wings drooping and its tail fanned out and held vertically.

CALL Its usual note is a rather hard 'tek-tek'. Its song is musical and varied.

REPRODUCTION From May onwards. The nest is built in bushy vegetation close to the ground. Four or five grey-white or greenish-white eggs with brown speckles and blotches are laid. The female alone incubates. Further information is unavailable.

FOOD Insects and larvae: also worms.

DISTRIBUTION AND MOVEMENTS Breeds in southern Iberia (has also bred in southern France), the southern Balkans, Asia Minor and the Middle East east to Afghanistan. Also breeds in central Africa. Winters in the south of the breeding range and beyond as far south as Kenya. Accidental in Britain and Ireland.

SUB-SPECIES *C.g. syriacus:* southeast Europe. Other sub-species are present in Africa and Asia.

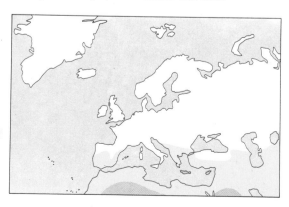

(Left) Breeding areas (yellow) and areas where the Rufous Bush Chat may be seen on passage (pink). (Facing page bottom) Rufous Bush (far left) and the sub-species *C.g. syriacus* (near left)

Wheatears in flight

1: DESERT WHEATEAR *(Oenanthe deserti)* During the winter the plumage of males and females is similar (a). In spring the male's underwing, cheeks and throat become black (b). Figure (c) shows the juvenile seen from above. The tail (d) is almost completely black, a distinguishing feature of this species.

2: ISABELLINE WHEATEAR *(Oenanthe isabellina)* The female's underwing, seen from below (a) is mostly white. The upper parts (b) are sand coloured. The black tail band (c) is almost rectangular. Striking fluttering display flight, although like most wheatears flight is flitting.

3: FINSCH'S WHEATEAR *(Oenanthe finschii)* The male, seen from below (a), could easily be mistaken for the male Desert Wheatear though the black coloration on its tail is less extensive; seen from above (b) its pale back contrasts with its black wings. The female, seen from above (c), is hard to distinguish from the female Pied Wheatear; however distinguishable from

Black-eared Wheatear by its white outer tail feathers (d).

4: RED-TAILED WHEATEAR *(Oenanthe xanthoprymna)* In winter, the male (a) has rufous underparts which distinguish it from the other species of the genus *Oenanthe* in which the black coloration of the throat merges with the underwing. Seen from above (b), it is grey-brown with a reddish rump and tail coverts and a dark terminal band on the tail (c). In winter, the female (d) has pale underparts and its upper parts (e) are like the male's but paler.

5: RED-RUMPED WHEATEAR *(Oenanthe moesta)* In winter, the male's throat and tail are dark (a). Seen from below the wings are pale. Seen from above (b), there are white carpal patches on the wings and the rump and head are pale. Its tail (c) is like the Desert Wheatear's but the lesser coverts are rufous rather than white. The overall coloration of the female (d) is lighter than that of the male, with less conspicuous carpal patches. Also easily distinguished by her rufous head.

(Right) Desert Wheatear
Oenanthe deserti

6: PIED WHEATEAR *(Oenanthe pleschanka)* The female (a) is very similar to the female Wheatear but its belly is whiter and its underwing is slightly paler. Seen from below, the male in summer plumage (b) has dark wings, a black throat and breast, and a white tail (with black terminal band) and belly. Seen from above (c) its crown, rump and tail coverts are white, its wings and back are black, and its tail (d) has a T-shaped terminal band. In the autumn (e) its crown and rump are brownish and its wing coverts have paler borders. In spring (f) its crown is white with black speckles.

7: BLACK-EARED WHEATER *(Oenanthe hispanica)* This species is divided into two sub-species, both of which are found in Europe. They differ particularly in the plumage of the males. Each sub-species has two types of summer plumage in the males—one with a white throat and the other with a black throat. Figure (a) shows a white-throated type and (b) shows a black-throated type belonging to the sub-species *Oenanthe hispanica melanoleuca.* The white-throated individuals of the nominate sub-species *O.h. hispanica* may have rufous on their heads (c) or dark markings (d). Figure (e)

shows a male of the sub-species *O.h. hispanica,* seen from below, in winter plumage. Figure (f) shows a male of the sub-species *O.h. melanoleuca* in spring plumage, seen from above. There is no dimorphism in the female (g). In the winter, both sexes seen from above (h) have the same plumage. Males and females differ in the pattern of their tails, with considerably less black in the male (i) than in the female (l).

8: BLACK WHEATEAR *(Oenanthe leucura)* Seen from below (a), its white tail with a black terminal bar and its pale underwing contrast markedly with its very dark plumage. Seen from above (b), the black tail pattern in the form of an upturned 'T' is conspicuous (c). Its head (d) is black in the male and brown in the female.

9: WHEATEAR *(Oenanthe oenanthe)* The male in summer plumage (a) has a grey back and blackish wings; its tail (b) is black and white. The breeding male's head pattern (black cheeks, white eyestripe and grey crown) is also distinctive. The female, seen from below (c), has a distinctive pattern on its underwing: from above (d) in winter plumage has a brownish back.

(Right) Black Wheatear
Oenanthe leucura

Thrushes in flight

1: DUSKY THRUSH *(Turdus naumanni eunomus)* The male, seen from below, has a chestnut underwing, dark tail, pale throat and supercilium and a blackish breast.

2: FIELDFARE *(Turdus pilaris)* Seen from below (a), its breast is a yellowish-rufous colour, the tail is black and the wing coverts are white. The head is grey. Seen from above (b) the back is reddish, rump grey and the tail black. The white underwing flashes, like the Mistle Thrush's, are conspicuous in flight.

3: MISTLE THRUSH *(Turdus viscivorus)* Seen from below, it shows white on its underwing like the Fieldfare. There are numerous large, dark spots on its breast and flanks; light-coloured tail with white tips to the tail feathers. Shares characteristic flight with the Fieldfare: wings are held closed at regular intervals, but this does not produce marked undulations.

4: WHITE'S THRUSH *(Zoothera dauma)* The black and white bands on its underwing and the pale plumage with dark tips to the feathers are distinctive features. Flight is markedly undulating.

5: BLACK-THROATED THRUSH *(Turdus ruficollis atrogularis)* There are two sub-species which differ most in the coloration of the throat: *Turdus ruficollis ruficollis* (known as the Red-throated Thrush) has a reddish throat and tail (a) and the Black-throated Thrush *T.r. atrogularis* (b) has a black throat and a dark brown tail. Both show rufous beneath the wings in flight.

6: SIBERIAN THRUSH *(Turdus sibiricus)* The female (a) has buff underparts with brown markings and the male (b) is greyish. Both sexes show a distinctive white bar on the underwing in flight.

7: GREY-CHEEKED THRUSH *(Catharus minimus)* It has grey cheeks and a narrow white eye-ring (a). The upper parts (b) are grey-brown. In flight it is difficult to distinguish from the Olive-backed Thrush.

8: OLIVE-BACKED THRUSH *(Catharus ustulatus)* Distinguishable from the Grey-cheeked Thrush by the rufous eye ring and buff tinge to the breast. However, these features are difficult to note from any distance.

9: HERMIT THRUSH *(Catharus guttatus)* It differs from the other species of the genus *Catharus* in having a distinctly reddish tinge to its tail.

10: TICKELL'S THRUSH *(Turdus unicolor)* This is an Asiatic species from the Himalayas, and its inclusion among species found accidentally in Europe is not acknowledged by all authorities. Seen from below Tickell's Thrush has a greyish breast and belly, dark tail and white undertail.

11: SONG THRUSH *(Turdus philomelos)* Its breast is a yellowish-rufous colour with dark distinct spots which extend to its flanks; buff underwing. Flight is more direct than that of the Mistle Thrush.

12: REDWING *(Turdus iliacus)* The chestnut coloration under its wings and on the flanks is distinctive. Its breast and flanks are marked with dark spots.

13: EYE-BROWED THRUSH *(Turdus obscurus)* Grey head and underwing, white belly and undertail. Rufous unstreaked breast: some rufous coloration extends to the sides.

14: AMERICAN ROBIN *(Turdus migratorius)* Black head, distinctive red breast, belly and under-wing coverts: white undertail and black tail. It has longer wings than other thrushes.

15: BLACKBIRD *(Turdus merula)* The male (a), seen from below, is unmistakable because of its dark coloration: it is almost totally black, apart from its flight feathers which are not so dark. The bill is yellow. The female (b) is also dark, but is a uniform brownish colour, not black. Flight is direct: has a flicking motion of the wings and flips up its tail when alighting.

16: RING OUZEL *(Turdus torquatus)* The male in winter plumage (illustrated at right) has white margins to its feathers. In summer plumage it is completely black except for its white collar which remains unchanged throughout the year. The female is browner, with a narrower collar which is a dirty white colour. In flight, the Ring Ouzel's wings appear longer and narrower than the Blackbird's.

FAMILY PARADOXORNITHIDAE: Parrotbills

Bruce Coleman

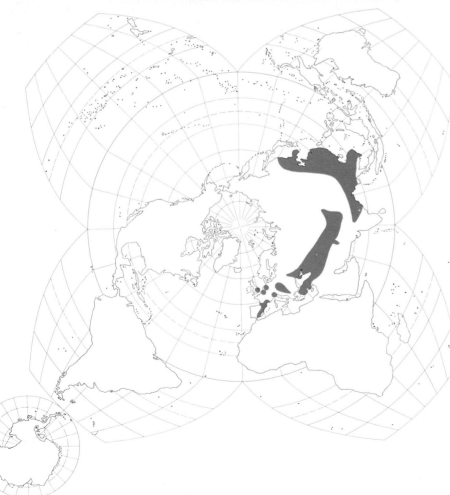

According to some authorities, the nineteen species comprising the family Paradoxornithidae or Parrotbills should be classified as a sub-family within the complex of the family Muscicapidae. However, it is treated here as a distinct family.

Parrotbills are birds of small or medium size, resembling tits in general appearance, with the exception of the bill which differs from that of any other birds of the order Passeriformes. The bill is very short, laterally compressed and is strongly convex in shape; the culmen (the upper part) is curved for its whole length and the gonys (the under part) curves up at the end, while the edges of the mandibles are irregularly wave-shaped.

The plumage is copious and soft and the nostrils are covered with bristle-shaped feathers. Both sexes are similar and there is little difference between juveniles and adults. Parrotbills are gregarious birds, constantly foraging for food among bushes, tall plants and reeds, in dense groups. Their calls help them to remain in contact with one another in the tangled undergrowth which they inhabit.

Most of the species are found in the Oriental faunal region (excluding the Malayan sub-region). Some species have a more extensive range and are found in the Palearctic region, while one, the Bearded Reedling *Panurus biarmicus*, is exclusively Palearctic. It is also known as the Bearded Tit and is the only small European reed-bed bird with a long tail.

Parrotbills feed mainly on insects and grass seeds; only the larger species regularly supplement their diet with berries and fruits. The rarity of many of the species means that little is known about their nesting habits, but the nest is apparently always built fairly close to the ground and is cup-shaped and carefully constructed. The eggs, two to four in each clutch, are unmarked blue or clay-coloured, with variously-coloured irregular markings.

Parrotbills are grouped in three genera, two of which are monotypic. One of these latter contains the giant of the family, the Great Parrotbill *Conostoma oemodium* of the Himalayas and south-eastern China, which is over thirty centimetres long. The other monotypic species is the Bearded Reedling, a delicately coloured species which may be said to constitute an aberrant form (but without any phylogenetic implications) of the Yangtze Crowtit *Paradoxornis heudei* which is found only over a limited stretch of the Yangtze River. All the other species are classified in the genus *Paradoxornis*, the largest of them being the Three-toed Parrotbill *Paradoxornis paradoxus* of southwestern China which, among other features, has the outer toe reduced to a sort of clawless stump adhering to the middle toe.

Avon & Tilford/Ardea

(Left) Female Bearded Reedling *Panurus biarmicus* and (below) male Bearded Reedling. The male is easily distinguished by the striking black 'moustaches'. (Facing page) Male Bearded Reedling and (below) world distribution of the family Paradoxornithidae

F. Balat/Ardea

French: MÉSANGE À MOUSTACHES
Italian: BASETTINO
Spanish: BIGOTUDO
German: BARTMEISE

Bearded Reedling
Panurus biarmicus

HABITAT Extensive reedbeds, sedge and marshy vegetation.

IDENTIFICATION Length: 16 cm. Male has pearl-grey head with black 'moustaches', bright yellow bill, rufous rump and long tail also rufous. Female paler, with rufous head lacking 'moustaches' and greenish-yellow bill. Adults: primaries brown-black barred white and rufous, secondaries black edged red and white; central tail-feathers yellowish, outer tail-feathers with black and white markings. Juveniles: part of tail and rump black. Wing coverts black in male, brown in female.

Climbs up reed-stalks and down again very rapidly, disappearing at ground level. An agile runner on the ground. Flies low over reed tops with rapidly whirring wings and the long tail held out behind. Sociable, lives in groups. Individuals will scratch one another, erecting feathers of head. During courtship flight rises slowly and then drops abruptly back to earth.

CALL A metallic 'ching' and a 'tzu-tzu'.

REPRODUCTION From late April. The nest is built a few centimetres off the ground, on broken reeds or among stems. It is cup-shaped, made of reeds and other plants and lined inside with reed-flower heads and sometimes feathers. Both male and female build the nest. Eggs: five to seven, sometimes up to twelve, whitish, irregularly streaked and spotted brown-black. Both male and female incubate for eleven to thirteen days. The young are tended by both parents. There are normally two broods, sometimes possibly three.

FOOD Insects, larvae, small molluscs and seeds.

DISTRIBUTION AND MOVEMENTS Breeds in western Europe from Britain, the Netherlands, southern France and Spain east across south and central Europe to central and western Asia. In Britain it is a scarce resident breeder which has markedly recovered from near extinction in 1947. In recent years small colonies have been established (although perhaps not permanently) outside its Norfolk and Suffolk strongholds.

SUB-SPECIES *P.b. russicus:* central and southeast Europe, southern USSR and Asia Minor.

(Left) Female Bearded Reedling and male (top).
(Below) Areas where the Bearded Reedling may be seen all year round (orange)

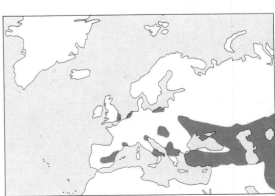

FURTHER READING
General Works

Cramp, S. and Simmons, K. E. L. *Handbook of the Birds of Europe, the Middle East and North Africa*, Vol. I, 1977, Oxford University Press, Oxford.

Dementiev, G. P. *et al. The Birds of the Soviet Union*, 1966, Israel Program for Scientific Translations, Jerusalem.

Etchécopar, R. D. and Hüe, F. *Birds of North Africa*, 1967, Oliver & Boyd, Edinburgh.

Gooders, John *Birds—An Illustrated Survey of the Bird Families of the World*, 1975, Hamlyn, London.

Hüe, F. and Etchécopar, R. D. *Les Oiseaux du Proche et du Moyen Orient*, 1970, Boubée, Paris.

Landsborough Thomson, Sir A. (Ed.) *A New Dictionary of Birds*, 1964, Nelson, London.

Vaurie, Charles *The Birds of the Palearctic Fauna*, 2 vols., 1959 and 1965, Witherby, London.

Voous, K. H. *Atlas of European Birds*, 1960, Nelson, London.

Witherby, H. F. *et al. The Handbook of British Birds*, 5 vols., 1938–1941, Witherby, London.

Specialist Works

Burton, John A. (Ed.) *Owls of the World*, 1973, Lowe, London.

Goodwin, Derek *Pigeons and Doves of the World*, 1967, British Museum, London.

Greenway, J. C. *Extinct and Vanishing Birds of the World*, 1967, Dover, New York.

Murton, R. K. *The Wood Pigeon*, 1965, Collins, London.

Smith, Stuart *The Yellow Wagtail*, 1950, Collins, London.

Stuart Baker, E. C. *Cuckoo Problems*, 1942, Witherby, London.

Yapp, W. B. *Birds and Woods*, 1962, Oxford University Press, Oxford.

Index

The main reference for each bird is printed in bold type; picture references are in italics.